Praise for *The Go Point*

"Great decisions are the hallmark of a successful executive. In *The Go Point*, Michael Useem provides invaluable insight into how to make the critical call."

—Larry Bossidy, retired chairman and CEO of Honeywell International and coauthor of *Execution* and *Confronting Reality*

"*The Go Point* is a tour de force of a tour through battlefields and boardrooms, illuminating the differences between brilliant and tragic decisions. Michael Useem is a wise, witty, and understanding guide whose insights can dramatically improve leadership and decision-making skills. Go for it!"

—Rosabeth Moss Kanter, Harvard Business School, bestselling author of *Confidence: How Winning Streaks & Losing Streaks Begin and End*

"Michael Useem has studied the qualities of leadership more thoroughly than anyone I know. He knows what it takes to be an effective leader—in the boardroom or on the slopes of Mt. Everest—and, in *The Go Point*, he spells out in plain English the consequences of making hard and fast decisions, when they matter most and impact teams of people. There are plenty of books on leadership but few that explain how to take a team from one place to the next. This one is the best."

—Maria Bartiromo, journalist and CNBC anchor

"This exciting book is a valuable guide to effective decision making. *The Go Point*'s great strength is to put the reader inside the heads of fascinating, often heroic people as they seek to 'get it right,' under pressure and with incomplete information."

—Steven Kerr, managing director and chief learning officer, Goldman Sachs & Co.

"A hallmark of any successful leader is *decisiveness*. Part instinct, part studied judgment, it is knowing when a decision must be made—and making it. Sometimes events allow thoughtful, full consideration. Other times, however, circumstance dictates an immediate choice, in the face of daunting uncertainty. In *The Go Point,* Michael Useem identifies the essence of what it takes to prepare for moments of decision. He draws from an array of compelling accounts to help us appreciate what is essential for decisive decision making when it really counts."

—PETER M. DAWKINS, vice chairman, Citigroup Global Wealth Management, U.S. Army Brigadier General (Ret.)

"Ralph Waldo Emerson famously wrote of Napoleon: 'Here was a man who, in each moment and emergency, knew what to do next . . . he never for a moment lost sight of his way onward, in the dazzle and uproar of the present circumstance. He knew what to do, and he flew to his mark.' How did such a man develop? How does any leader know what to do and when to do it? Here Michael Useem, one of America's foremost thinkers about leadership, unravels that mystery in a fast-paced, well-written, and unforgettable book. Highly recommended for everyone with courage for the arena!"

—DAVID GERGEN, professor of public service, director, Center for Public Leadership, John F. Kennedy School of Government, Harvard University

"It doesn't matter how much talent, intelligence, creativity, or reputation you possess, at some point you must put it all at risk and make a decision. At this point—the *go point*—all your intricate analyses and intentions crystallize into action and you create the future. It's a scary moment, a moment that both challenges you and defines you. In his latest book, Michael Useem walks you up close to it, and, with examples from some of the most pivotal go points in human endeavor, shows you how to master it. This is by far the most practical book on decision making I have ever read."

—MARCUS BUCKINGHAM, author of *First, Break All the Rules; Now, Discover Your Strengths;* and *The One Thing You Need to Know*

THE
GO
POINT

THE
GO
POINT

When It's Time to Decide

*Knowing What to Do
and When to Do It*

MICHAEL USEEM

THREE RIVERS PRESS
NEW YORK

THREE RIVERS PRESS and the Tugboat design are registered trademarks of
Random House, Inc.

Originally published in hardcover in the United States by Crown Business, an imprint of
the Crown Publishing Group, a division of Random House, Inc., New York, in 2006.

Some material in Chapter 1 appeared in different form in *Fortune* (Michael Useem,
"In the Heat of the Moment: A Case Study in Life-and-Death Decision Making,"
June 27, 2005, 125–33) and in collaboration with James Cook and Larry Sutton in
Academy of Management Learning and Education (Michael Useem, James Cook, and
Larry Sutton, "Developing Leaders for Decision Making Under Duress: Wildland
Firefighters in the South Canyon Fire and Its Aftermath," December 2005, 461–85).

Some material in Chapter 7 appeared in different form in collaboration with Jerry Useem
in *Fortune* (Michael Useem and Jerry Useem, "The Board That Conquered Everest,"
October 27, 2003, 73–74; "Great Escapes: Nine Decision-Making Pitfalls—and Nine
Simple Devices to Beat Them," June 27, 2005, 97–102). © 2006 Time Inc.
All rights reserved.

Library of Congress Cataloging-in-Publication Data

Useem, Michael.
  The go point : when it's time to decide—knowing what to do and when to do it /
Michael Useem.—1st ed.
     p. cm.
  Includes bibliographical references and index.
  1. Decision making. 2. Leadership. I. Title.
  HD30.23.U82 2006
  658.4'03—dc22   2006013293

ISBN 978-1-4000-8299-5

Printed in the United States of America

Design by Lee Fukui and Mauna Eichner

10 9 8 7 6 5 4 3 2 1

First Paperback Edition

CONTENTS

THE
GO
POINT

Imagine for a moment that you are taken out of your normal day-to-day life and thrust as a wildland firefighter into the midst of a raging Colorado fire, becoming the de facto leader of a crew whose goal is to stop it from spreading. With scant information available about weather conditions, you urgently have to decide where your crew should go—up the mountain or down—and your forced choice has potential life-and-death consequences.

Or you are now on the bond trading floor at Lehman Brothers and you have to make multimillion-dollar buy or sell decisions that will have huge consequences not only for the profitability of your firm but also for your year-end bonus.

Or perhaps you are the new chief executive of Hewlett-Packard forced to clean up the mess left by your predecessor, who pushed through a decision to merge Compaq Computer company with your own struggling computer operation. Jobs are going to be cut, perhaps entire divisions dissolved. How do you decide who goes and what stays?

All of these are go points, times to decide, moments for saying yes or no, instants for jumping in one direction or another when the fate of others depends on it. How should you do it?

To master the art and practice of being decisive, our account will take you to some of the most daunting terrains on Earth—from a burning mountain in Montana to the highest mountain in the Himalayas, from a corporate boardroom to a Civil War battlefield, from troubled Tyco to surging Lenovo. But we will also witness people making less time-bound or momentous decisions: training astronauts, writing poetry, prepping a quarterback, leading a church, taking a job. And we will make four decisions of our own by applying what we have learned from those who have staked their companies, their careers, their countries on reaching the right decision.

The Go Point takes you inside the heart and head of people at their go point. And from their experience and that of our own we will build a decision-making template, the principles and tools for being decisive at times when it really counts: using small steps to make hard decisions, building a network of counselors for testing ideas, keeping options open until they must be closed.

This book is built on more than a hundred interviews and observations of leading decision makers, mostly conducted between 2002 and 2006. For the interviews, my approach has been to ask individuals to describe and analyze decisions they have made with consequences for those around and dependent upon them. What were their best and worst decisions, their most challenging ones? How did they reach them? What factors brought them to their individual go points? What would they change and what have they learned? During the interviews, generally sixty minutes in length but sometimes shorter and other times far longer, I kept detailed notes and often a digital recording.

I sought interviews with people from a broad cross section of professions and callings: a NASA astronaut, a Marine colonel, a thoracic surgeon, an Episcopal bishop, schoolteachers, corporate executives, Chinese entrepreneurs. A full listing follows. Many are not explicitly referenced in the book's text, but their experience and thinking are reflected throughout the book. The settings for the interviews ranged from executive suites to classrooms, trailsides, and training centers. I accompanied a wildland fire team as it fought a blaze in California, spent hours on the trading floor of an investment bank, and joined a daylong briefing by those who run the training program for astronauts at Houston's Johnson Space Center.

At times, I have also observed decision makers as they described, analyzed, or even engaged in decisions with consequences for others. And in some cases I was able to both observe and interview the individuals in question, sometimes on multiple occasions. All moments of observation were accompanied by detailed note taking and in some instances audio and even video recording.

High-profile figures such as Cisco Systems CEO John Chambers; General Peter Pace, chairman of the U.S. Joint Chiefs of Staff; former Hewlett-Packard CEO Carly Fiorina; Pakistan's President Pervez Musharraf; and New York Times Company chairman Arthur O. Sulzberger Jr. have shared or conveyed their decision-making experiences, but I have also looked in more out-of-the-way corners, where the decisions taken or avoided had dramatic consequences for those involved. I hiked a fire zone on Colorado's Storm King Mountain with seventeen professional firefighters, seeking to understand the chain of go points that had led an earlier group to be engulfed by a lethal blowup in 1994, and I talked with a survivor of a well-known airplane crash in the Andes.

In addition to the interviews, I have devoted more than fifty days to the on-site study of decision making by the Civil War commanders who fought at Gettysburg. Time and again I have walked that hallowed battlefield with managers and MBA students, accompanied by U.S. National Park Service licensed battlefield guides William Bowling, Hans Henzel, and Charles Fennell and, during one of those days, Civil War historian James M. McPherson.

As part of Wharton Leadership Ventures, I have also observed managers and MBA students making hundreds of decisions on everything from route finding to program restructuring in venues as far-flung as Patagonia and even Antarctica. In conjunction with a leadership development program for the Philadelphia public school system, I have informally discussed with teachers and administrators how they go about making decisions. Lessons in decision making, in go pointing, can be found literally everywhere.

In all these interviews and observations, I have looked for both recurrent themes and unique experiences across a range of organizations and even national boundaries. I have sought to extract what is most enduringly important for decision makers when they carry responsibility for others, regardless of the context. I have also drawn upon a broad range of research studies and historical accounts, some but not all cited in the pages of this text. The decision principles and tools identified here bear a huge debt to all those who have lent me their time, their experience, and their intellect.

DECISION MAKERS INTERVIEWED

The roster below identifies many though not all of the individuals whose decision-making experience I have drawn upon. Their title or position is at the time of the interview. Interviews marked with an asterisk can be found on *The Go Point*'s Web page at http://leadership. wharton.upenn.edu/TheGoPoint.

Decision Maker	Title or Position	Date
Advani, Deepak*	Senior vice president and chief marketing officer, Lenovo (China)	August 23, 2005
Ashby, Jeffrey S.	NASA astronaut	October 29, 2003
Barr, John*	Founder, managing director, and chair, SG Barr Devlin, and president, the Poetry Foundation	January 26 and February 2, 2005
Behrman, Grant	Founder and managing partner, Behrman Capital	October 1, 2004, November 11, 2005, and numerous other times
Bennison, Charles E., Jr.	Bishop, Episcopal Diocese of Pennsylvania	May 27, 2004
Bernard, Joe	Lieutenant colonel U.S. Marine Corps, Officer Candidates School, Quantico, Virginia	May 21, 2004
Boatner, Tom	Group manager, Fire Operations, National Office of Fire and Aviation, National Interagency Fire Center	July 19, 2001, January 25 and February 16, 2005
Bogle, John C.	Founder and retired CEO, Vanguard Group	January 18, 2002
Boitano, Aldo	Vertica SA (Chile and U.S.); K2 mountaineer	Numerous times, 1997–2005
Breen, Edward D., Jr.	Chairman and CEO, Tyco International	September 29 and December 20, 2005
Brennan, John J.	Chairman and CEO, Vanguard Group	March 15, 2004, July 28, 2005, and September 9, 2005

Decision Maker	Title or Position	Date
Buch, Madhabi Puri	Senior general manager, Product and Technology Group, ICICI Bank (India)	January 28, 2006
California Inter-agency Hot Shot Superintendents	Ten leaders of dedicated U.S. wildland firefighting teams	February 18, 2003
Canessa, Roberto	Pediatric cardiologist, Montevideo, Uruguay; survivor of 1972 air crash in the Andes	February 10 and 11, 2005
Carter, Larry	Chief financial officer, Cisco Systems	March 28, 2003
Cattano, Michael	Managing director, Corporate Bond Trading, Lehman Brothers	March 1, 2004
Chambers, John T.	President and CEO, Cisco Systems	March 28, 2003
Christensen, Johannah	Program manager, World Economic Forum	March 3, 2005
Cook, Jim	Training projects coordinator, U.S. Forest Service Fire Safety Office, National Interagency Fire Center	July 23–26, 2004, and numerous other dates
Cook, Wayne	Incident commander, Meadow Fire, Yosemite National Park	July 25, 2004
Cooper, Daniel	Chief operating officer, Department of Surgery, Hospital of the University of Pennsylvania	March 19, 2004
Crisson, Mark	Director of utilities, Tacoma Public Utilities	March 29, 2004

Decision Maker	Title or Position	Date
Crooke, Michael W.*	President and CEO, Patagonia, Inc.	February 20, 2005
Dillon, Steve	Guidance/flight control/propulsion instructor, space flight training, United Space Alliance	October 29, 2003, and April 12, 2004
Doehring, Sarah	Smokejumper, U.S. Forest Service	April 22 and 28, 2005, and other dates
Druskin, Robert	President and CEO, Global Corporate and Investment Banking Group, Citigroup	June 3, 2004
Elachi, Charles*	Director, Jet Propulsion Laboratory	February 3 and March 23, 2004
Fiorina, Carly	CEO, Hewlett-Packard	August 13, 2002, and March 28, 2003
Fuld, Richard S., Jr.	Chairman and CEO, Lehman Brothers	January 20, 2006
Grangaard, Paul	Head, private client services, Piper Jaffray	January 30, 2004
Heifetz, Ronald A.	Codirector of the Center for Public Leadership, Kennedy School, Harvard University	June 2, 2005
Higgins, Nancy M.	Executive vice president of ethics and business conduct, MCI	February 2, 2005
Hillary, Peter	Explorer and author	January 9 and June 9, 2005
Hund-Mejean, Martina	Senior vice president and treasurer, Tyco International	October 13, 2005

Decision Maker	Title or Position	Date
Irick, Jaime A.	Vice president, sales, Homeland Protection, General Electric Co.	June 4, 2005
Jones, Thomas W.	Chairman and CEO, Global Investment Management, Citigroup	June 3, 2004
Jordan, Rodrigo	President, Vertical SA (Chile); K2 mountaineer	Numerous times 1997–2005, most recently September 1, 2005
Kaiser, Larry R.	Surgeon-in-chief, Hospital of the University of Pennsylvania	May 25, 2004
Kamath, K. V.*	CEO, ICICI Bank (India)	January 5 and 26, 2005
Khatu, Satish	General manager, IBM ASEAN/South Asia	March 12, 2004
King, Al	Planning section chief, Meadow Fire; safety and prevention specialist, National Park Service and National Interagency Fire Center, Yosemite National Park	July 25, 2004
Krol, John A.	Former CEO, Dupont; lead director, Tyco International	October 18, 2005
Kurtz, Eric	Deputy operations chief, Meadow Fire, Yosemite National Park	July 25, 2004
Lester, Mark	Vice president, Clinical Excellence, St. Mary's Hospital, Saginaw, Michigan	June 29, 2005
Li, Dongsheng	Chairman and CEO, TCL (China)	March 2005

Decision Maker	Title or Position	Date
Liu, Chuanzhi*	Chairman, Lenovo Group (China)	August 16 and 30, 2004
Livermore, Ann M.	Executive vice president, Technology Solutions Group, Hewlett-Packard Company	February 2, 2005
Lykketoft, Mogens	Former Danish foreign minister and finance minister, leader of Danish Social Democrats	March 4, 2004
McPherson, James M.	Civil War historian, Princeton University	April 27, 2003
Means, Robert	Operations chief, Meadow Fire, Yosemite National Park	July 25, 2004
Miller, Richard S.	Senior vice president, Global Sales Operations and Government Sales, Lucent Technologies	April 15, 2004
Pace, Peter	Chairman of the U.S. Joint Chiefs of Staff; former vice chairman of the Joint Chiefs	February 9, 2006, December 6, 2005, December 9, 2003, and other occasions in 1999–02
Peterson, Peter G.	Senior chairman, Blackstone Group	February 9, 2004
Petrie, Dave	Guidance/flight control/propulsion instructor, Space Flight Training, United Space Alliance	October 29, 2003; April 12, 2004
Pillmore, Eric M.	Senior vice president, Corporate Governance, Tyco International	Numerous times in 2002–05

Decision Maker	Title or Position	Date
Platt, Lewis*	Chairman and then lead director, Boeing Company; former CEO, Hewlett-Packard	January 30, 2004; July 18, 2005
Pottruck, David S.	Former CEO, Charles Schwab Corporation; director, Intel Corporation	Numerous times in 2001–05, most recently on October 1 and November 3, 2005
Poulsen, Soren Moller	Colonel, Danish Air Force	June 8, 2005
Purcell, Miguel	Manager, Portillo Hotel, Chile; K2 mountaineer	September 2, 2005
Rachal, Louis	Commander, Officer Candidates School, U.S. Marine Corps	April 21, 2004
Rieder, Rick	Head, Global Credit Trading, Lehman Brothers	February 4 and March 1, 2004
Rodek, Jeffrey R.	Executive chairman, Hyperion Solutions	April 23, 2004
Rosso, Brit	Superintendent, Arrowhead Interagency Hotshot Crew	July 25, 2004
Russell, Ian	CEO, Scottish Power	March 8, 2004
Rust, Randy	Safety Office, Meadow Fire, Yosemite National Park	July 25, 2004
Scully, Steve	Program manager, EBS Dealing Resources	May 27 and June 3, 2005
Sekijima, Yasuo	President, Hitachi Institute of Management Development	November 11, 2004

Decision Maker	Title or Position	Date
Sulzberger, Arthur O., Jr.	Chairman and publisher, the New York Times Company	January 3–10, 2004
Sutton, Larry	Training unit leader, U.S. Bureau of Land Management, National Interagency Fire Center	Numerous times in 2002–5
Thomson, Todd S.*	Chairman and CEO, Global Wealth Management Group, Citigroup; former CFO, Citigroup	Numerous times in 2004–6, most recently on January 28, 2006
Unruh, James A.	Chairman and CEO, Unisys Corporation	1995
Unwin, Roger	CEO, National Grid Transco	May 14, 2004
Watkins, Sherron	Former vice president, Enron Corporation	Numerous times in 2002–4
Willumstad, Robert B.	President and chief operating officer, Citigroup	June 4, 2004
Wuchner, Gary P.	Fire captain, Orange County Fire Authority; Information Officer, Meadow Fire, Yosemite National Park	July 25, 2004
Zhang, Ruimin*	Chairman and CEO, Haier Group Company	February 20, 2005

I have also participated in a wide range of instructional programs, company meetings, and conferences in the United States, Asia, Europe, and Latin America where the presentation or discussion topics included decision making that impacts other people. During these events, I have often engaged in one-on-one discussions with participants, asking them about their own decisions and those of others in their organization. I frequently compiled detailed notes on their observations and experiences. The organizations, groups, and companies that I had opportunity to observe or witness in such settings include:

Accenture

American Public Power
   Association

American Public Transportation
   Association

American Society of
   Ophthalmic Administrators

ASIS International

Association for Human
   Resources Management in
   International Organizations
   (United Nations)

AstraZeneca

Aventis

Aviva

Axcel Company

Bank of America

Behrman Capital

Berwind Group

Blank Rome LLP

Blockbuster

Brazilian medical doctors via
   Unimed

Cendant/Coldwell Banker

Centocor

CEO Academy

Checkpoint Systems

Chilean managers via
   Seminarium

Chinese Securities Association

Chubb

Cisco Systems

Coca-Cola

Coldwell Banker

Cooper Health Systems

Credit Union Executives Society

DaimlerChrysler

Danish Defense Forces

Danish managers via DIEU (Copenhagen, Denmark)

Degussa

Delta Dental

Deutsche Post World Net

Eli Lilly

Federated Department Stores

Fidelity Investments

General Cologne Re

General Mills

Girl Scouts of the USA

GlaxoSmithKline

Goldman Sachs Young Leaders Program

H&R Block

Hearst Corporation

ICICI (India)

ImBev

Indian School of Business

Institute for Private Investors

Institute of Business Travel Management

Johnson & Johnson

Kimberly-Clark

KPMG

LG Electronics

LIMRA International

McGraw-Hill

Merrill Lynch

Mexican managers via HSM

Michigan State University

Morgan Stanley

Pacific Coast Builders

Peruvian managers via Seminarium (Santiago, Chile)

Philadelphia public school teachers and administrators

Philips Medical Systems

Piper Jaffray

Pitney Bowes

PricewaterhouseCoopers

Principal Financial Group

Radian Group

Royal Dutch/Shell Group of Companies

Sanofi Aventis

Scotia Bank

Scottish Power

Seattle Pacific University

Securities Industry Association

Shanghai Municipal
    Government

Singapore General Hospital

Singapore Management
    University

State Farm Insurance

Stockholm School of
    Economics

TeleDenmark (TDC)

Textron

Thai managers via Sasin
    Graduate School of Business
    Administration of
    Chulalongkorn University

Thomson

Toyota

United Healthcare

University of Ulster

U.S. Marine Corps

U.S. Military Academy

U.S. Naval Academy

U.S. Veterans Administration

VF Corporation

Women's World Banking

World Economic Forum annual
    meetings in Davos,
    Switzerland

Wyeth

Yamanouchi

In addition, I have devoted a number of days to visiting and learning directly from a host of institutions that depend upon or train people on making decisions. These include the National Interagency Fire Center in Boise, Idaho; NASA's Johnson Space Center near Houston, Texas; Army War College at Carlisle, Pennsylvania; and the 2004 Meadow Fire in Yosemite National Park.

During the fall of 2004, collaborating with colleague Andy Zelleke, I conducted interviews with board chairs, nonexecutive directors, chief executives, chief financial officers, executive vice presidents, general counsels, and corporate secretaries of thirty-one large publicly traded companies. In these interviews, we focused on decision making in governing boards. Since we completed those interviews with a promise of confidentiality, neither the individuals nor their companies can be identified here, but their experience figures prominently in these pages as well.[1]

During the completion of this book, I also consulted with three companies on corporate governance—Tyco International in 2002, Fannie Mae in 2004, and HealthSouth in 2005—and those experiences provided helpful insights into how decisions are made in corner offices and boardrooms.

INTRODUCTION

Deciding with Consequences for Others

As a professor and director of the Center for Leadership and Change Management at the Wharton School of the University of Pennsylvania, I have spent more than a decade studying and interacting with influential men and women at the center of events, and I have become convinced that one of the most unexplored and underdeveloped aspects of leadership is the art and science of decision making: art because decision making depends upon hunches and intuition, science because it also needs to be disciplined and analytical.

We all want to make the best possible decisions, for ourselves and on behalf of others. That is obvious. Good decisions build our assets, boost our careers, burnish our reputations. In sports, natural talent can carry a quarterback to the National Football League, but good decision making—when to pass and when to pull the ball down and run for the sidelines—determines who starts and who watches from the bench. In a corporate setting, the ability to make clear, crisp, timely decisions can label us a go-to person, the individual that others rely upon to start a program or introduce a product.

Yet if no one wants to make bad decisions, plenty of us do, every day, in sometimes spectacular ways. We introduce an Edsel; we take the wrong job or hire an incompetent person for a critical post. Unforced errors spoil tennis victories and shared dreams; smart plays win games and build futures. The question is how best to prevent the unforced errors and make the right shots.

In my own classroom, I directly witness the tangible difference between good and bad decisions when I ask MBA students and midcareer managers to divide into teams, then build an airline through a computer simulation based on the real experience of a 1980s start-up phenom, People Express. The simulated experience requires participants to make just a handful of decisions—how many aircraft to acquire, what price to charge, how many employees to hire—over nine years, yet the cumulative effect of those few decisions is vast. When teams make too many poor decisions, they find themselves face-to-face with an abrupt collapse, much as the real People Express experienced. When their decisions are made well, they can build an airline worth hundreds of million of dollars. The best teams have managed to create an enterprise with a market value well over a billion dollars. Since the sole difference between prosperity and insolvency was decision quality, the results of good choices—and bad ones—become starkly evident.

DECIDING FOR MORE
THAN OURSELVES

For most of us, the decision-making equipment is generally pretty sound, at least in broad terms. We do not follow the lead lemming over a cliff. We cannot be fooled into thinking that a 99-cent lure is a meal. Nor do we try to catch car fenders with our teeth (although it was not a dog who launched New Coke).[1]

Where decisions are concerned, though, there are a few built-in bugs—design flaws of the mind—that can have big consequences.

People are overly optimistic, for instance, assigning zero probability to events that are merely unlikely, such as a massive iceberg in the path of a really big ship, or the rupturing of a levee in the aftermath of a category four hurricane. We see "patterns" in the random movements of stocks the way our ancestors saw bears and hunters in the scatterplot of the night sky. We make choices that justify our past choices and then look for data to support them. Not only do we make these errors, we make them reliably. But that is the good news. Predictable errors are preventable errors. And the simple principles and tools developed in these pages can help us steer clear of the most common wrong turns.

The tools that follow are applicable to most decisions, from those that affect only individuals (what doctor to see, whether to buy a house) to those that determine the fate of entire nations (whether to invade or hold back). But the principles have been derived primarily by focusing on *decisions that have consequences for others,* those moments when an individual with responsibility faces a discrete, tangible, and realistic opportunity to commit enterprise resources to one course or another on behalf of collective objectives, or alternatively to make no commitment at all, a nondecision that is also a choice whether consciously recognized or not. These are the moments when the stakes are highest and when the most useful ideas emerge, and for that reason it is where I have chosen to focus attention.

The Go Point

Ultimately, every decision comes down to a *go point*—that decisive moment when the essential information has been gathered, the pros and cons are weighed, and the time has come to get off the fence. The go point is not always a matter of "getting to yes." If the managers at Morton Thiokol had gotten to no back in 1986 when they debated whether the O-rings in their booster rockets would work in cold weather, a New Hampshire schoolteacher and six fellow astronauts on

Challenger most likely would have launched on a later, warmer mission date. Rather, the go point is that instant when the choice gets made, whether no or yes, and the commitment moves from consideration to action. How you jump at that moment can make a vast difference, not only for yourself but also for all around you.[2]

People "make their own history," Karl Marx famously observed, yet "they do not make it under circumstances chosen by themselves, but under circumstances directly encountered, given and transmitted from the past." True enough. Every decision arguably is to a greater or lesser degree a product of our history, of the culture we exist in, and of other circumstances not wholly of our making. Within those constraints, though, go points present us with the opportunity to shape our own destiny, sometimes dramatically so. In Robert Frost's well-known verse "Two roads diverged in a wood, and I— / I took the one less traveled by, / And that has made all the difference."[3]

Astronauts Christa McAuliffe, Ellison Onizuka, and Gregory Jarvis on their way to the *Challenger.*

At times, our go points can even constitute points of divergence that change the fate of institutions and nations. Would Orlando be anything like it is today without Disney World? What if Al Gore had won in Florida? Or imagine what America and Russia and the planet itself might be like today if Nikita Khrushchev had chosen not to turn back Soviet ships at the height of the Cuban missile crisis.

No wonder authors as divergent as Philip Roth *(The Plot Against America),* Robert Harris *(Fatherland),* and Harry Turtledove *(The Guns of the South)* have found the alternative history such an appealing fiction form. All those what-if's—if Robert E. Lee had won at Gettysburg, Franklin Delano Roosevelt had kept the United States neutral in World War II, Lee Harvey Oswald had never pulled the trigger, the 9/11 attackers had been stopped by airport security—remind us how vital reaching the right decision can be, especially when it carries consequences for others.[4]

URGENT DECISIONS

All decisions entail reaching a go point, but getting there depends upon the nature of the terrain. As with orienteering, the beginning of go point wisdom is recognizing where you are. Like any continuum, the decision terrain has virtually endless gradations, but many decisions bunch into two big clusters, each imposing a distinct set of demands. The first cluster includes decisions imposed by deadlines not of one's own choosing; the second, decisions without clear deadlines at all.

Many decisions must be taken *now*. When there is no choice but to make a choice, the ticking of the clock concentrates the mind and forces resolution. Imagine that you're facing tennis pro Andy Roddick as he is delivering his serve at better than 150 miles an hour. The ball crosses the net as fast as an Indy racer but is small enough to fit into an Indy tailpipe. But speed is only one factor. Which part of the court is the ball heading toward? And which way is it spinning? Will it bounce high or low, kick left or right? Think of anything else as you are waiting to receive it, let yourself be distracted by the slightest stray thought, and you will never see the ball skid by.

Bond traders face a similar go point measured in just seconds. Delay an extra tick to make the call, and the price of a bond is out of reach. Jump too soon and you miss a market rally. One bond trader that I interviewed for this book instructed her family never to phone during trading hours since she was incapable of focusing on anything but the tiny, fleeting spreads on the screen in front of her.[5]

Now imagine that you are responsible for a whole floor of bond traders, any of whom can make or lose you millions with a click of the mouse. Orchestrated well, their instant decisions are the stuff of a great quarter; led poorly, their actions can become a company disaster. Investment banker Rick Rieder arrives at his midtown Manhattan office by 6 a.m. most days, responsible for fixed-income trading at Lehman Brothers. There he oversees a vast trading operation, with more than 125 traders betting billions on bond movements every day. So extreme is his day's concentration that on his evening commute home Rieder used to sometimes find himself flummoxed by thruway tollbooths. After twelve hours of total absorption in rapid-fire decision making with fortunes on the table, Rieder had trouble mustering himself to dig out the few coins needed for passage. E-ZPass, he said, saved the day.

Or try imagining yourself working in a business that supports millisecond decisions. Created by a consortium of a dozen premier banks, EBS provides more than two thousand foreign-exchange and precious-metal traders in forty countries with the technology to trade $110 billion in foreign currencies every day. The statistics are startling: more than half of the fifty thousand daily transactions—averaging $2 million per trade but some reaching $100 million—are completed in less than half a second, 95 percent within one second. The typical trade, in fact, requires just 485 milliseconds to complete. In a small fraction of the trades, a black box makes the decision automatically, without human intervention, but most deals still remain the province of people who are having to place huge bets in seconds or less. A big day for a single trader can occasionally entail total deal making of more than $5 billion. To service this world of near-instant human decision making, EBS reports a completed transaction to its customers—say, the price of swapping a big batch of dollars for euros—within 170 milliseconds. In response to one bank's request, the company is working to shave another 20 milliseconds from even that wafer-thin time slice.[6]

These urgent, flick-of-a-switch decisions—the first big cluster—

are time-driven, recurrent, and unrelenting. They require an ability to live by the clock, execute rapidly, and remain steadfast under intense stress.

DELIBERATIVE CALLS

At the other end of the spectrum are decisions with ambiguous deadlines, or even none at all: to alter a career plan, or launch a new product, or transform a policy. The go point cannot be deferred forever, but it can be reached today or put off until tomorrow or put on ice for weeks, even months or years. One rising manager told me that he knew another division at his company was being woefully underled and was certain he could do a better job. Getting the job, though, meant he had to not only evict a longtime colleague but also master an unfamiliar market. With no cutoff date looming and with hard work and unpleasant confrontations blocking his path, the manager needed six months to finally reach the go point on this career change.

On the surface, these slow-to-emerge decisions seem like the easier ones to make. The results can be just as consequential as clock-driven choices, but there is no heat of the moment to force the action. Instead, time exists to study all the angles, hear from all the stakeholders. As we have all experienced, though, the luxury of consideration also can turn into a trap. Absent natural triggers, the situation we are hoping to resolve festers around us until something—often unpleasant—finally forces us to action.

L. Paul Bremer III, the U.S. administrator in Iraq, faced just such a situation in the spring of 2003 following the ouster of Saddam Hussein's brutal regime. Bremer's ultimate goal was the creation of a constitution that would lead to democratic self-rule for the Iraqi people, but for months upon months, the Iraqi Governing Council found itself unable to agree even on a procedure for drafting the new constitution. Given the turbulent and oft-violent aftermath of Saddam's removal, the lack of agreement came as no surprise, but without a document to build a new government on, there was no way to move toward self-rule. Finally, Bremer created an artificial go point. On November 15, 2003, he declared that the United States would transfer sovereignty to Iraq seven and a half months later, on June 30, 2004. By implication, the quarreling factions would have to reconcile their differences by then and get on with the task of writing the constitution and deciding how to govern.[7]

Learning by Witnessing

How does anyone master the art and science of good and timely decisions? One fruitful path is to study the standard pitfalls of decision making—what two researchers have aptly termed "decision traps." A mound of research, for example, tells us that sunk costs should not stand in the way of clearheaded thinking about the future. Studying the classic tools involved in making good decisions—what other researchers have termed "smart choices"—is a fertile companion path. Again, numerous studies show that quality information is vital to good judgment when reaching a go point. Less obviously, research also shows that intuition informed by past experience—basically, educated guesses—can be an equally reliable guide for action, especially when the pressure is on.[8]

A second learning path is to make decisions and then unflinchingly reflect upon then. This method is used to great advantage by the U.S. Marine Corps in preparing its next generation of leadership. During months of intense training in the vast Marine base at Quantico, Virginia, future officers are asked to take hundreds of decisions and then to dissect, parse, and inspect them in after-action reviews. If too many choices are disastrously made, the candidates wash out. For those who survive, this relentless preparation in making, reviewing, and learning from their decisions prepares officers for the solemn responsibility of leading others into combat.[9]

A third course is to witness or review what others have done in reaching their decisions and then extract what is most useful from them. Why, for example, did Robert E. Lee decide on the eve of July 3, 1863, to order what became known as Pickett's Charge—a desperate race across an open field with Union muskets and cannons blazing from behind a stone wall? Only Lee himself, of course, could have said for sure, but by dissecting his choice, we see the stakes of decision making in profound relief at one of the great turning points of American history.[10]

All three methods have validity, and I draw on each in these pages. But the dozens of MBA courses that I have taught and the management programs on leadership and decision making I have led have convinced me that one of the most powerful and enduring ways to learn decision making is to study what others have done—on location whenever and wherever possible, walking the very decision terrain that others have walked before us—and then to take lessons from that experience for oneself.

I have accompanied groups into the Himalayas as we have tried to understand the choices that led to great conquests and great suffering in the desperately thin air above 20,000 feet. We have studied such moments in management programs that I have undertaken in Argentina and Chile and Brazil, in China, India, and Japan. And in the company of executives from companies such as AstraZeneca, General Mills, and Merrill Lynch, I have walked the very ground Pickett's men charged across, probing how such a consummate field general as Lee could have made such a disastrous call. Along with professionals from a host of U.S. agencies, I have also walked ground zero and mission control. And always I have found that this hands-on learning drives home the lessons of decision making most effectively and best arms participants with the necessary principles and tools for making their own decisions.[11]

EXPERIENCE COUNTS

Today, Tom Boatner is responsible for sending thousands of firefighters across the United States to attack forest and grassland fires, but virtually every choice he makes in the swirl of combating one of nature's most unpredictable and dangerous phenomena traces back to a time more than a quarter century earlier when a raging fire threatened an Alaskan farming community.

It was June 1977 when Boatner jumped down from the back of a truck, not far from three fast-moving forest fires in an area bordering Delta Junction, a remote hamlet in the shadow of the Alaska Range. The fires had erupted when violent winds from the range swept across slash-pile fires set by local residents, scattering burning embers into nearby forests.

Tom Boatner.

Called in to stop the fires' spread, Boatner and his dozen fellow firefighters arrived near 5 p.m. with their trademark axe, the Pulaski, at the ready. "We were all incredibly excited and wound up because it was the first fire of the year, and we heard the wind was blowing hard and the fires were really moving," Boatner told me as he reconstructed events. A darkened sky swirled with dust, smoke, and cinders as the firefighters clambered out of their trucks in the middle of a recently cleared field. Some residents were rushing off in broken-down pickups; others dashed over to help.

"I was filled with adrenaline. I wanted to grab my Pulaski and haul ass to the nearest smoke and start to cut a line and fight the fire," Boatner said. Still a college student, just twenty years old, he had worked one prior summer as a firefighter, but he was about to meet a seasoned fire hand who would change forever his decision-making matrix for evaluating and fighting a wildland blaze.

Robert Burritt.

The fire supervisor was Robert Burritt, all of twenty-nine years old himself but already a veteran of the business. His steady demeanor, Boatner remembers of first seeing him, stood in complete contrast to the eager but inexperienced firefighters rushing around him—and the fires surging around them. "He was very quiet and he was very calm, and he was looking around and he wasn't saying much," Boatner recalled. "I just wanted to scream at him and say, 'Come on, let's go, we gotta do something!' "

Burritt was witness to the same frenzied scene and could sense the anxiety flowing around him, but he carried a decision template that pointed to a vastly different response. Rather than rush to attack the blaze, the supervisor meticulously extracted the data he felt he needed from the crew and residents, and then methodically planned how best to suppress the blaze.

"Bill," he instructed one crew leader, "you take your crew to that spiral over there on the hilltop, anchor in, and have your crew start flanking. Scout the fire and call me in fifteen minutes with an update on what's happening and what we need to catch the fire." And then to another, "Joe, you take your crew to that fire on the bottom of this field and do the same thing." And to a third, "Fred, you go tie in with that [bull]dozer and that volunteer fire department and see where they're at on that third fire." After several further instructions to still other crews, Burritt finally gave the nod: "Okay, go to work and call me when you have better information!"

Burritt had taken barely fifteen minutes to steady the team, appraise the fire, and plan the attack. By doing so, Boatner remembers, he "had turned this totally chaotic, frenzied group into a very calm, deliberate group of people who all knew the same information about what was going on, what the plan was for everybody, and what their own part was in the plan." Backed by a good strategy and Burritt's continued steady guidance, Boatner and his fellow firefighters aggressively fought the blazes through the night and well into the next day. Just twenty-four hours after arriving, they had reduced the inferno to smoldering ash.

For Tom Boatner, it proved an indelible incident. Nearly two decades later, in June 1996, he was back in Alaska, now responsible for operations on what became known as the Miller's Reach Fire, an enormous blaze requiring the deployment of more than fifteen hundred firefighters and nearly two dozen helicopters and air tankers. During his first hours on the ground, Boatner concluded that it was the most hazardous assignment that he had ever received; the potential for fatalities had never been greater. But, harking back to Burritt's behavior years earlier, he remembered, "I needed to transmit to all of the people engaged in the firefight how critical it was to be calm and to be confident and to be very deliberate in what we were doing. It was an incredibly dangerous situation we were in. If we weren't totally on top of our game, people would die."[12]

By the time this fire was brought under control two weeks later, it had destroyed more than 37,000 acres and 350 homes. But thanks to Tom Boatner's go point methods that had first been shaped by Robert Burritt all those years earlier, his firefighters did stay on top of their game, evacuating more than three thousand residents with no fatalities or even serious injuries and finally suppressing one of the worst blazes in Alaskan history.

During nearly thirty years of public service, Tom Boatner has led crews into well over 250 wildland fires of virtually every possible description. And during them all, the image of Robert Burritt coolly making decisions on a hot Alaskan field was never far from Boatner's mind when he faced his own decision point.

There is a world of education to be had in walking with Tom Boatner over the terrains where he has battled blazes—an education in how decision making can be both urgent *and* deliberate, and one that extends far beyond the rarefied work of firefighters. That cannot be done literally through the medium of a book, but I will do my best in these pages to put readers where the action is—where the decisions are taken—and allow you to see events unfold through the eyes of the participants.

DECISION TEMPLATES: PRINCIPLES AND TOOLS YOU CAN USE

Robert Burritt arrived on the battlefield with a well-developed decision template, a set of personal concepts for making consequential decisions. That template is what Tom Boatner glimpsed momentarily that first time in Alaska and then embraced forever. Boatner saw Burritt calmly assaying the pandemonium around him and conveying that the plan of attack should come from deliberate decisions, not a flick of the switch, and he made it a life principle.

By looking closely at decisions being made under sometimes extraordinary conditions and by digging out the principles, good and bad, that emerge from such tangible experience, we can begin to build our own decision templates for guiding our own go points.

One size does not fit all in templates any more than it does in suits or shoes. To be truly useful, a decision template should be generic enough to apply to many situations, yet specific enough to provide real guidance with real-life choices. More than a step-by-step guide to action, the template provides a set of prompts, reminders of what to keep in mind when facing a range of consequential decisions. But a truly useful decision template also needs to reflect the history and culture and predilections of its bearer. I will provide the broad outline in the chapters that follow, but readers should use my templates as a starter menu for refining their own, personal collections.

To be most informative and to take root at the deepest level, decision templates need to be accompanied by two special features. First, each of the template principles should be rooted in tangible experience, for that often serves as the most enduring and powerful trigger. Years later, Tom Boatner still anchors his own calmness and his determination not to rush to judgment in the image of the motionless Robert Burritt among the enveloping chaos. My own experience with hands-on learning as well as volumes of research confirm that principles such as these are best retained and recalled when discovered during moments of intense emotion and acute stress. Embedded in experience, they remain unforgettable.

Second, each of the decision principles should also be accompanied by decision tools, tactical steps that transform ideas into action. Tom Boatner recognized that the principle of staying cool and analytic required translation into what he did on the ground. And here he came to appreciate that unruffled demeanor at a crisis moment calmed others in ways that words could not; it was a tool that helped him convert his mental concept into his actual behavior.

These decision principles and tools, I am convinced, are essential vehicles for translating ideas into action, one of the most challenging features of human behavior, especially in making decisions with consequences for others. Too often, we understand and voice high-minded management concepts such as thinking strategically, then forget to do so when faced with a tangible decision.

Organizational researchers Jeffrey Pfeffer and Robert Sutton have termed this disconnect between concept and behavior the "knowing-doing gap." They write that company managers "say so many smart things about how to achieve performance, work so hard, yet are trapped in firms that do so many things they know will undermine performance." People recurrently "knew what to do, but didn't do," and the gap between knowing and doing, they conclude, is "one of the most important and vexing barriers to organizational performance." I believe that the same barrier applies to reaching a go point, and I hope this book will help readers leap it.[13]

THE ENRON TRAP

I can recall so vividly when Kenneth Lay spoke of the lessons of his leadership and decision making at the World Economic Forum in Davos, Switzerland, on February 3, 1997. Joining the chairman and chief executive officer of Enron Corporation were luminaries from the apex of European business: Percy Barnevik of the Swiss engineering firm ABB Asea Brown Boveri, Heinrich von Pierer of the German manufacturing firm Siemens, and Cor A. J. Herkstroter of the great energy firm Royal Dutch Petroleum Company.

As a personal witness to the event, I was deeply impressed by Lay's account of how he had transformed Enron from a small pipeline company into a powerhouse energy provider. Others in the audience seemed particularly attentive to the concepts that he offered as well. Lay's star was so ascendant that he seemed to walk on the same water as did Microsoft's Bill Gates, Intel's Andy Grove, and other celebrities who graced the hallways in Davos that year.

In early 2001, Lay passed his CEO title on to Jeffrey Skilling, while remaining executive chairman. Impressed by what we were hearing about Enron's creative methods and remarkable growth, I and several faculty colleagues invited Skilling to serve as an exemplary subject in a required leadership course that we offered our incoming MBA students in the fall of 2001. All eight hundred students were to read about Lay, Skilling, and the rise of Enron, and then Skilling would visit the school for a day, tell his story, and serve as a living case from which our students would learn leadership. From our perspective, this seemed a golden moment in the making. *Fortune* magazine had recently named Enron as one of the world's twenty-five most admired companies, and number one for innovativeness.[14]

When Jeffrey Skilling resigned from Enron on August 14, 2001, his office cryptically notified us that he would be unable to come to Wharton in the fall. We were stunned, since we had already prepared the course syllabus with Skilling's visit featured as one of its highlights. Little did I appreciate in Switzerland in early 1997 or even in the United States in early 2001 that behind Lay's and Skilling's public leadership and decision accounts were entirely contrary behaviors. While they stressed integrity and touted Enron's ethics code as exemplary, they were at the very same time asking the Enron board to suspend its code of ethics to permit the formation of the special-purpose entities that would bring the company to bankruptcy on December 2, 2001.[15]

I suspect that Lay and Skilling believed in their code of ethics as a concept, but their actions did not reflect that understanding. They and their company suffered from an acute knowing-doing gap that helped bring the house down. For me, learning about that gap strengthened an item on my own decision template, namely, the need to check to make sure that reality matches appearance before making a decision based on the latter. For all of us, though, I think, Enron and Kenneth Lay and Jeffrey Skilling are, in effect, a kind of continuing morality play about the power of wrong decisions to destroy lives—in this instance their own and those of Enron's ill-fated shareholders and employees—and the need to build templates that can help us get beyond moments of temptation to the high decision ground of what really matters in business and in life.

The organizational theorist John Van Maanen likes to talk about the value of allegory as a message "being conveyed in writing through the narration of a most concrete set of events." Literary theorists have described allegory as symbols rising vertically from the narrative and moving horizontally through it. This book walks much the same ground. I have used narratives of characters and events—as close as we can come to directly experiencing the events within the pages of a book—to make the decision principles and tools as indelible and tangible as possible for getting to the right go points.[16]

1

In the Heat of the Moment

At 4 p.m. on August 5, 1949, Wagner Dodge and his crew of sixteen parachuted into the remote Montana wilderness at Mann Gulch to combat what seemed to be a routine forest fire. By 5:56 p.m., all but three of the firefighters were dead, fatally burned—then the worst disaster in the history of the U.S. Forest Service and one caught memorably by Norman Maclean in *Young Men and Fire*.[1]

Forty-five years later, on July 6, 1994, Donald Mackey was helping to oversee a team of forty-nine firefighters spread out on Storm King Mountain in Colorado. Some of the group had parachuted onto the mountain that day; others had come by helicopter, still others by foot. Again, it looked like a routine fire, and again, the fire proved that it is always a mistake to treat any backcountry blaze as routine. By four o'clock in the afternoon of July 6, the Mann Gulch disaster seemed about to repeat itself.

In both cases, bad luck and a fatal confluence of environmental factors contributed to the flaming ambush of the firefighters, but individual decisions were critical in each instance. At Mann Gulch as at Storm King, those most directly responsible on site faced a sequence of decision points during their fateful hours in the fire zone, and their decisions at those moments helped take their teams to the brink of disaster and beyond.

Wildland fires are a special circumstance, and wildland firefighters— the men and women who parachute, helicopter, or trek in to fight them—a special breed. But while the conditions are unique, the experience of those who fight fires in the outdoors has much to teach us all about decision making indoors, especially when there is little room for error or delay. The go points their crew leaders reach and the consequences that follow are unusually clear-cut and consequential for the goals of the enterprise. And like so many critical business decisions, fire decisions brutally punish those who do not keep both the big picture and small detail well in mind.

The blaze that raged over Colorado's Storm King Mountain on July 5 and 6, 1994, in what has come to be known as the South Canyon fire, has been the subject of extensive official study and secondary analysis, including one by Norman Maclean's son, John, who chronicled the fire's course and the efforts to combat it in *Fire on the Mountain*. Thus, we have an exceptionally well-documented record of the decisions taken by those responsible for the firefighters on the mountain.[2]

In analyzing the record, I do not seek to criticize anyone involved or to affix blame for the disaster that occurred on any one individual. Whether they survived the blaze or not, the wildland firefighters who assembled on Storm King Mountain were heroes: they placed themselves in harm's way to protect others, and some paid the ultimate price. But firefighters also feel it is their duty to unflinchingly examine past tragedies to determine what decisions went wrong so they can prevent similar calamities in the future. In that spirit and from their bravery come enduring lessons in the art and science of decision making whatever the zone.

THE BASICS: SAFETY, SPEED, AND SUPPRESSION

In attacking wilderness fires, firefighters traditionally form into crews ranging from three to twenty members. The crews are rapidly deployed, combining with other crews to combat larger fires and then just as quickly breaking up and redeploying to other incidents. As might be expected of their organizational chart, crew leaders operate both collaboratively and independently, but during multiple-crew blazes, as was the case in the South Canyon fire, one individual of necessity should assume clear and authoritative responsibility. As we shall shortly see, that did not happen on Storm King Mountain.

"On any incident, large or small," states one of the basic fire service manuals, "the Incident Commander has ultimate responsibility for the effective and safe execution" of all aspects of the attack. The commander's duties place a premium on ensuring that decisions optimally contribute to the three primary goals of firefighting: safety, speed, and suppression.[3]

Always, the premier criterion for decision making by fire crew leaders and incident commanders is the safety of their team. Even though physical peril looms large whenever crews are called in, fatal injuries are no more tolerable in firefighting than is fraudulent accounting in business or bogus stories in journalism. Yet since risk is always present, wildland fire leaders must be able to appraise it and take appropriate steps toward mitigation.

The second criterion for crew leaders and incident commanders is speed. Firefighting is a world of decision urgency. Hesitation and equivocation can do more than delay a solution: they can radically compound the problem. In product markets, the short term can be months; in stock markets, days; in fire zones, hours or even less. A 10-acre fire—small potatoes in the wildfire playbook—if not quickly suppressed can explode in minutes into a 1,000-acre conflagration. "Make sound and timely decisions," the official firefighters' manual exhorts, with good cause.[4]

The final criterion for decision making in a fire zone is a set of technical considerations to actually suppress the fire: How many firefighters are required? Where should a fire line be constructed? What aerial reconnaissance is needed? On such technical calls can hang the fate of both the zone's natural resources and the men and women who seek to preserve them.

Winding around all these matters and never separate from them are the shifting conditions of the wilderness fires. It is not in the nature of blazes to sit still, and each new shift in the fire can create new and dangerous microclimates—powerful winds, intense heat—that further complicate suppression. An incident commander or crew leader who makes the right choices, handles them quickly, and anticipates correctly where the fire might suddenly go and where his crew should subsequently be achieves the primary purpose of the business: "fight fire aggressively but provide for safety first." Make the wrong choices, make them too late, and all hell can break loose.[5]

WHEN "CAN DO" IS NOT ENOUGH: PREPARING FOR DECISION MAKING

Wildland firefighters often assume leadership roles with little warning, in venues that are always new. Military leaders, of course, are called to do the same: freshly commissioned officers commanding soldiers in combat, for example, or seasoned officers taking troops onto an unknown battlefield. But unlike graduates of the military academies or war colleges, where leadership decisions have a central place in the curriculum, newly appointed wildfire incident commanders traditionally have taken charge with little or no formal preparation in leadership decisions. Indeed, prior to the South Canyon fire, the responsible federal agencies offered virtually no coursework in how to make decisions when lives depend on them.[6]

Poor preparation predictably leads to poor choices. Consider one large adversary of good decisions: overconfidence, a moment when a responsible decision maker believes that a decision outcome is more likely than the factual situation would predict. Business studies have found that excessive audacity is most prevalent when managers face decisions on products and markets with which they are least familiar. In one such study, two researchers examined confidence among product managers of small computer software and hardware firms when they introduced radically new products to the market. The more pioneering the new products—and thus the less familiar the market— the more the product managers were likely to view the prospects for success through rose-colored glasses.[7]

Firefighters constantly forced to make snap decisions in unfamiliar terrain face the same challenges. The less they have been prepared for a responsible decision-making role, the more a natural can-do attitude takes over. Without a pool of experience to back them up— experience in firefighting *and* in decision making—incident commanders sometimes latch onto a flawed firefighting strategy, certain that "we can make it work." In the rapidly changing world of a racing fire, a can-do attitude is both essential and potentially dangerous.

In the Heat of the Moment: Acute Stress and Decision Making

Wildland fires can reach 2,500 degrees Fahrenheit, race forward at speeds up to 25 miles per hour—a gold-medal speed in the Olympics'

100-meter event—and leap overhead without warning. At their most dangerous, such fires are said to "blow up," an inflection point when they acquire a manic momentum of their own. Like avalanches and tornadoes, a blowup is one of nature's most terrifying spectacles, one reason tension is ever present in a fire zone. For crew leaders and incident commanders, those who carry personal responsibility for the lives of others, the resulting tension can become acute. The more severe the stress, the less optimal decisions are likely to be just at a time when they are becoming most consequential.

Research confirms that individuals under time pressure or performing simultaneous multiple tasks are more prone to indulge in poor decision making for a host of reasons including a reluctance to search for relevant information. Studies also demonstrate that the adverse effects of underpreparation on decision making become most pronounced in the most severe conditions. In short, the two enemies of optimal decisions—poor preparation and great stress—are particularly pernicious when combined.[8]

In studying urban firefighter captains and lieutenants, Fred Fiedler found that while seasoned officers actually improved their performance under the stress of a fire, less prepared ones went in the opposite direction. The same is true of responsible officers on aircraft carrier flight decks. According to research by Karl Weick and Karlene Roberts, the officers were more likely to commit errors during stressful landing episodes when their collective mindfulness and mutual heedfulness were insufficiently developed or became impaired by the rush of events. John Salka, a battalion chief with the New York Fire Department, spoke from his own twenty-five years on the front lines when he urged fire managers to pay particular attention to their inner voice—if well educated—when taking decisions under stress. For "making the right call when the heat is on," Salka writes, "intuition is really your subconscious trying to offer up the benefits of a lifetime's worth of experience."[9]

Drawing on extensive investigation of those facing difficult decision points, Gary Klein concluded likewise that intuition—if well honed and informed by experience—improves decision making, especially in the heat of the moment. Note the "well-honed" and "informed" part of that. Decision experience helps one compile a mental reference library that sends up a special alert when conditions look bad. It is what you call on when the ground is shifting beneath your feet and there is little time left to reason things out for yourself and for those depending on you. Unfortunately, in South Canyon on July 6, 1994, well-honed and informed decision capacities were in short supply.[10]

WHO'S IN CHARGE? AMBIGUOUS AUTHORITY AND LEADERSHIP DECISIONS

The decision-making burden on fire leaders is made even greater by three organizational factors that are especially prevalent in combating wildland blazes. First, crew leaders guide a workforce that is largely seasonal since fires are by far the most common in the dry summer months. Second, leaders are required to collaborate with other agencies over which they have no control. And third, as fire crews meld into temporary amalgamations on larger blazes, crew leaders and incident commanders find themselves working with, reporting to, or instructing other crews and leaders whom they have never previously met or barely know.

All three sources of ambiguous authority work to undermine optimal decision making. The seasonal crews are often underdeveloped as teams. Although they are forced to work together in ad hoc organizations, the various parties also bring self-interested agendas to bear, and crew leaders and incident commanders must coordinate unknown quantities and unfamiliar personalities. (Think of an orchestra conductor taking the podium for the first time in front of a brass section from Cleveland, strings from San Francisco, reeds from Denver, and percussion from Seattle.) The weak relations among the various parties also tend to result in information hoarding as much as sharing. Incident commanders are sometimes called upon to make critical decisions based on less knowledge than is available within the teams themselves.

Add the parts up—a reduced flow of information to the fire leader, a weakened commitment by the leader to exercise authority, and diminished team compliance with the leader's instructions—and you have the ready makings of a decision crisis. All that is needed is an unpredictable fire to spark it.

THE SOUTH CANYON FIRE

"Okay, everybody out of the canyon!" Don Mackey radioed to his beleaguered firefighters. For hours, they had been clearing a corridor on Storm King Mountain to thwart a spreading wildfire. Now that path had become the crew's only way out. Eighteen people were sprinting for their lives. Could they reach safety?

The summer of '94 baked central Colorado in a heat rarely seen on the mountains. Drought dried out the earth, leaving it gasping for moisture and ripe for ignition. On the morning of July 2, Storm King Mountain began to burn. By July 4 the fire had spread to perhaps 3 acres, a relatively small and slow-moving blaze and one, local officials decided, that could wait while they put out dozens of more serious ones.

Not until the morning of July 5 did the first firefighters venture up to contain it. Less than thirty-six hours later, fourteen of them were dead. Elite members of a caste of itinerant warriors who battle in hard hats and chain saws against one of humanity's oldest enemies, these ten men and four women were consumed by a wall of fire that moved faster than the fastest could run.

The crisis on Storm King Mountain was not only a natural disaster; it was also a decision failure, a result of miscalculation. Firefighter Don Mackey made several of the big decisions—some good, others less so, at least one of them heroic—but Mackey was not acting alone. He was a product, arguably a victim, of a system that had failed to teach him how to make good decisions.

For years the agencies responsible for wildland firefighting had focused on fire behavior rather than human behavior, akin to a business that concentrates on engineering rather than customers. Even when earlier fire tragedies had hinged on human error, the recommendations sent forth from them were usually technical ones. The result was that Mackey and others hit the mountain with state-of-the-art gear but scant training in how to make urgent choices under intense pressure.

As in most disasters, no single decision was responsible for the outcome at South Canyon; instead, it was the result of a cascading series of smaller ones. One of the tragedies of the conflagration is that the errors could have been avoided. Excessive optimism, untested assumptions, unheeded warnings, poor intelligence, failure to clarify authority: at Storm King, nearly all the great enemies of good decision making were present in abundance. The "collapse in decision making" was "almost automatic," a U.S. Forest Service researcher argued afterward.[11]

At NASA, it took a second space shuttle explosion to convince the agency that its problems were not just technical but also organizational. And it took Storm King Mountain and the South Canyon Fire to change the way forest fires are fought. Today, wildland firefighters are schooled extensively in how to make timely decisions under complex and stressful conditions. Trainees walk in the footsteps of Don Mackey. They pause at the spot where he yelled his final instruction. They sprint uphill while a stopwatch runs. They imagine what a wall of flame must look like when it is moving at 20 miles an hour. And they often end up, panting, at a granite cross marking the spot where Mackey was overtaken by the flames he could not outrun.[12]

The Decision Trail

As a business school professor, I tend to conduct my research into leadership and decision making in rather formal surroundings: private offices, executive suites, even boardrooms. Not this time. In the company of seventeen wildland firefighters, I walked the slopes of the 9,000-foot Storm King Mountain, located 40 miles northwest of Aspen, to try to understand what had happened on those fateful days in 1994 and to tease out lessons that can help people make the right calls, however extreme the circumstances. What follows is a reconstruction, drawn from interviews, research, and reports, of the events that led to one of the worst days in the history of wildland firefighting.[13]

As first light dawned on July 5, Butch Blanco, a veteran firefighter with the U.S. Bureau of Land Management, hiked up the mountain to evaluate the situation. Just a few months before, Blanco had qualified as an incident commander, the person who takes charge of a blaze. A former city firefighter, he was known for giving a long leash to his crews when it came to getting the job done.

Presently, he and his team of seven began digging a line around the slow-moving fire. Using picks, shovels, and saws, they scraped the earth clean—one person rooting out the vegetation, another chucking it to the side. The idea was to create a fire line—a thin strip where the flames have nothing to feed on and thus cannot cross. But this blaze was more tenacious than Blanco expected, and at 8:19 a.m. he radioed for help.

Since Blanco's fire was still not a priority—there were many bigger ones in the tinder-dry region—it was not until 5:20 p.m. that an eight-person crew of smokejumpers, some of the best-trained wildland firefighters in the country, finally boarded a small plane. Among them was Don Mackey. Thirty-four years old and the father of two, Mackey had eight seasons of smokejumping under his belt and had also served as an instructor. Strong and well built, with the look of a mountain man, Mackey was regarded as a good smokejumper. Seated next to him was Sarah Doehring, a slightly built but strong woman from up-state New York whom Mackey had helped train.

"He was easygoing, a likable guy, the kind of guy we enjoyed being around," she said of Mackey. And as a firefighter, "he was very competent." Doehring remembers thinking that it "could be difficult down there" but was reassured by her teammate's confident demeanor.

At 5:45 p.m. the smokejumpers left the plane. Because Mackey happened to be sitting in the seat nearest the door, he leaped and landed first. That made him, in accord with a protocol that interpreted leadership in the most literal sense, the "jumper in charge." He would coordinate the landing and prepare the crew to go into fire combat. The fire itself was still Blanco's responsibility as incident commander, but the lines of authority would soon begin to blur.

From One Boss to Several

Unequipped for a night on the mountain and hampered by chain saw malfunctions, Blanco and his crew descended to the town of Glen-wood Springs for the evening not long before Mackey and his fellow smokejumpers arrived. Within hours, the flames had crossed the fire line Blanco's crew had cut, growing from 30 acres to 50. With that, Don Mackey went into action against the blaze.

"We all thought we were going to dig a line around it by mid-night" to contain the fire, Doehring remembered. But it continued to spread, and Mackey realized he needed more firefighters. In Blanco's absence, he took the initiative, radioing a request at 11:30 p.m. for two more fire crews (decision 1 in the timeline below).

The cold mountain ridge permitted only fitful rest. Wide awake at 2 a.m., Mackey worried that the fire was burning especially hot for that

Anatomy of a Tragedy

It started as a routine forest fire; there were dozens of more serious blazes in Colorado in the drought-ridden summer of '94. But Storm King ended up as the deadliest. Smokejumper Don Mackey made nine key decisions on that terrible day.

16.5 HOURS ◄Time until blowup

Area on fire

Main ridge fire line

Decision 1
At 11:30 P.M. on July 5, with the fire intensifying, Don Mackey radios a request for two more firefighting crews.

10.5 HOURS

2 Around dawn on July 6, Mackey asks for continuous aerial surveillance of the fire. The request is denied.

6.5 HOURS

Fire growth

3 At 9:30 A.M., Mackey and Butch Blanco, leader of another crew, conduct their own reconnaissance in a helicopter assigned to the fire.

6 HOURS

West flank fire line

4 Mackey proposes to cut a fire line below the flames on the west flank of the ridge—a risky strategy to which Blanco agrees.

2 HOURS

5 Mackey wonders who is in command but does not clarify the situation. One possible result: No lookout is posted.

1.5 HOURS

Strong winds

6 A local weather forecast predicts strong winds but no rain; Mackey does not receive or ask for the forecast.

30 MIN.

Doehring to ridge   Flare-ups

7 Mackey orders Sarah Doehring to the top of the main ridge. Thanks to this order, she survives.

6 MIN.

Lunchspot ■

8 Sensing an imminent blowup, Mackey directs eight firefighters to Lunchspot Ridge. They all survive.

Decision timeline in the South Canyon fire.

time of night. As dawn broke on July 6, he again took the initiative, asking for aerial surveillance (decision 2), a fixed-wing aircraft that would serve as a full-time "eye in the sky." Officials informed Mackey that none was available; instead he got the services of a light helicopter that would have to do double duty ferrying gear as well as monitoring the fire. Whether Mackey would have had more luck if his authority had been clearer or if he had better known the people of whom he was making the request is unknowable, but the effect of being denied his full-time eye in the sky was to leave him partially blind at a time when the blaze was threatening to morph into something far larger.

Early on the morning of July 6, Butch Blanco reappeared on the ridge with a fire crew of eleven. In his absence, Mackey had made all the right moves: he had tracked the fire vigilantly, secured more crew, and requested aerial intelligence. Now he and Blanco huddled. Deciding they needed more information before settling on a strategy, they boarded the helicopter at 9:30 a.m. to get a better sense of the fire (decision 3). What they saw was worrisome. The blaze had expanded to 125 acres and was creeping down the west flank of the ridge. Mackey now proposed a bold plan (decision 4). He wanted to cut a fire line very close to the flames—though below them, since fire can climb up a slope faster than a person can—on the west flank of the ridge. Before turning left and extending horizontally across the slope, the line would cut sharply downhill for its first 300 feet: a 55 percent gradient, equal to a one-foot drop in elevation for every two feet forward.

Blanco agreed with the strategy, and Mackey prepared for action. In retrospect, this was a crucial moment in which two important things happened. First, Blanco effectively—though not officially— ceded some of his incident commander authority to Mackey, who now became the point man on how to deal with the downhill fire line. And second, both men committed themselves to a strategy at odds with several established rules.

"Downhill fire line construction is hazardous in steep terrain, fast-burning fuels, or rapidly changing weather," warns the wildland firefighters' manual. All three conditions prevailed in the canyon. The manual also cautions against relying on a steep uphill escape route, but Mackey's plan created just that. Since the crews were already on top of the ridge and could not readily redeploy to the bottom, however, cutting a downhill fire line seemed the pragmatic way to go.

Nonetheless, some of Mackey's team clearly considered this a dangerous call. "You sure you want us to do that?" one radioed back. "Go down that side?" Mackey reaffirmed the decision, only to be challenged again: "Are there any safe spots down there?" Mackey

responded, "It doesn't look too bad." Again, his smokejumpers hesitated. "We're going to wait for you to come down here and explain
some stuff to us," said one.

Face-to-face with his crew, Mackey noted that the vegetation became sparser down the hill. In any case, he argued, the fire would run
back uphill—above the proposed fire line—in the unlikely event it
surged out of control. "Let me have a big crew and we'll do this. We'll
do fine," he said. Mackey's confidence got the crew moving. At 11:30
a.m., armed with saws, axes, and shovels, they began to cut and scrape
a new fire line.

Just as researchers have found in other circumstances, so it was at
South Canyon. In the absence of an experienced decision maker, a
can-do attitude had trumped. Don Mackey was serving as a de facto
incident commander—something he had never done before. Although he had years of experience in fighting city fires, Butch Blanco
was also new to a wildland command. Neither man brought the kind
of experience that gives a sense of how the worst can happen if conditions are wrong. Standard operating procedures are intended to guard
against just such leaps of faith, but there was no veteran in authority
to insist on such caution.

Muddling the Lines of Authority

An hour later, eight additional smokejumpers floated down onto the
ridge. More than two dozen firefighters were now deployed on the
mountain: Blanco's eleven, Mackey's eight, and the eight newcomers.
The ad hoc melding of crews from diverse locales and several agencies
became further exacerbated at 1 p.m. when a team of twenty hotshots
from Prineville, Oregon, supervised by Tom Shepard, began arriving
on the ridge by helicopter. Like smokejumpers, hotshots are among the
most highly trained and esteemed wildland firefighters in the business.

On the mountain now with one mission were three crew leaders with firefighters from five states:

Crew type	Smokejumpers	Local firefighters	Hotshots
Crew leader	Don Mackey	Butch Blanco	Tom Shepard
Federal agency	U.S. Forest Service	U.S. Forest Service and Bureau of Land Management	U.S. Forest Service
Members and location	Sixteen from Idaho, Montana, and Washington	Eleven from Colorado	Twenty from Oregon

Inevitably, the question of who exactly was in charge became harder to sort out with each new addition. Mackey was now directly supervising twenty-four people, including the hotshots, over whom he had no authority, formal or otherwise. Did that mean the fire was his? At 2 p.m. he asked the question of fellow smokejumper Kevin Erickson: was the incident commander Butch Blanco or Mackey himself? "I don't know," Erickson responded. "Neither do I," said Mackey. But he took no steps to clarify the issue (decision 5).

The lingering ambiguity may also explain why Don Mackey ignored standard firefighting procedures that call for lookouts to ensure that no flames are burning below a fire line. Incident commanders are expected to be aware of the entire environment as it evolves. Unequivocal acceptance of that responsibility here would have dictated the assignment of a fire lookout, radio contact with all parties, and a personal inspection of the situation. "Look up, down, and around," commands the fire manual. Quite possibly because he was still confused about who was in charge, Mackey did not, and the result was disastrous. Concealed behind a vertical cleavage known as Lunchspot Ridge, the fire had already burned down below the level of the fire line. Had there

Firefighters cut a fire line on Storm King Mountain, July 6, 2005.

been a well-posted lookout—or the surveillance plane Mackey never got—the radios would have been crackling with warnings.

Seeing the Forest and the Trees

Because Blanco concentrated on controlling the fire at the top of the ridge and Mackey on completing the fire line lower down, neither had an overall view of the developing situation. Thus neither sensed that the canyon could be on the cusp of a blowup, that frightening phenomenon when a fire suddenly bursts across the landscape. Nor did Mackey, Blanco, or their crews know that nature was just then creating the catalyst for a catastrophe.

The local meteorologist predicted that a cold front would surge through around 3 p.m., generating no rain but plenty of wind. This was, of course, crucial information under the circumstances, but it failed to reach the front line. Bureaucratic bungling had bottled up the alert, and without warning lights flashing in the back of his head or prior training to alert him to its need, Mackey never asked for a weather forecast (decision 6). Both failures—not to clarify his leadership responsibilities and not to ask for weather updates—were closely connected. If Mackey had been certain that he was in charge, he might have felt compelled to seek the data, and then he would have known to protect those on the fire line from the anticipated currents.

By 3:30 p.m., the perilous conditions were becoming palpable, forecast or not. Taking note of the rising winds, Mackey assigned Sarah Doehring to patrol the west flank's fire line for burning debris and hot spots. He also sat a few minutes with her for a bite to eat. Though outwardly relaxed, he seemed to have much on his mind, Doehring remembered. "What should I do if the wind comes up?" she asked. "Go down," Mackey instructed. As they stood, though, and Doehring began to resume her patrol toward the far end of the fire line, Mackey changed his mind and ordered her back to the top of the ridge (decision 7). Tense about the worsening conditions, Doehring was relieved to turn around—an act that saved her life. Most of the other firefighters on the fire line remained at work, from 1,450 to 1,880 feet below the ridge top.

"Go Up!"

By 4 p.m., smoke swirled, flames churned, air thundered—all the classic signs of a blowup. A 1998 Forest Service analysis said, "The fire began burning through the live fuel canopy as a continuous flaming front." The front came surging from both below and the far end of the fire line. In an instant Mackey stopped fighting the fire and raced to survive it. Grasping the gravity of the situation, he told eight nearby firefighters to run directly up Lunchspot Ridge to an area where he knew there was sufficient ground cover to serve as a safe zone. "Go up!" he shouted. "There's good black farther up" (decision 8). And indeed, they would find the "good black" and survive by huddling on it inside their portable fire shelters.

Mackey did not follow the eight firefighters up the ridge. Instead he radioed ahead: "Okay, everybody out of the canyon!" Then he dashed back along the fire line, urging the remaining firefighters to flee (decision 9). For Mackey, it was the decision maker's final and hardest choice. At a moment when his self-preservation must have screamed, "Run!"—a moment when he still had a chance to save his own life— he instead returned to assist those yet in jeopardy.

Fire
started here

Main ridge fire line

Lunchspot ridge

With the front of flames accelerating, 12 firefighters, with Mackey at the rear, are overcome
by the fire less than 100 yards from the ridge.

■ Lunchspot

West flank fire line

0
MIN.

Wind-driven flame front

9 The fire blows up and Mackey, only 100 feet from the Lunchspot, decides to risk his own life to hurry the 18-member crew working along the west flank fire line to safety on the main ridge.

Donald Mackey's final decision.

With Mackey's urging, six firefighters crested the ridge top with seconds to spare. One of them was Brad Haugh. "The fire blew up behind a little ridge below me," Haugh told author Sebastian Junger for his book *Fire.* "People were yelling into their radios, 'Run! Run! Run!' I was roughly 150 feet from the top of the hill, and the fire got there in ten or twelve seconds. I made it over the top and just tumbled and rolled down the other side, and when I turned around, there was just this incredible wall of flame."[14]

Mackey and the rest were not far behind, but the steepness of the hill meant that they were not moving fast enough—perhaps just 1 to 3 feet per second. The fire, meanwhile, was coming at 9 feet per second. At 4:16 it caught up with them. A surging 300-foot wall of flame overtook nine of the Oregon hotshots and three smokejumpers, including Mackey. They were less than 100 yards short of safety.

It took five more days to bring the fire under control. The final death toll reached fourteen—two died elsewhere on the mountain— making it one of the deadliest forest fires in U.S. history.

Decision Makers and Breakers

Although he was not the only leader on the mountain, Don Mackey's decisions had a decisive impact on the firefighters' experience during the South Canyon fire. To be sure, he was dealt a poor hand by the government agency that dispatched him to Storm King Mountain. Firefighting resources arrived late or in inadequate measure to combat the blaze. Federal agencies failed to unequivocally designate an incident commander. A critical weather warning never made it to the front line, where the personal stakes were highest. Nor was Mackey sufficiently trained in the essence of incident leadership. Butch Blanco and Tom Shepard added their own important decisions to the matrix, as did off-site officials. Still, Mackey's nine decisions became critical on the ground. Their impact is summarized below:

			Nine Decisions by Don Mackey During the South Canyon Fire on July 5–6, 1994		
No.	Decision by Donald Mackey	Time	Source of Suboptimal Decision Making	Appraisal	Result
1	Requested two additional crews for the next day	July 5, 11:30 p.m.		Effective assessment and prompt decision	Acquired the additional personnel required
2	Requested continuous fixed-wing aerial surveillance	July 6, 5:30 a.m.	Ambiguous authority	Right decision but thwarted by poor interagency coordination	Prevented appraisal of fire's rapid downhill spread
3	Conducted own aerial surveillance	9:30 a.m.		Acquired good overview of fire	Enhanced intelligence on the fire's growth
4	Started building downhill west flank fire line without lookout	10:00 a.m.—proposed; 11:30 a.m.—started	Under-preparation and ambiguous authority	Aggressive and unsafe	Placed firefighters in peril
5	Did not clarify who was in charge of incident	2:00 p.m.	Under-preparation, acute stress, and ambiguous authority	Left authority ambiguous when it should have been unequivocal	Absence of full situational awareness plus a lack of clarity among followers as to who was in charge

No.	Decision by Donald Mackey	Time	Source of Suboptimal Decision Making	Appraisal	Result
6	Did not secure weather update	2:30 p.m.	Under-preparation and ambiguous authority	Left Mackey unaware of the worsening conditions	Firefighters continued fire line work despite imminent arrival of a cold front with high winds
7	Sent Sarah Doehring to top of ridge	3:30 p.m.		A sub-conscious response to an increasingly alarming situation	Saved Doehring's life
8	Sent eight smokejumpers up Lunchspot Ridge to safe area	4:00 p.m.		Clear-minded instruction during increasingly stressful moments	The eight smokejumpers survived
9	Evacuated west flank fire line	4:06 p.m.		Placed crew safety ahead of personal risk	Helped save six firefighters, but too late for eleven others and himself

What Worked, What Did Not

We lack the controlled elegance of a laboratory experiment or the sta-tistical value of a sample, but drawing on the detailed record of first-person accounts and subsequent analyses, five of Mackey's nine decisions proved relatively optimal while the other four were less so, in some cases far less so. Those that improved the likelihood Mackey and his team would swiftly and safely suppress the South Canyon fire were:

Decision 1 at 11:30 p.m. on July 5 to request two additional elite crews, which secured the firefighters necessary to combat a rapidly expanding fire

Decision 3 at 9:30 a.m. on July 6 to conduct aerial surveillance, which significantly improved Mackey's information on the environment

Decision 7 at 3:30 p.m. to send Sarah Doehring to the top of the ridge, a decision that saved her life

Decision 8 at 4:00 p.m. to dispatch eight smokejumpers up Lunchspot Ridge, successfully moving them into a safe area

Decision 9 at 4:06 p.m. to evacuate the west flank fire line, thus helping to move six firefighters toward another safe area, and plac-ing team survival ahead of personal safety

Weighing against Mackey's five successful decisions were four that lessened the likelihood that he and his team would halt the fire or even come out of it alive. In each case, the suboptimality of the choice can be explained at least in part by one or more of the three factors identi-fied at the outset as potentially undermining effective decision mak-ing: underpreparation, acute stress, and ambiguous authority.

Decision 2 at 5:30 a.m. on July 6, requesting continuous aerial surveillance. The intent behind this decision was sound: Mackey sought an eye in the sky so he would have real-time data on areas of the fire that he could not see directly. The fact that he was unable to obtain the resource may have seemed unremarkable at the time since firefighters are often denied such requests because of competing priorities, safety concerns, or resource constraints. But by neither achieving his goal nor insisting up the ranks on the need for the best aerial surveillance, Mackey limited his available information and knowledge of the fire. Almost certainly contributing to the rejection and to Mackey's seeming reticence about pursuing the matter further was the fact that he was not the formal incident commander. With more clearly delineated authority, Mackey might well have secured the overview he sought of the fire instead of being blind to it at a time when it was dangerously expanding.

Decision 4 taken at 10 a.m. and implemented at 11:30 a.m. to construct the downhill west flank fire line. We cannot be certain that a better-trained supervisor would have made a safer decision under the stress of the moment, but a more thoroughly prepared decision maker might have been less sanguine about transgressing standard operating procedures and more likely to take extra measures to guard against downhill dangers. A more experienced and better-trained leader also might have been more uncomfortable predicating this prime strategy on an essential resource not yet firmly in hand: the "big crew" that Mackey required if his line was to "do fine" but which never did materialize. Finally, a leader with unequivocal authority for making decisions might have been more successful in deploying the big crew that was required.

Decision 5 at 2 p.m. not to clarify who was in command of the incident. The ambiguity of authority stemming from the diverse units on the mountain, the stress of firefighting, and sheer fatigue were all contributing factors. So too was underpreparation: with greater experience and training comes greater appreciation for the requirement of unequivocal clarity in who carries ultimate responsibility on the line.

Decision 6 at 2:30 p.m. not to secure a weather forecast. Again, the uncertainty of whether Mackey was incident commander was a likely factor, especially in combination with his underpreparation and other preoccupations. The fire was becoming more threatening, Mackey had far more firefighters under his wing with the arrival of the hotshots, and absent the intuition that comes from leadership experience, the danger of a missing weather forecast was not necessarily at the top of his mind. Still, by not acting—by deciding through default to fly blind on the weather front, too—Mackey left the west flank of his fire line painfully vulnerable to the blowup that ensued.

DEVELOPING DECISION MAKING

Some of the nation's most elite wildland firefighters were on Storm King Mountain on July 6, 1994. Hotshot crews and smokejumpers are among the best-prepared of the nation's vast corps of wildland firefighters. Nonetheless, fourteen of them lost their lives in what most qualified observers have concluded was a preventable disaster. If even those most technically adept at fire suppression were caught by a blowup, a lack of formal firefighting skills cannot be the dominant cause. The disaster, rather, derived in large part from an underdeveloped capacity for making rapid decisions under demanding conditions. Simply put, good people were left on their own to reach subpar go points.

Donald Mackey parachuted into the fire zone as a crew member, became jumper in charge on the ground, and soon assumed virtual command of a multiple-crew firefighting incident. His decision-making responsibilities had escalated overnight, and he willingly rose to the occasion. Organizations often depend upon people such as Mackey to get a job done. But if the job is to be done well and crews protected as best they can be from the manifold dangers of the work, then training and development in the essence of urgent decision making is a priority. To understand everything about fire behavior but little about human behavior is to have only half the decision equipment an incident commander requires, yet prior to 1994, that is precisely what government training practices had produced.

It took the tragedy of South Canyon to lay bare that shortfall, but fortunately, future fire decision makers should be far better prepared for their own crisis moments than Don Mackey and Butch Blanco were. In 2001, the National Wildfire Coordinating Group, a consortium of federal and state wildland firefighting agencies, established the Wildland Fire Leadership Development Program explicitly to enhance decision-making skills so that responsible firefighters could "make sound and timely decisions." If "snap judgments can be educated and controlled," Malcolm Gladwell concluded in *Blink,* they "can be every bit as good as decisions made cautiously and deliberately." The challenge now is how to educate and control those judgments. In the wake of South Canyon, the nation's firefighting agencies have been working to achieve just that.[15]

Learning How to Decide

A decade after the South Canyon fire, an array of courses had been established to provide in-depth training in decision making under tension in fast-changing, unfamiliar, and complex environments. The courses are designed in accord with one of the main principles that now guide all wildland fire leadership development: take good and timely decisions.[16]

In a first-level course for all firefighters, "Human Factors on the

Fire Line," the focus is on situational awareness and decision making with an emphasis on ensuring that personal stress and private attitudes do not undermine clear-mindedness. In one exercise, participants are provided information on trends in temperature, humidity, and clouds over a particular terrain as a cold front approaches, then asked to forecast the way the wind will shift and what slope will become most dangerous. The consequences for fire crew deployment and redeployment are obvious.

A second-level course entitled "Followership to Leadership" emphasizes such skills as ethical decision making. Participants devote a day in the field to making decisions in small teams. "Fire Line Leadership," the level-three program, is designed for those responsible for a fire crew and emphasizes communicating intent and managing stress. Here participants study models of decision making, engage in tactical decision simulations adapted from the Marine Corps, and master after-action reviews of key decisions.

The next-level course is "Incident Leadership," for "leaders of leaders"—those who would serve as commanders for several fire crews during an extended attack. This time the focus is on identifying how ambiguous authority can undermine effective decisions, how decision errors can be detected early, and how decision tempo can be maintained. Participants engage in role playing and computer simulations of fire combat. This is the training course that Don Mackey should have had but did not, for the uncomplicated reason that it simply did not exist then.

A capstone course for "leaders of organizations"—those who run incident management teams that oversee dozens of units on a major fire—focuses on integrating information from numerous sources to reach knowledgeable and timely decisions, and on communicating strategic intent to the field in a way that enables front-line leaders to take appropriate decisions. Had Don Mackey been properly trained before his dispatch to Storm King Mountain and had he then swiftly and safely suppressed that fire, this course would have qualified him for a promotion.[17]

Running through all these courses is an emphasis on building the right decision-making skills for safety, speed, and suppression in a fire zone. Acquiring and analyzing the right data, allocating people and resources to the essential tasks, implementing in a timely fashion, and focusing on the goals of the enterprise regardless of personal concerns are central to the curriculum. The coursework also emphasizes learning to cope with ambiguous authority and personal stress. While those sources of suboptimal decision making can never be entirely eliminated, the federal initiative is intended to reduce the third cause of suboptimal decisions: underpreparation for making leadership decisions, especially when authority is uncertain and stress is intense.

Virtually every major element of these new programs points to the decision challenges that firefighters faced on Storm King Mountain. Trained well, incident commanders should now be better able to reach the right go point when in a fire zone—good news for the men and women who willingly trust their lives to the readiness of those who lead them into fire combat.

From Knowing to Doing

To reinforce the classroom lessons, the Wildland Fire Leadership Development Program has also created a set of out-of-classroom learning experiences that draw on the concept of the battlefield "staff ride." Long used by the armed forces to teach military strategy, staff rides reconstruct key decisions on the ground at sites such as Gettysburg and Normandy.[18]

In the fire leadership program, the rides offer hands-on study of the strategies used by incident commanders during several dozen fires. While walking the terrain, participants evaluate what decisions they would have taken had they been in the shoes of the incident commander.[19]

Not surprisingly, the South Canyon fire terrain is one of the most frequently visited. Numerous groups have walked the west flank fire line on Storm King Mountain to review the leadership decisions of Don Mackey and others. A hotshot fire crew from Redding, California, even reoriented its entire training program around leadership decision making, using an extended walk in the fire zone as the culmination of its six-week program. One participant reported that it "was without a doubt . . . the most beneficial training and learning experience of my fire career." Said another, "It enabled me to identify the error chains and hopefully given me the strength to break them before something like this happens again." And for a third, it "was one of the most moving and educational experiences of my firefighting career."

I have taken "staff rides" in this and many other decision venues, with everyone from battle-tested military officers to midcareer desk jockeys, never without being intensely moved by the experience. Personal engagements of this kind can cut through the fog of abstraction and connect theory with practice more powerfully than virtually any other learning event.

Classrooms are an excellent vehicle for acquiring decision theory; tangible venues are the indelible vehicles for remembering how to apply it.[20]

Race to the Top

As their walk on the mountain came to end, one group of Redding firefighters stood near the end of the fire line where Don Mackey had shouted, "Okay, everybody out of the canyon!" The facilitators then asked the firefighters to race against Mackey's clock to reach safety. Many ran along the same fire line that Mackey had built and used, while others bolted directly for the top, but whatever the path, most failed to reach the safety of the ridge top within the few minutes that remained for most of Mackey's crew. As "I ran up the west flank fire line," one said, "I was able to imagine the fire, the smoke, and the heat below me, and even experienced a few chaotic thoughts while I second-guessed my decision to take the west flank escape route."[21]

Another of the Redding hotshots said that as he neared the area where many of the fire victims perished, just several hundred feet from the top of the ridge, he was overcome by emotion. "A pair of skis formed an X over a cross marking the spot where one of the firefighters died," he recalled. "I immediately became paralyzed and stunned," appreciating that if "I had been on the mountain in 1994, I too would have perished." All hotshot firefighters, he said, should "climb that mountain to see and experience the emotional connections." In the clinical language of researcher Max Bazerman, an "event that evokes emotions and is vivid, easily imagined, and specific" will have greater hold on an individual's memory than unemotional and bland events and thus be more able to inform one's future decisions.[22]

However you word it, the odds are good that anyone who has been through the Wildland Fire Leadership Development Program will be far better prepared to deal with two of the three root causes of the suboptimal decisions that plagued leaders on Storm Mountain in July 1994: inadequate preparation for decision making and high stress. Separately, the fire service has attacked the third root cause—ambiguity of authority—by sharpening and better instilling the principles of unequivocal responsibility when on a fire line.

Today, in the aftermath of South Canyon and largely because of what happened there, the rules are different. No longer is the first smokejumper on the ground automatically in charge, analogous to handing a product launch to the first junior executive through the door. Now authority goes to the most experienced person. Firefighters are also trained to decide against taking excessive risk, a seemingly basic precaution that too often got lost in the can-do ethos of men and women accustomed to laying their lives on the line without adequately trained incident leadership.

The firefighting decisions taken on Storm King Mountain are a reminder that personal audacity is essential for making many decisions. With only ambiguous authority and little training, Don Mackey took charge and made swift decisions in his final moments that saved lives while sacrificing his own. His extraordinary courage helped fifteen firefighters escape, and it is now instructing a new generation of fire leaders on how to make the right decisions when lives depend on them.

The Decision Template for Urgent Decisions

In this account, we have seen how a constellation of discrete decisions, some good and others less so, can have in the aggregate a profound, even tragic effect. To avert adverse outcomes in the future, whether in a fire zone, school zone, or office zone, it is useful to extract decision principles and tools from the events on Storm King Mountain to serve as a starting template for reaching the right go points whatever the venue.

As suggested previously, I am convinced that such template building can go a long way toward closing the knowing-doing gap and translating ideas into action, decision theory into decision making. The process is akin to the way Tom Boatner extracted items for his decision template from the firefighter he witnessed in Alaska. With the Colorado fire fresh in mind, this is a good moment to extract lessons from that experience to create your own guide for making urgent decisions. It is certainly what we would have done in the classroom for MBA students or as part of the program for midcareer managers looking to improve their decision making.

I am also convinced that the principles and tools will be mastered most effectively and be most readily available in the event of an individual crisis if they are first mined by the reader. My own principles and tools from walking the terrain of the South Canyon fire are listed on the next page, but I urge you to generate your own before examining my template. By joining what you create with what I have extracted, and by continuing to do so in subsequent chapters, you will build a well-elaborated set of decision principles with a tool kit to match. In the meantime, it is a good idea to begin testing the template at your workplace and in your community during the days ahead.

Principle	Tool	Illustration
1. Prepare for decisions under stress.	a. Acquire and digest decision experience. b. Obtain formal instruction.	a. Mackey brought experience to his task but had not reviewed it. b. No training program in decision making was available to him.
2. Build situational awareness.	a. Survey the environment. b. Assign others to help.	a. Mackey flew over the fire. b. Mackey posted no lookout.
3. Sharpen responsibility.	a. Clarify authority with others. b. Identify implications of responsibility.	a. Mackey's authority was ambiguous and remained so. b. Mackey did not obtain a weather report.
4. Establish clear priorities.	Review priorities on eve of urgent decisions.	Mackey dispatched 15 firefighters to safety on the cusp of the blowup.
5. Adhere to operating principles.	Review operating procedures.	Mackey built a downhill fire line even though fire manuals caution against it.
6. Revise operating principles.	Change rules that undermine decision making.	U.S. no longer assigns first smokejumper on the ground to take charge.
7. Make well-timed decisions.	Track developments and take swift action when the clock demands.	Appreciating that time was short, Mackey dispatched Doehring and eight others to safety.
8. Overcome self-interest.	Reaffirm that responsibility to others supersedes self-interest.	Mackey sacrificed himself to rush others off the fire line.

2

Getting into the Decision Game

To launch or delay? Fire or hire? Take a promotion or let it be? A marriage counselor or a divorce lawyer? How about surgery or what physicians call watchful waiting? Decisions come in all shapes and sizes, with every sort of consequence in between. Some decisions are fleeting, the difference between a social grace and a faux pas. Others are fearsome, keeping us restless and awake for hours. At the extreme, they can become what F. Scott Fitzgerald described in *The Crack-Up* as the "real dark night of the soul" when "it is always three o'clock in the morning, day after day."[1]

At work, at home, in the community, we make decisions all the time, a constant barrage of them. Or we fail to make them, put off to tomorrow, let things slide, opt out of the game. Some decisions are as trivial as ordering whole wheat or rye, while others are as consequential as standing in silence or blowing the whistle when witness to company malfeasance.

The exercise of tough choices might be one of the most universal of all experiences. In a national survey taken in 2000, four out of five respondents said decision making was very important in their current or most recent job. What's more, the capacity to make choices—the willingness to jump into the decision game and play it well—is arguably one of the great discriminators and predictors of ultimate success or failure. "Managers at every level," warned former General Electric chief executive Jack Welch, have to be ready to make many "hard decisions." Those who can do so rise high; those who cannot manage it tread water or sink.[2]

GUSTAVUS WHO?

We have all known the fortunate few for whom decisions seem effortless. They glide through one judgment call after another, flummoxed by none, content with most, never breaking a sweat. Ernest Hemingway called it grace under pressure. We have also known the opposite, the equivocators who cannot get off the fence, the contemplators who consider a choice from every angle, the freezers who simply lock up at a consequential moment.[3]

More than 135 years after his death, Robert E. Lee has some fifty public schools across the South named after him. Gustavus Woodson Smith has none; indeed, his name is virtually unknown outside a small circle of Civil War buffs and historians. Yet on May 31, 1862, with the Union Army under George McClellan

Confederate general
Gustavus W. Smith.

knocking on Richmond's gates and threatening to make short work of the new Confederacy, it was Smith, not Lee, to whom Confederate president Jefferson Davis turned.

So alarmed was Davis by the 125,000-man enemy force advancing on his capital that he had ridden out to the front lines that day to consult with Joseph E. Johnston, the general in charge of Richmond's defense. Davis had almost reached his general when shrapnel and a bullet knocked Johnston from his horse and took him out of action. With that, Davis extended a battlefield promotion to Johnston's ranking subordinate, the forty-year-old Gustavus W. Smith, and handed over to him the defense of Richmond and, by extension, the fate of the Confederacy.[4]

There was no question of Smith's pedigree. Born in Kentucky and educated at the U.S. Military Academy at West Point, he graduated eighth in the Class of 1842, a group that included such future Civil War luminaries as Abner Doubleday and James Longstreet. Nor was there any question of Smith's personal bravery or military acumen. Like Jefferson Davis, he had fought with distinction in the Mexican-American War in 1846–47 and served briefly on the faculty of West Point before involving himself in New York City politics. He had a blustery style, one that seemed to suggest that this was a general not easily fazed. Yet when Davis summoned him to greatness, Smith shrank from the task.

At a meeting with Davis and his military aide, Robert E. Lee, at 8:30 p.m. on May 31, Smith appeared at a loss. When Davis pressed him for his plans for the defense of Richmond, the newly appointed commander of the Army of Northern Virginia responded by asking his president what *he* knew about the day's battle. Smith confessed that he "could not determine" without more information "what was best to be done." The next day, after his army had achieved little on the battlefield, Smith took ill and appeared on the verge of a nervous breakdown. No question of "personal courage could be raised by anyone who had seen him battle," observed one historian, but "responsibility it was that shattered his nerves." At 2 p.m. on June 1, 1862, Jefferson Davis relieved Smith of his command and gave the assignment to Lee.[5]

DECIDOPHOBIA

Handed a momentous assignment at a critical juncture in the greatest crisis of the American experiment, Gustavus Smith served as commander of the Army of Northern Virginia for less than twenty-four hours. Robert E. Lee, by contrast, would turn McClellan back from the gates of Richmond and subsequently lead the South's biggest army brilliantly through the epic battles at Antietam, Chancellorsville, and Fredericksburg until he reached his own mistaken go point at Gettysburg. For Lee, major decisions came readily, but for Smith they did not. When faced with consequential decisions, most people would prefer to be more like Lee than Smith, but the reality for many can be just the opposite.

So many individuals are so averse to making decisions, especially when they impact so many others, that clinical psychologists have even come up with a name for it—or rather two names for two related conditions: decidophobia and its close cousin hypengyophobia, an abnormal and persistent fear of responsibility. Save for the most natural of decision makers, most people have edged up against those clinical conditions at one time or another. Almost all have experienced that sinking feeling when a particularly vexing decision is finally reached after days or even months of circling the issue.

For most, the natural business of making choices is hardly natural at all. But then again neither is speaking Arabic, designing airframes, or playing the tuba. All are learned skills, mastered through observation and practice, and honed by experience. So it is with decision making, too.

A THOUSAND EMERGENCIES

Even the most seasoned decision makers report that it never gets easy. Unisys Corporation CEO James Unruh was speaking to one of my executive MBA groups at the Wharton School when a student asked about the experience of arriving in the morning at the corner office of a large corporation facing epic challenges. Unisys at the time—the mid-1990s—employed forty thousand people, down from eighty thousand just a few years earlier. The first minutes of his workday at headquarters were delightful, Unruh said. The security guard and office assistant greeted him warmly, and nothing had defined his day so far except a cup of coffee and a morning newspaper. But from that point on the CEO's experience went steadily downhill. All the easier decisions at the company already had been made by his subordinates; only the intractable and wrenching issues were left for him to decide. Unruh's senior staff members were soon traipsing through his office, laying on his desk one thorny decision after another that they had been unable to resolve themselves. The easy ones never bubbled up that high.[6]

I obtained a similar taste of life on the other side of the executive's desk when I visited Rick Rieder at his Lehman Brothers office

while researching this book. The chief of fixed-income trading, Rieder started his day with a relaxing breakfast in Lehman's executive dining room high in its gleaming new headquarters on New York's Seventh Avenue, just around the corner from Times Square. Sleek, modern, and richly appointed, the building had been acquired from Morgan Stanley soon after 9/11 when Morgan Stanley decided to

Rick Rieder.

disperse its workforce and sell the brand-new custom-built high-rise.

The dining room décor and breakfast service were exquisite, the conversation relaxed. But as Rieder rode the elevator down to his office floor, his morning descended with it. Rieder's comfortable, glass-walled office oversees the trading floor, where 125 bond traders were already riveted on computer screens blinking buy and sell quotes while the traders took orders from customers around the world. It looked to be a productive and profitable day, but then Rieder took an early call from one of his senior managers, expecting it to be the usual update on some arcane development in the bond market. Not so. The manager announced that he was quitting that morning and going to work for a crosstown rival by afternoon. For Rieder, it stood to be a huge loss, though one that was maybe still reversible if he and Lehman acted quickly and decisively enough. His decision point clear, the stakes defined, Rieder began his workday by calling other executives at the bank, seeking help in talking a prized human asset out of resignation.[7]

Todd Thomson, the former chief financial officer of Citigroup and now CEO of its Global Wealth Management division, says that his workday almost invariably starts with a host of tough decisions. "When I come to the office in the morning, I have a thousand emergencies" is how he characterized it. General Peter Pace, now chairman of the U.S. Joint Chiefs of Staff, said the same of his arrival at the Pentagon in his previous post as vice chairman. Waiting on his desk every morning were dozens of overnight reports on potential terrorism. Pace's task: to decide on a daily basis which warnings deserved his attention and which did not.[8]

James Unruh, Rick Rieder, Todd Thomson, and Peter Pace all know the pain of decision making. They know what it is like to start each day faced with a multitude of crises, most with resonances and implications that reach far beyond the office. All four know that in the decision game, you have to play to win, and unlike Gustavus Smith, they thrive on the challenge rather than freeze in the face of it. We depend on such people to produce our technologies, grow our port-folios, and defend our security. Their go points are, in a very real sense, our go points, too. Fortunately, despite the emergencies and pressures they personally confront every day, they have chosen to stay in the fray.

GETTING INTO THE
ULTIMATE GAME

We humans are biologically and chemically programmed to survive sometimes astounding conditions. Faced with extreme cold, the body begins to shut down circulation to the extremities, then to the lesser organs, until finally all that remains is the blood flow between heart and brain. Call it an involuntary will to live. Yet learned responses can be key to survival as well.

Training, inventiveness, clear-mindedness—they all help us en-dure the extreme hardships of arctic cold, desert heat, and thin air. In his study of how humans survive such inhospitable environments as the Amazon, high seas, and outer space, medical doctor Kenneth Kamler found that by learning from experience, "humans demonstrate enormous adaptability" to the extremes. Through a mix of creativity and will, adventurers have free-dived to 531 feet beneath the sea and free-climbed to 29,035 feet above sea level.[9]

Even the greatest preparation is not always enough. On October 12, 2002, free-diver Audrey Mestre descended to 561 feet off the coast of the Dominican Republic, holding her breath for 1 minute and 42 seconds while exceed-ing the prior depth record by 30 feet. However, as Mestre began her ascent up a guiding wire, an air bag that was to propel her quickly to the surface failed to

Audrey Mestre.

inflate. She remained extraordinarily self-disciplined during what had to be an excruciating 7-minute struggle to regain the surface. In the end, though, Mestre's 8 minutes 38 seconds under water simply outstripped the limits of what her body would endure, maybe of what any human could withstand.[10]

Great determination, though, sometimes can spell the difference, even when others have written you off for dead. Twenty-six thousand feet above sea level, close to the near-airless summit of Mt. Everest, Beck Weathers faced his own high-altitude version of the conditions that finally claimed Audrey Mestre. Trapped in a severe storm with a windchill factor of almost 100 degrees below zero and without shelter or oxygen, Weathers slipped into a coma and was left behind by other climbers, including a physician who deemed him beyond recovery. Yet hours after being abandoned, Weathers regained consciousness and, despite frozen extremities and extreme hypothermia, climbed down the mountain. "Beck's survival," concluded Kenneth Kamler, the first doctor to treat him high on the Everest slopes, "transcends the laws of medicine."[11]

For Beck Weathers, the roots of the miracle were clear: it was animated by an overwhelming drive to live, to endure. Like Mestre, he had no gray areas left to stumble through. His go point was one-dimensional, his decision honed down to a simple choice: rise or die. He decided to stand up, and he did survive.

Do or Die

Roberto Canessa deserves a special place in the annals of survival decision making since his decisions saved not only himself but fourteen companions as well. What is more, in making his decisions, Canessa repeatedly demonstrated an unflinching determination to get into the game so that he and his associates could get out alive.

Canessa was a nineteen-year-old medical student from Monte-

Roberto Canessa, 1972.   **Roberto Canessa, 2002.**

video, Uruguay, when he boarded a flight out of Mendoza, Argentina, on October 13, 1972, with his rugby team and followers. The group was bound for three days of sport and partying in Santiago, Chile, but when the pilot became disoriented and strayed from his prescribed route over the cloud-shrouded Andes, the Fairchild F-227 clipped a mountain cliff. Canessa and twenty-eight others of the forty-five on board miraculously survived the crash when the fuselage slid to a stop on a snow field. Many of the survivors were severely injured and no one was prepared for the bitter cold, but in the hours that followed, everyone anticipated rescue momentarily. It never came. Search planes and helicopters crisscrossed the terrain for ten days but spotted neither the fuselage nor the survivors.[12]

Canessa and his fellow survivors built a makeshift shelter against the extreme temperatures and huddled together for warmth. For water, they funneled sun-melted snow into a bottle. The uninjured among them salvaged a few chocolate bars and wine bottles from the ruined aircraft, but what little nourishment there was quickly ran out. Confined to an isolated snow field 11,500 feet up in the Andes, they were without any source of food, and within a week, many of the twenty-seven remaining survivors approached starvation. On day ten, just as the air search was being called off, Roberto Canessa reached his first go point.

Cognizant of how their bodies were being drained of energy and reaching a point of no return, Canessa concluded that the only means of survival was to consume those who had already perished. As a medical student, he argued the case as clinically as he could, asserting that what they were so horrified to consider as a food source was simply protein, and without protein they would soon perish. "Every time you move," he said, "you use up part of your own body. Soon we shall be so weak that we won't have the strength even to cut the meat that is lying there before our eyes."[13]

Canessa also argued as personally as he could, contending that they had to live to tell the world of their epic survival against the odds. The only way to do so was to consume their deceased associates.

"It is meat," he insisted. "That is all it is. The souls have left their bodies and are in heaven with God. All that is left here are carcasses, which are no more human beings than the dead flesh of the cattle we eat at home."[14]

On October 22, Canessa made the first cuts of flesh with a piece of broken glass and then ingested what he had removed. Slowly, haltingly, with great distress, one by one his fellow survivors resorted to the same. Their cannibalism enabled them to reverse their otherwise terminal path toward sure starvation. By deciding and then persuading others to do the same, Canessa had prolonged the lives of them all, but they were still no closer to civilization. Nor were they out of more immediate danger.

End Game

On the evening of October 29, sixteen days after the air crash and a week after the survivors had first tasted human flesh, an avalanche swept into the fuselage, swallowing up many of the occupants including Canessa. The medical student was close to suffocation when one of those not buried by the snow dug him out, but seven others, including the person who had been sitting next to Canessa when the avalanche struck, could not be saved.

By early December, almost two months into their ordeal, the group had been reduced from an initial group of forty-five to sixteen emaciated survivors. A November 28 newscast overheard on a transistor radio carried by one of the traveling party promised that the air search would soon be resumed, but Canessa knew the chances of the searchers finding the group were small—the pilot, after all, had strayed from his assigned flight path. They could be anywhere.

At one level, there was nothing to do but wait. The group had food, albeit a grisly source. Perhaps the air search would succeed, some thought. One of the survivors kept contending that helicopters could pick out a golf ball from 5,000 feet. What's more, the alternative— hiking out through the extremely rugged mountain terrain—seemed all but impossible, especially given their weakened condition. Yet Roberto Canessa could see that they were playing an end game. Spotting the survivors from the high overflights was akin to spotting a needle in a vast haystack. Eventually, their special protein source would exhaust itself. Even with the food they still had, the day was coming when they would become too weak to attempt to rescue themselves.

To Canessa, a second and more critical go point had arrived. He began to press the group to mount its own rescue by organizing a small party to walk out of the Andes. "The helicopters would rescue us," Canessa argued, but first "we must go tell them where we are." Despite the hardships and dangers sure to be encountered along the way, he also decided that he himself had to be one of those who set out in search of help. Canessa reasoned that he was among the best conditioned and least injured of the survivors, some of whom were still debilitated with fractured limbs. "I realized that my legs belonged to the group," he recalled. "I had to put aside personal advantage for group advantage."

Two other survivors volunteered to join Canessa on the expedition, but not the one who, along with Canessa, had advocated most strenuously for the strategy. "He was always a good visionary," recalled Canessa, "but he did not follow through." Canessa shared the vision but not the reticence. He had closed the knowing-doing gap and reached his own go point for getting out.

"You Can Only Look Ahead"

To overcome his inertia in facing the daunting trek ahead, Canessa began telling himself that the climb out would require only a hundred thousand steps. If he began by taking just a few steps and then a few more, he could eventually take them all. Beyond that, he simply listened to what his own inner voice was telling him. "Some people have a good sense for when it's time to go," he remembered years later. For Canessa the time had come.

Thirteen remained behind as Roberto Canessa and two companions commenced their climb on December 12 across extremely treacherous mountain terrain. They walked westward, theorizing that they were closer to the Chilean lowlands than the Argentine pampas. One expeditionary, Antonio Vizintin, turned back after two days so that the other two—Canessa and Nando Parrado—would have additional food for what appeared by then to be a far lengthier climb than expected. The two remaining trekkers understood that they had reached a go-for-broke moment: if they turned back themselves or were swallowed by a chasm along the way, the entire band was unlikely to survive. If they reached civilization, all of them would be celebrating the Christmas holidays with family in Montevideo.

It proved a harrowing journey from the start. They endured bitterly cold nights, surmounted a 13,500-foot ridge, and caromed down icy slopes. But Canessa never doubted his decision to go. "There are moments in life when you make a decision and you must not look back," he thought as they progressed toward the Chilean lowlands. "You can only look ahead."

On the sixth day of their journey, Canessa and Parrado walked onto soil with flowers and grass for the first time in more than two months, and for the first time in their ordeal Canessa became certain

Roberto Canessa's Days of Decisions in the Andes, 1972	
Date	**Decision**
October 13	Aircraft crashes in Andes with Roberto Canessa and forty-four others on board.
October 22	Go point one: Canessa convinces fellow survivors to begin eating the dead.
October 23	Survivors learn that search-and-rescue operations have been suspended.
October 29	Twenty-seven are still alive, but massive snow avalanche buries fuselage and kills eight.
December 12	Go point two: Canessa convinces the group that it must try to save itself, and he and two others decide to climb across the Andes to Chile.
December 18	Canessa and companion Nando Parrado reach a snow-free valley.
December 20	Canessa and Parrado see three Chileans across a river.
December 21	Canessa and Parrado report their ordeal to a Chilean, who contacts officials.
December 22	Helicopters rescue fourteen survivors from the fuselage.

they would prevail. Two days later, on December 20, they came upon several Chilean horsemen who had ridden high in the valley, but the ordeal still was not over. A raging river separated the two groups, too powerful to cross and too loud to shout over. The Uruguayans cried for help, but they received back only a faintly heard "tomorrow." The next day, one of the Chileans returned and threw a rock with an attached note across the river, asking what they wanted. Parrado returned the rock with a written explanation: "I come from a plane that crashed in the mountains. I'm Uruguayan. We've been walking for ten days. I have an injured friend up in the valley. There are fourteen injured people in the plane. We have to get out of here soon and we don't know how. We have no more food. We're weak." The note ended: "When are you going to come for us up here? Please we can't even walk. Where are we?"

That day, one of the Chileans relayed word of the survivors to the outside world, and on December 22, helicopters airlifted the others off the mountain. By making the decision to walk out of the Andes and by forcing his will on the group, Roberto Canessa had given everyone a chance to live.

DECISION PRINCIPLES FROM THE ANDES

Roberto Canessa was guided by five decision principles during his Andean ordeal—principles that continue to inform his decision making more than three decades later.

1. *Stay focused.* In the days immediately following his near death when the avalanche swept through the fuselage, Canessa reports that he was terrified by every new sound that suggested a recurrence. But as time went on, he disciplined himself to suppress his

anxieties before they undermined his resolve and capacity to make clear-minded decisions.

"If I have to die, what the heck!" he declared. "But that doesn't mean that I'm not fighting for my life. No way! I'm doing my best." The bravado might have been manufactured in part, but it served the purpose of focusing his attention solely on the tasks ahead, not the tragedies behind. The experience of the avalanche had the effect of reaffirming his resolve to stay in the game. "If you're very afraid," he warned himself, "you won't give your all," and he believed that a successful descent into Chile would require everything he had left.

2. *Set the bar high.* Canessa says that he resolved early on that he would make decisions on behalf of others in ways that would allow him to take pride in his actions and not be disappointed in his own behavior. In deciding to become an expeditionary, he recognized that he was one of the most physically able survivors, and he concluded that he could not live with himself if he did not volunteer for the climb out to Chile.

The criterion for that conclusion came, of course, from the culture and society of which he was part, and the self-conscious embodiment of its moral prescriptions provided the implicit underpinning for reaching decisions of which he would be proud. "The more miserable the human condition," Canessa recalled of his own response to their worsening plight, "the more people got out of themselves to help others."

3. *Get back to basics.* "I wanted to do the proper thing" in initiating the climb toward Chile, Canessa says now, even though "all the odds were against us." For deciding what was proper, he came to rely upon what he terms "basic truths," seemingly irrefutable axioms that helped steady his hand. One of them served in effect

as his mantra when he set out for Chile: "To the west, there's life, and where there's life, there's hope."

4. *No second-guessing.* Canessa decided that he would not second-guess or obsess about the decisions already made and roads not taken. To do otherwise was to blur a clear-minded focus on the decisions that lay ahead. "When you make a risky decision such as the one to become an expeditionary," he explained, "you must do it and not be looking back all the time." Otherwise, "you will lose the power and confidence of what you are doing."

5. *Stay cold and calculating to maximize your chances of success.* Once the decision had been made to attempt the expedition into Chile, Canessa says he was bursting to leave, but at the insistence of one of the survivors, Arturo Nogueira, Canessa first spent hours studying in great detail maps that had been salvaged from the plane. (Nogueira, whose legs had been broken and who suffered more than most from the severe temperatures, would die of his injuries and pneumonia not long before the rescue helicopters arrived at the snow field.) Before the flight across the Andes, Canessa had also read a book that recommended against making decisions after 7 p.m. since the day's weariness can make for suboptimal thinking. Whether the principle held validity or not in the circumstance, Canessa insisted that it be followed.

In reflecting on the Andean experience some thirty-three years later, Canessa reported that he no longer thought about the ordeal every day. He had put it behind him, completed medical school, and become one of Montevideo's leading pediatric cardiologists. Still, he said, his experience had furnished him a lifelong guiding principle: "You must be persistent, you must be ready for the unpredictable things that happen, and you cannot do more than your best."

FROM RETICENCE
TO RESPONSIBILITY

Because the stakes are so high, the causes of suboptimal decision making have been well studied by economists. Indeed, one of the pioneers
in the field, Daniel Kahneman, received the 2002 Nobel Prize in economics for his work. Behavioral psychologists and related researchers
have trailed behind, but not by much. Edward Russo and Paul Schoemaker, for example, have identified ten dangerous blunders that people commonly make, such as plunging into a decision too quickly,
being overconfident in their own judgment, and failing to learn from
past mistakes. We are not well wired to avoid such shortcomings,
Russo and Schoemaker warn, even though the failures can cause
havoc. Worse, the blunders can feed upon themselves. Fearing suboptimality and even havoc, we tend to hedge our bets when the decision
outcome will affect others, especially when we are likely to hear about
our errors from them.[15]

The good news according to another researcher, Max Bazerman,
is that "we all have plenty of room to improve our judgment," and
consciously learning how to make better decisions is a proven avenue
for doing so. Decidophilia—a zest for decision making—may be rare
in nature, but it can be mastered, and if it is, it becomes a foundation
for accepting greater responsibility for our own lives and the lives of
others.[16]

When Reuven Dar, Dan Ariely, and Hanan Frenk studied forty
soldiers who had been injured during military service, they found that
the most seriously wounded—crushed bones, amputated limbs, and
severe burns—had developed a significantly higher tolerance for pain
than those who had suffered a variety of light injuries ranging from
torn ligaments to broken hands. The three researchers measured pain
by the length of time the veterans waited until yanking their finger
from hot water. The lightly injured veterans withdrew on average in

twenty-seven seconds, while the severely hurt waited fifty-eight seconds. The same is true of decision making: The incremental acceptance of greater decision responsibility tends to increase our tolerance for the greater hardship that comes with each new territory. The decisions themselves do not necessarily get easier, but the more we engage, the less anxiety and sleeplessness result.[17]

Once the initial barriers are surmounted, decision making can even become a desirable end in itself. Mark Lester, a surgeon who became a hospital clinical director in 2004 after years in the operating room, observed that by putting his own career on the line in taking responsibility as senior administrator for other physicians, his decision points became more tangible and engaging. This is one reason why doctors frequently prefer to follow their own guidance rather than a formal protocol in diagnosing patients even though research shows that such protocols often offer more correct guidance. As one physician put it, "It's much more gratifying to come up with a decision on your own."[18]

SMALL STEPS MAKE
HARD DECISIONS EASIER

Roberto Canessa set out to reach Chile—the most daunting challenge of his life—by telling himself that it would require only a hundred thousand steps. If he took several now, followed by another small batch, and another, in time they would add up. The figure was only theoretical, but by breaking the seemingly impossible down into achievable segments, he triggered his go point, and in ten days' time, he arrived where few would have given him any chance of reaching.

This device of breaking a big achievement into numerous small steps comes in many guises. Royal Robbins, one of America's premier early rock climbers and now a clothing manufacturer, had become discouraged during his 1968 solo attempt of one of the celebrated rock faces of Yosemite National Park, the Muir Wall of El Capitan. After seven days, Robbins had concluded that he had insufficient energy and willpower to continue the difficult technical ascent up another 1,000 feet to the top of the 3,000-foot vertical granite face.

Robbins was on the verge of rappelling down when he told himself that he should go up at least a few more feet before descending. "Why don't you climb the next five feet?" he silently cajoled. "You can get down just as easily from five feet higher as from where you are, and you'll have a new high point and a little more honor." He made those five feet, then the next five feet, and then five more. After two more days of five feet at a time, he could finally see the top, and that tangibility was enough to take over as the driving force of his ascent. But getting there required hundreds of five-foot steps, each a proximate goal to the larger one.

"How do you climb a mountain when you can't see the summit?" he asked himself. "By setting targets you can see and hit." They are the small "steps to the dream." Without them he would have fallen short of what became one of the celebrated moments of Yosemite climbing history.[19]

SURMOUNTING THE INSURMOUNTABLE

Another variation of getting into the game through proximate goals is offered by Dean Karnazes, one of the most extreme runners of his era. Karnazes regularly competes in 100-mile events and once completed a marathon to the South Pole. One of the greatest challenges he ever set for himself came in a 199-mile race called The Relay. The event is intended for teams of twelve runners who take turns completing thirty-six segments of 5½ miles each, but Karnazes decided to run it entirely himself. Cheered on by other contestants as the one-runner "Dean Team," he started the race at 5 p.m. on a Friday at the northern end of the Napa Valley of California and ran through the night, all day Saturday, and well into Sunday on his way to the finish line in Santa Cruz.

By 3 a.m. on Sunday, though, Karnazes had lost the will to go on. He sat slumped on a curb at mile 155 in Silicon Valley after nearly being hit by a vehicle. When he told himself he had to get running again despite his utter exhaustion, his muscles would not respond. He thought he might have to call 911, and he decided that he wanted to be standing when the police arrived. "If I can just rise to my feet," he said to himself, "I'll be satisfied. Baby steps, I thought. Just stand up." He did, and then he told himself to reach a reflector some 20 feet up the road, and then a bush 50 feet ahead. His momentum restored, Karnazes crossed the finish line Sunday afternoon, 46 hours and 17 minutes after his start on Friday. The concept of running one 199-mile course would stop virtually everybody, but the idea of running thousands of small increments of a few dozen feet powered him through at the end.[20]

A still different incarnation of the same device carried Johannah Christensen through the arduous yearlong task of assembling a program for the World Economic Forum in Davos, Switzerland, the annual event that since 1970 has been bringing together many of the world's premier business and political luminaries for five days of discussion and debate on leading economic, political, and technological issues. As program manager, Christensen held responsibility for helping to create a lineup of speakers, panels, and workshops on topics ranging from world trade to nuclear proliferation, from microfinance to corporate governance, from religious faith to global terrorism.

The 2005 meeting was typical of the challenge. The agenda included 217 separate sessions and events for a total audience of some three thousand attendees, many top executives of the globe's leading companies or ranking officials of the world's major countries. In attendance were Microsoft founder Bill Gates, then Hewlett-Packard CEO Carly Fiorina, and Citigroup CEO Charles Prince; British prime minister Tony Blair, former U.S. president Bill Clinton, and Ukrainian president Viktor Yushchenko; and actors Angelina Jolie, Richard Gere,

and Sharon Stone. Adding to Johannah Christensen's travails was intense jockeying among many of the powerful for prominent speaking
roles at the best times during the five-day affair. The forum arranged,
for instance, to give French president Jacques Chirac and German
chancellor Gerhard Schröder solo speaking slots on a prime afternoon.

Planning for the annual meeting commences a year in advance.
Laid out on charts and tables in Christensen's office in the World Economic Forum's headquarters in Geneva, the event initially looks simply "insurmountable," she said. But her tactic for getting from
objective to reality is to break the vast scale of the enterprise again into
hundreds of small, definable steps and then to remind herself constantly from past experience that the participants "will all show up,
they'll have a great time, and then they'll leave." By proceeding in small
increments without losing sight of the larger goal, Christensen helped
herself stay in the game. Some three thousand mostly powerful personalities did arrive in Davos in January and were met with a well-
orchestrated program of sessions and speakers. The "insurmountable"
task of orchestrating a hydra-like gathering point for what the British
call "the great and the good" came off well.[21]

STAYING OUT OF THE GAME

While you have to play to win, not every game is worth playing. You
may not yet be prepared to embrace a position of decision responsibility. The position may come with untenable constraints. The deck may
be stacked against responsible decision making.

Carefully vetting in-house candidates for high company positions
is, or should be, a basic human resources function. At one large financial services company, for example, the chief executive appointed a senior HR executive whose charge was to evaluate the readiness of each
of the company's top three hundred managers for promotion. Serving
as an internal headhunter, she worked to ensure that the candidates

were rotated through roles of increasing responsibility, but she also tried to be certain that they were not appointed to positions that were still over their head. Executives should be able to stretch—that is, enter a bigger game—but not stretch too much, and the HR manager's rule of thumb was the stretch should be around 30 percent. That had no real anchoring in measurable attributes, but it did serve as a useful reminder of the need to stretch but not too far.[22]

Executive search firms seek to do much the same with external candidates, appraising the job and then the candidate to make sure the latter can rise to the former. Companies want someone who can do the job, and candidates want to know that they are capable of filling the shoes that have been proffered. But candidates should also want to know that the shoes do not have any hidden nails.

Doing Due Diligence

G. Richard Thoman.

IBM chief financial officer G. Richard Thoman failed to spot the nails when he accepted Xerox Corporation's offer to become its president and chief operating officer in June 1997. Like Gustavus Smith, Thoman's bloodlines were impeccable. He had been serving as the ranking executive at IBM behind Louis Gerstner, the talented outsider who had been recruited to turn Big Blue around. Now Xerox needed its own turnaround. Recruited by search firm Ramsey Beirne Associates, Thoman had seemed to fit the ticket. Before Big Blue, he had held senior posts at American Express and RJR Nabisco, and at IBM he had led the successful restructuring of its personal computer division.

"We were looking for a change agent," said CEO Paul Allaire, "and he seemed to be a perfect match." Wall Street agreed. Xerox shares rose $2 when Thoman's appointment was announced. Thoman agreed, too. He told a reporter that he saw himself as a "leader, someone who can size up a situation and act on it quickly." He was ready to take charge and make the hard decisions required of the corner office.

But what Thoman had not sized up before accepting the position was Xerox's resistant culture and Allaire's continuing presence. When Thoman challenged the company's belief that it had achieved world-class manufacturing standards, management pushed back. When he asked for swift cutbacks in the employment rolls, management studied the options for six months. When he moved to reorganize the sales force, opposition flared. Still, Xerox elevated Thoman to chief executive in April 1998, just as planned. "I'll always remember it as a summit moment," he recalled, "a feeling of arrival."

To make room for Thoman, Paul Allaire took leave of the corner office but remained chairman of the board, and he asked two Xerox executives who had been passed over in favor of Thoman—William Buehler and CFO Barry Romeril—to join the board as vice chairmen. Allaire also asked to attend management meetings with Thoman on the assurance that the chairman would remain mute. Still, as one executive recalled, "the line of eyes around the table would keep focusing on Paul even though Rick was doing all the talking." When Thoman considered ousting the two executives who had lost the succession struggle to him, he hesitated because of their seats on the board and long-standing friendship with Allaire. His free hand with the turnaround was quickly turning into something closer to status quo handcuffs.

In mid-1999 Xerox reported an 11 percent decline in income when growth had been expected. Wall Street reacted with fury to the surprise, stripping away a quarter of the company's market value in a single day. Soon, the two vice chairmen who reported as executives to

Thoman were complaining about him directly to chairman Allaire. On May 10, 2000, Allaire summoned Thomas to his office to tell him the board had decided to fire him the next day. Allaire later explained, "The problem Rick had was he did not connect well enough with people to get a good feel of what was going on in the organization and what was and wasn't possible."

For Thoman, the sacking was the abrupt and humiliating end of what had been until that moment a spectacular career. On the surface, the board had handed him a mandate to streamline and transform a legendary company that had become bogged down in old ways, much the same way Thoman's mentor Gerstner had been given a mandate to turn around a hidebound IBM. But Gerstner enjoyed the free hand denied his protégé. Surrounded by executives who had built the world he set out to dismantle, Thoman found himself first thwarted, then squeezed out altogether. Better for him that he had never sat down at the table in the first place. Better, too, that he had appreciated the hidden rules of the game before he picked up his cards.[23]

WHEN ALL ELSE FAILS

In centuries past, rulers nearing a decision point often turned to seers and oracles. The question would be put, and then a goat or chicken would be sacrificed and the entrails used for divination. For those still on the cusp of deciding whether to get into or stay out of the game, there is a useful modern counterpart: prophetic signs. Omens have no predictive value, but in getting to go, they help bring out underlying decision preferences.

When President Bill Clinton appointed Mickey Kantor to be U.S. trade representative in 1993, Kantor turned to Washington lawyer Charlene Barshefsky and asked her to serve as his deputy. Barshefsky knew that the post would provide an opportunity to shape U.S. trade

policy at a time of rapid glob-
alization in investment and
trade, especially with China
itching to join the World
Trade Organization. But she
already served as a partner in a
prominent law firm, cochair-
ing its international practice,
and she earned several times
what she would receive in government. With her husband,

Charlene Barshefsky (left) with U.S.
secretary of state Madeline Albright.

who also worked, she was raising two young daughters, ages four and
nine. Would serving in the Clinton administration be the right decision for her family or a dreadful mistake? Barshefsky became "paralyzed," she said, and days passed without resolution while Mickey
Kantor increasingly pressed her to make up her mind.

A week and a half after being asked, Barshefsky decided that she
had to decide even though she was still utterly irresolute. Driving to
work in downtown Washington with her husband, she announced
that she had to say yes or no that very day. She wished for some kind of
sign, she said. Several minutes later, as another car overtook hers, she
noticed that its vanity plate read GO4IT. It proved the omen she
needed. "I'm going to say yes!" she told her husband. Shortly after arriving in her office, she called Kantor to accept a job that would place
her on the forefront of negotiating China's entry into the WTO and
transforming America's arm's-length relations with the world's most
populous nation.[24]

In the spring of 2000, Rick Pitino was caught by much the same
moment of indecision as he sat on the porch of a rented house in
Louisville, Kentucky. Pitino was then coaching the Boston Celtics of
the professional National Basketball Association after a remarkable

college coaching career that included taking two teams—Kentucky and Providence—to the Final Four of the National Collegiate Athletic Association's annual tournament. The Kentucky Derby had brought Pitino to Louisville, but he had a second reason for being in town as well: an attractive offer to leave the NBA and become coach of the University of Louisville Cardinals.

Pitino was sitting on the porch talking the offer over with his friend Ralph Willard, the coach for Holy Cross. Willard said it would be tough to return to collegiate basketball. Pitino had done just about all he could do at that level. Moreover, there would be bitter feelings up the road at the University of Kentucky if its ex-coach signed on with its in-state archrival. At that very moment, Pitino recalled, a red cardinal landed on the table between them, almost as if it was a prophecy. In January 2001 Pitino resigned from the Celtics and three months later became the Cardinals' coach. When you are stuck at a decision point, it pays to listen to the small signs that can help reveal what you are thinking deep down inside.[25]

THE DECISION TEMPLATE FOR GETTING INTO THE DECISION GAME

Once again, I encourage the reader to extract the main lessons from the experiences that we have just witnessed. Keep in mind, too, that the resulting principles and tools are best remembered and invoked at a go point if they remain embedded in those experiences. When faced with a wrenching decision, remember Roberto Canessa as he resolved to walk out of the Andes to civilization; when faced with a promotion decision, recall the experiences of Gustavus Smith and Richard Thoman as they reached high; when faced with a seemingly undoable task, recall Dean Karnazes, Johannah Christensen, and Royal Robbins as they broke the grand task into hundreds of smaller decisions.

Principle	Tool	Illustration
1. Suppress your natural fears about making hard decisions.	Focus on ultimate goals for which decisions are intermediate steps.	Though nearly buried alive in an avalanche, Roberto Canessa refused to let fear of a recurrence dictate his actions.
2. To achieve daunting ends, focus on basic truths.	Use simple axioms to keep the ultimate goal clear.	Canessa constantly told himself "to the west, there's life, and where there's life, there's hope."
3. Look to the future instead of rethinking the past.	Channel thought and vision on what lies ahead.	Once on his climb to Chile, Canessa never questioned that it was the right course.
4. Combine dispassionate assessment with passionate commitment.	Embrace a goal but carefully analyze the means for achieving it.	Canessa studied the maps assiduously after pledging to climb toward Chile.
5. Take on the difficult decisions of the game.	Recognize that decision anxiety and even shocks are inherent in holding responsibility.	Rick Rieder reacted to the loss of a key human asset by setting out to win him back, not by giving in to anger or despair.
6. Prepare oneself to get into a bigger game.	Incrementally engage in decisions now to anticipate greater responsibility in the future.	Despite an excellent pedigree, Gustavus Smith proved unready for his battlefield promotion to army commander.
7. Break hard decisions into smaller steps.	Set proximate goals and tangible targets that add up to larger aims.	Royal Robbins, Dean Karnazes, and Johannah Christensen focused on the dozens of small steps ahead.

Principle	Tool	Illustration
8. Stay away from games where decisions are improperly constrained.	Conduct due diligence to detect hidden limitations on the power to decide.	Richard Thoman did not appreciate the constraints of having the former CEO on the board and his protégés in the ranks.
9. Trust your intuition if it is well informed.	Look for an omen that will bring out your intuition.	Charlene Barshefsky used a license plate of a passing car to trigger a decision to accept a demanding position.

3

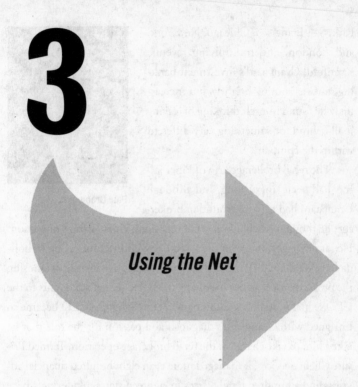

Using the Net

Paul D. Grangaard began his career with a bachelor's degree in economics from Stanford University and an MBA in finance and international business from the University of Chicago. Following a training stint in the Chicago headquarters and then the Frankfurt, Germany, branch of The First National Bank of Chicago—it would later merge into JPMorgan Chase—Grangaard joined Piper Jaffray in 1986. A midsized financial services company, Piper Jaffray offered investment services to both individual and institutional investors, including brokerage, investment banking, and asset management.

In 1995, at the relatively young age of thirty-seven, Grangaard was promoted to run the investment banking arm of Piper Jaffray. For the next five years he grew the franchise, opening offices in Menlo

Park, San Francisco, Chicago, New York, and London, and multiplying revenue sevenfold. Grangaard's investment banking star was shining brightly, but increasingly he found himself thinking of leaving it all behind for something very different within the company.

Paul Grangaard.

The retail brokerage arm of Piper Jaffray had been languishing, and although Grangaard had no background in brokerage, he thought he could see what was ailing Piper Jaffray's operation. He sat down at home over the three-day Martin Luther King Jr. holiday weekend in 2001 and banged out a seven-page memo, diagnosing the problems with an eye to solving them. He took his thoughts to the CEO's chief of staff at the company. Before long, the CEO became so intrigued with Grangaard's diagnosis and passion for the role that he asked him to take charge of the retail brokerage operation. Termed Private Client Services, it managed more than eight hundred financial advisors and a hundred retail offices in eighteen states, rendering advice to wealthy clients on how to allocate assets and prepare for retirement.

Grangaard knew the job was a stretch for him, but he also had some basic truths to work from. One was his personal philosophy that managers, above all himself, should take charge, rise to the next challenge, and then, to paraphrase one of Jim Collins' axioms in *Good to Great,* get the right people on the bus and the wrong ones off. The CEO was leading the entire company to embrace Jim Collins' concepts, and Grangaard had a boss willing to talk through the issues with him and to encourage change, a critical element in reaching the right go point.[1]

When Grangaard made the leap in October 2001, he knew he had a significant uphill climb, as an outsider to that side of the company, to establish the level of credibility necessary to lead brokers through significant change. He was therefore fully determined to get the right people around him as a leadership team. Even so, implementing change proved to be the toughest challenge of his career.[2]

GREATER RESPONSIBILITY, LARGER NET

Paul Grangaard is certainly not alone. Time and again during the interviewing for this book, I would ask people to name their most difficult decision, and as often as not, the answer would be deciding to accept a new position with amplified responsibilities. Greater stature brings more prestige, to be sure, but it also brings more demands, more stress, and more risk. The monetary rewards are higher in the more competitive bracket, as they should be, but so is the impact on others. Choosing to go after the brass ring alters more than the title and the office; it can impact many lives. The best way to get such consequential decisions right is not to make the leap alone.

Mark V. Hurd, another rising corporate star, took an even greater leap. Hurd had joined NCR in 1980 and rose quickly through its sales-and-marketing ranks. One executive who knew him well in those days recalls that Hurd was not particularly strong in public speaking, but he was drawn to "make hard decisions other people wouldn't make." That proved enough to propel Hurd to the company's apex in 2003. By early 2005, at age forty-eight, he was presiding over a publicly traded company with $6 billion in annual sales and 24,500 employees. For most, it might have been accomplishment enough for a lifetime, but Mark Hurd's world was about to become far larger.

Hewlett-Packard had just fired its celebrity CEO Carly Fiorina. Now, board chair Patricia Dunn called Hurd to ask if he would take over the troubled firm. On March 29, 2005, Hurd arrived at company headquarters in Palo Alto, California. Three days later, he officially assumed the helm of one of America's great technology franchises.

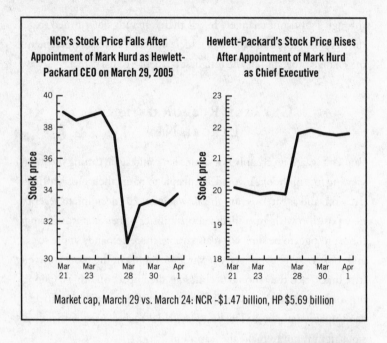

NCR's Stock Price Falls After Appointment of Mark Hurd as Hewlett-Packard CEO on March 29, 2005

Hewlett-Packard's Stock Price Rises After Appointment of Mark Hurd as Chief Executive

Market cap, March 29 vs. March 24: NCR -$1.47 billion, HP $5.69 billion

Hurd's ultimate superiors—the stockholders—placed big bets that his decisions would be worth billions to Hewlett-Packard. On the day he was announced as the new CEO, the market value of NCR plummeted by more than $1 billion compared to just two days earlier, while HP's soared by more than $5 billion.

Mark V. Hurd.

The pattern is not unusual. Just two months after Hurd's appointment, another troubled corporate icon, Boeing, forced out its own CEO for ethical lapses and brought in 3M chief executive James McNerney Jr. Within hours, investors had stripped $3 billion from the value of 3M and added $3 billion to Boeing. Nor is it unusual for investors to take back some of their initial enthusiasm in the

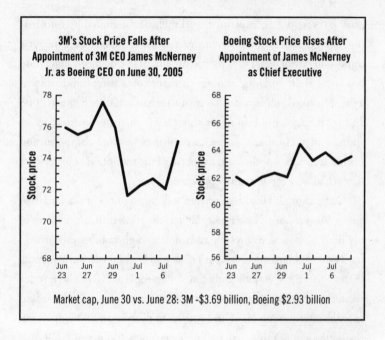

3M's Stock Price Falls After Appointment of 3M CEO James McNerney Jr. as Boeing CEO on June 30, 2005

Boeing Stock Price Rises After Appointment of James McNerney as Chief Executive

Market cap, June 30 vs. June 28: 3M -$3.69 billion, Boeing $2.93 billion

days that follow, as happened with both HP and Boeing. But the professional investors and equity analysts who drive these kind of stock gyrations place, in effect, multibillion-dollar wagers on the new executives' decision-making skills. And demonstrating early that the bet is well placed can be essential. "Being a CEO is like being a product," Hurd said of his jump to HP. "If you get out of the gate poorly, it's hard to recover."

James McNerney Jr.

ACQUIRING A NET

To make sure he got out of the gate well, Hurd sought advice from Hewlett-Packard's trenches. "I personally like to understand how the businesses work," he explained, and then he vacuumed up information and guidance from front-line managers, seasoned executives, and important customers. Hurd turned his e-mail in-box into a suggestion box and soon found it brimming with more than three hundred ideas a day. He asked employees what the business should look like in 2008 and what they would do in his shoes. One manager insisted, in response, that Hurd should recombine the personal computer and printer business. Another said to get rid of the mountain of paperwork that stood between him and customer calls.

Even though Hurd had proven willing to jump into a far larger game, his was not an easy move. "It was the most difficult decision of my life," he later said, a refrain common to high-ranking executives I interviewed. Hurd's decisions at HP would be far more consequential than at NCR. HP employed six times the people as NCR, and revenue was thirteen times greater. In one of his first major actions, just four months after joining HP, Hurd moved to dismiss 14,500 employees, the equivalent of more than half of the entire workforce at NCR.[3]

Rick Thoman had made a similar leap—from a senior post at IBM to the top operating slot at Xerox—without fully sizing up the terrain he was leaping to and without setting up a network of trusted advisors within Xerox once he arrived. Instead of a triumphant reign, Thoman came under constant sniper fire from below until his abrupt and humiliating removal from above. Mark Hurd did it differently. Early on at Hewlett-Packard, he made big, company-changing decisions, and he consulted with those whom he could trust before acting, listened before shooting.

Like Paul Grangaard, Hurd also made sure he got the wrong people off the bus and the right ones on it. And unlike Rick Thoman, who never could escape Paul Allaire's long shadow at Xerox or create his own shadow below, Hurd swiftly established his own net at the top. All that, in fact, is consistent with an array of research that points to the quality of a company's top team as a better predictor of the firm's fate than the capacity of any single executive. Equity analysts say the same thing when they insist on meeting not just with the CEO but the entire top tier before deciding whether to recommend or downgrade a stock.[4]

Developing and managing your network—both the inner and outer parts—can be vital for the hard, fateful decisions ahead.

CONSULTING THE INNER CIRCLE

At the center of an effective decision-making net is a small band of trusted advisors. In her study of computer hardware and software companies in Silicon Valley, Kathleen Eisenhardt found that one of the key distinguishing factors between companies that moved swiftly and those that plodded along was whether their managers sought advice from experienced and unbiased counselors before reaching decisions. The advisors, generally inside the company rather than outside consultants, served as sounding board, advice givers, and confidence boosters. The best of them knew much about the business but did not want the boss's job, and thus were willing and able to provide catholic, non-self-serving guidance. When consulting with such counselors, the research suggests, company managers became more comfortable in reaching major decisions, often in half the time.[5]

The value of such counseling was much in evidence at Internet equipment manufacturer Cisco Systems as it rode the technology wave during the late 1990s and early 2000s. Like other high-tech companies, Cisco took a big hit when the Internet bubble burst in 2000, but over the ten years beginning in 1995, Cisco grew from 4,000 employees and revenues of $2 billion to 34,000 employees and revenue of $24 billion.

Much of Cisco's growth came through acquisitions of firms that had developed new technologies. In 2000, for instance, it spent $355 million to pick up Growth Networks, a 1998 start-up that had created a new form of silicon that would help Cisco build extremely fast switches and routers. Because Cisco was an end game sought by many Silicon Valley entrepreneurs, such buyout offers arrived by the dozens on the desk of John Chambers, who had run the company's marketing, manufacturing, and research operations before taking over as CEO in 1995. But even though Chambers chose few—only one in ten on average during the first decade of his service as CEO—his hit rate was extraordinarily high.[6]

How did he manage, I asked, to make consistently good acquisition calls and to do so in the fast time frame required? The first person he pointed to was John P. Morgridge, who had served as Cisco's CEO from 1988, when the firm employed just thirty-four people and booked only $5 million, until 1995, when he became nonexecutive chairman of the board and yielded the corner office to Chambers. The second person was Larry Carter, his financial officer, who happened to be standing next to him at the time.[7]

Both men, Chambers said, provided fast and unbiased evaluations of proposed purchases. They needed no briefing on the firm's interests, and they gave him candid advice on whether a proposed acquisition was in Cisco's interest. What he did not have to add was that neither man wanted his title: Morgridge had already had it and Carter was of an age—six years senior to Chambers—that would prevent it.

CONSULTING AN ORACLE

An informed counselor comes in many guises: work associate, significant other, college friend, board member. Early in his life, the Dalai Lama further stretched the boundaries.

The Dalai Lama's life story is well known. Born in a village in northeastern Tibet in 1935 and identified by Buddhist monks at age two as the reincarnation of the thirteenth Dalai Lama, he became the newest Buddha of Compassion before he could spell or even comprehend the honor. The Dalai Lama was still only a teenager when China's People's Liberation Army invaded Tibet in 1950, creating a political crisis that led to his sudden elevation as head of state for a vast territory with six million citizens.

The Dalai Lama and his mother shortly after entering exile in India.

For the next decade, the young Dalai Lama strove to protect Tibet's autonomy against China's rising encroachment. He traveled to Beijing at age nineteen to seek a solution from China's leadership. Two years later, in March 1957, he was returning from a meeting with the Indian prime minister when he saw red banners proclaiming the People's Republic of China flapping beside the traditional prayer flags of his own people. More ominous still, a People's Liberation Army general had come to meet him at the Tibetan border.

"Although he was a good and sincere man," the Dalai Lama recalled, "I could not help thinking of him in terms of the military uniform he wore, rather than in terms of 'liberation.' "[8]

Two more years of political tension and military repression in Tibet led to open revolt in early 1959. Eight Chinese divisions with 150,000 well-armed soldiers had earlier arrived to suppress roving bands of mountain insurgents; now they turned their attention to the new urban uprisings as well.

Amidst these momentous developments, the ranking Chinese general in Tibet, Tan Kuan-sen, insisted that the Dalai Lama view a performance on March 10 of a visiting dance troupe at the Chinese military headquarters, and that he come without his own soldiers or armed bodyguards. To avoid affront, the Dalai Lama agreed to attend, but as word spread of his impending visit, thousands filled the streets, spurred to action by rumors that their spiritual and political leader could be personally endangered. The next day, with protesting women filling the streets of the capital, Lhasa, the Chinese command issued an ultimatum that all demonstrators must disband. Tibetan officials responded that they would no longer recognize Chinese authority if General Tan's troops moved to crush the protests.

"Go! Go! Tonight!"

"What was I to do?" the Dalai Lama wondered. In fact, his tradition contained a distinctive device for finding out. For counsel in this most delicate of diplomatic relationships, the Dalai Lama often turned to a revered member of his net, the state oracle. He asked the oracle if he should remain in Lhasa or flee toward India. The oracle advised him to remain and continue a dialogue with General Tan. Three days later, however, the Dalai Lama learned that the Chinese general was commencing preparations for an attack on the Lhasa street protestors. The Dalai Lama feared thousands of casualties, but again, he said, "I was at a loss as to what to do next." On March 17, he once again sought the counsel of the oracle. This time he heard an alarming response: "Go! Go! Tonight!"

The Dalai Lama delayed a day, but on the following evening he reread a passage from the Buddha's sutras emphasizing the need for "confidence and courage," and in disguise, with a rifle slung over his shoulder, the twenty-three-year-old spiritual leader and head of state slipped quietly out a side door. Following an arduous and sometimes terrifying escape, the Dalai Lama crossed into India on March 31. More than eighty thousand Tibetans would follow him into exile.

Taking up residence in Dharamsala, a hilly city in the Himalayan foothills of northern India, the Dalai Lama has presided in the decades since over a Tibetan government in exile and served as inspirational leader of not only Tibetan Buddhists but also those of many faiths around the world. His book *The Art of Happiness* has sold more than a million copies since its publication in 1998. Having exited his first calling, the Dalai Lama opted to pursue an even larger one. His decision to flee Tibet had been the fateful moment, and he had come to that go point through dialogue with one of the most trusted members of his inner circle. Informed advice can be drawn from many points in the net.[9]

CONSULTING THE OUTER CIRCLE

A trusted inner circle is an invaluable source of counsel in making decisions. Who knows us better, after all, than those who stand by our side? Yet research and experience also tell us that the best advice does not always come from those closest to us. Intimates support and advise us, but they may think too much like us and bring forth too little intelligence from distant points.

Researcher Mark Granovetter noticed that in finding new jobs, engineers often developed better leads through acquaintances than friends. Because the former are more socially remote from the job seeker, they reached further afield and thus spied more openings. In Granovetter's phrasing, those anxious to secure work elsewhere found particular strength in their "weak ties," receiving most from those they knew least.[10]

The same applies to decision making. With less directly invested in the outcome, our weak ties can be more skeptical of a proposed course of action, or they may have unique information that bears on the decision. Their outsider status can help them see concerns that the inner circle cannot. The wider and more diverse the outer net, the better the chance that *all* the stakes will be factored into the decision before it is too late.

Irving Janis argued the case so well in 1972 that not only has his article become a minor classic of the business school repertoire, but its title—"Groupthink"—has also entered our everyday language. In its assessment of the failure of U.S. spy agencies to correctly identify whether Iraq possessed weapons of mass destruction, for instance, the U.S. Senate Intelligence Committee attributed the problem partly to groupthink that led the "Intelligence Community analysts, collectors, and managers to both interpret ambiguous evidence as conclusively indicative of a WMD program as well as ignore or minimize evidence that Iraq did not have active and expanding weapons of mass destruction programs." So strong was this presumption of doomsday arms, said the Senate investigators, that a host of customary methods for "challeng[ing] assumptions and group think were not utilized."[11]

Groupthink, Janis argued, stemmed from "group norms that bolster morale at the expense of critical thinking." In other words, when the inner circle feels compelled to go along to get along, its analytic capacities are left at the door. That, Janis argued, explained many suboptimal national decisions, from John F. Kennedy's support for an invasion of Cuba at the Bay of Pigs to Lyndon Johnson's decision to escalate military action in Vietnam. One simple but critical corrective, he urged, was to bring outsiders into the inner circle.[12]

Weak Ties, Strong Results

Academic studies confirm the importance of expanding the net well beyond one's personal counselor or spiritual advisor. In one investigation, researchers Mark S. Mizruchi and Linda Brewster Stearns studied how managers at a large commercial bank closed deals with their corporate customers. Since completing such deals is subject to considerable uncertainty, the researchers hypothesized that the strength of a banker's relations with his or her colleagues would affect the likelihood of successfully doing a deal. They were right, but not exactly in the way they expected.

Working with some fourteen hundred multinational corporate

customers, the bankers offered four main products: commercial lend-
ing such as lines of credit and project finance, trading services including derivatives and currency exchange, capital market services, and
transactional services such as cash management. The bankers endured
tough competition from other banks in all four areas, and they also
faced an internal hurdle: final authorization for any deal had to come
from at least three bank executives, including a senior credit officer.
The bank had imposed this approval process to ensure that deals meet
its criteria for acceptable rates of return and levels of risk.

The researchers evaluated the uncertainty factor in a given deal by
asking the responsible banker to assess the risk to the bank's capital and
whether the banker trusted the customer's key executive behind the
deal. When uncertainty in a deal was large—high risk and low trust—
the researchers expected that the bankers were more likely to turn for
advice to colleagues with whom they had already established strong
working relationships. They found what they anticipated: the greater
the uncertainty in the 137 deals studied, the greater a banker's reliance
on trusted colleagues.

But Mizruchi and Sterns then discovered an ironic outcome: the
greater the reliance of a banker on a familiar circle of associates within
the bank, the more likely those contacts were to know one another and
thus the less likely the banker was to receive a diverse range of views
and feedback on a deal and to win approval for it. In the final analysis,
relying upon strong ties without also turning to weak ones proved a
source of weakness, not strength.[13]

None of this is to minimize the importance of catholic input from
trusted associates in making a decision. Our inner circle functions in a
sense as our collective memory and private sounding board. But too
close can also be too limiting. Decision makers wisely turn not only to
their inner circle but also to a diverse range of associates in their outer
circle—Granovetter's "weak ties"—to get as complete a picture as possible before reaching a good and binding decision.

DEVOLVING AND
RETAINING DECISIONS

Not only is the outer circle likely to possess vital information, but it might also be better equipped to make front-line decisions than the central figure. Denizens of the outer circle are often closer to the action and can better appreciate the tangible context of a decision. Devolution of the decision making to them makes good sense—providing those on the front line have been well schooled in how to make good decisions consistent with the enterprise's objectives.

The U.S. Marine Corps is a seasoned practitioner of the art of devolving decision making. Commanders define the mission, but of battlefield necessity, teams of Marines make most of the field decisions during focused and fast-moving assaults. As Marine Corps general Peter Pace puts it, commanders should tell subordinates, "Look, if it's not dying or burning, don't call me." Officers who cannot or will not yield their powers find their outer circles less able to achieve missions and their own careers often cut short in consequence.[14]

Zhang Ruimin has used the same pattern of devolving decisions to transform Chinese home appliance giant Haier into a global player, but the practice emerged slowly as the terrain gradually broadened under Zhang's feet.

"Twenty years ago when Haier started," he recalled, "it was a small factory on the verge of bankruptcy, with only 600 people. At that time, the top priority for the leaders was to make quick, tough decisions and ask subordinates to execute them accurately. Our management style had to be top-down. We worked like marshals and generals and asked people to carry out our instructions," he said. "We

Zhang Ruimin.

needed to hold ourselves accountable for all our decisions, and we required our people to execute them very quickly."[15]

Two decades later, with 15,000 manufactured products and 50,000 employees spread across 160 countries, Zhang of necessity has decentralized the structure. He decided to let subordinates make their own calls—though always within a disciplined and demanding regime that he imposed. "It is impossible today to rely upon a single person or just one management team to make decisions responding to the challenges in the global market," he explained.

Mini-Mini Corporations

To push more decisions down, Zhang flattened the organization and created mini-mini corporations—MMCs—within the company to make decisions on their own. "These MMCs can respond more swiftly to the needs of their respective markets and win more customers by independent innovations," he told me.

Zhang instructed the manager of his American operations, for instance, that he had to compete head to head with home appliance giants General Electric and Whirlpool. To do so, he said, the manager would have to win over American customers by making his or her own local marketing choices. The American manager and his team have "to make every detailed decision themselves," Zhang explained. "We don't want [our] managers to keep coming back and asking questions about why and how they should do something. We want them to find solutions that can increase our competitiveness in that market. In other words, we set up a target, but they have to decide themselves—in their context—on how to reach it and by what innovative approach."

Today, Haier is China's largest producer of appliances, including microwaves, televisions, even wine cellars and beer dispensers. Thousands of American college students chill snacks in their dormitory rooms with Haier's portable refrigerators. Much of that growth can be attributed to Zhang's devolution of decision making, but not all. As anxious as he has been to put power in the hands of Haier's front-line managers, Zhang has retained for himself the very biggest decisions, such as his 2005 attempt to acquire America's third-largest appliance maker, Maytag. Building and managing a net is not about abdicating decision-making responsibility. It is about gathering input from many angles and then assigning the decision to the person best advantaged to reach the right go point.

Giving Everyone Some Say

Devolving and retaining decisions might sound like polar opposites, but they should not be viewed as alternatives or mutually exclusive. Often it is a matter of doing both at the same time, making a decision but not before consulting those most affected by it. Consider mountaineer Arlene Blum, who organized the 1978 Women's Himalayan Expedition to climb one of the world's highest and most dangerous peaks, Annapurna. Its summit pierced the sky at 26,545 feet. To reach it, the expedition would have to dodge the killer avalanches that regularly caromed down its precipitous slopes. To prepare the world-class climbers she had recruited for the assault, Blum brought in a consulting psychologist, who asked the group what qualities they wanted to see in their leader. "Someone who's strong and decisive, who makes firm decisions and sticks to them," offered one of the mountaineers. Yet another countered, "But we all want to be part of the decision-making process."

Decisions, in short, were expected of Arlene Blum, but so was consultation. Her high-octane mountaineers understandably were looking for both, but how to reconcile them, how both to devolve and to retain decision making? "I couldn't help wondering what it meant to be the strong leader of twelve tough-minded women, each of whom

Arlene Blum.

wanted to contribute to each decision," recalled Blum. "I was a bit flummoxed about how I was going to meet this challenge." Mindful of the need for clear direction among the many dangers they would face in the Himalayas, she resolved to be a "model of decisiveness."[16]

From the outset, Arlene Blum knew that her most fateful decision would be to select from the eight climbers the two who would go for the summit. The logic was clear: a two-woman assault would require six climbers to provide the vital support base. Try to send everyone up, and no one was likely to succeed. Intellectually, the veteran climbers all understood the principle. Emotionally, though, each wanted a crack at the top. "Although everyone agreed that if anyone reached the top it would be a victory for us all," Blum said, each climber wanted to be that "anyone." In the end, after extensive consultation with each member of the group, Blum made the call she knew she had to retain for herself, and the two she selected did reach the summit, a crowning moment for both her expedition and women's mountaineering. Her go point was both decisive and consultative.[17]

Retrieving Decisions

Sometimes a decision sent out to the front lines for the best of reasons has to be reeled back in. The stakes may have been miscalculated. More often, circumstances have changed. What seemed of mild consequence under the old calculus may no longer appear that way in a reconfigured world. Instead of leaving delegated responsibility vested in the ranks, it is time to retrieve it.

Norman Pearlstine, editor in chief of Time Inc. since 1994, faced such a moment in 2005. *Time* magazine reporter Matthew Cooper had run an article in which an unidentified government source named Valerie Plame as a CIA agent. When Cooper refused to name his informant during a grand jury investigation of the leak, U.S. prosecutor Patrick J. Fitzgerald threatened incarceration, and with that, Time's general counsel's office began gearing up for a public fight. *New York Times* reporter Judith Miller found herself facing the same fate for a similar refusal to cooperate.

Time Inc. is both a vast enterprise in its own right, including its flagship magazine and a stable of other publications, and a part of Time Warner, whose holdings stretch out to include AOL, HBO, filmmaking, and cable television. As a key player in a megacorporation, Pearlstine's first instinct was to let the process work as planned. He might advise, but the general counsel would decide. The more he considered the case, though, the more Pearlstine became convinced this one was different. His world had changed.

Pearlstine had worked his way up the corporate ladder as an editor, but he had been trained as an attorney, and that is what he called on now. When federal Judge Thomas F. Hogan held both Cooper and

Norman Pearlstine.

the magazine in contempt for refusing to give Cooper's interview notes to the grand jury, Pearlstine started delving into prior cases of how editors had responded when court orders had gone against them.

In part, the issue was legal: What were the applicable statutes? Had they complied? In part, it was personal: Cooper, after all, would have to bear the burden of the company's stance. But in part, the issue was also corporate. Pearlstine felt deeply that he had to protect the editorial independence of the magazine, but his obligation was not just to *Time*'s editors and reporters; it was also to Time Warner's shareholders. In the end, letting the decision happen somewhere else just felt wrong. The stakes were too large. It was time to reverse the devolution and bite the bullet in his own office.

"As editor in chief, I am totally responsible not only for the editorial independence of this division, but decisions like these," Pearlstine said. When the U.S. Supreme Court refused on June 27, 2005, to hear an appeal of the judge's decision, Pearlstein decided that his magazine and reporter would have to cooperate with the court. Cooper himself and many *Time* reporters criticized Pearlstine for making it far more difficult for them to protect and thus learn from anonymous sources, but Pearlstine stood his ground. "Thinking we're above the law rings wrong to me," he explained.[18]

Sometimes bottom-line conditions leave little choice except for the top decision maker to retrieve the authority. Witness General Motors' chief executive Richard Wagoner's response when his biggest operation, the North American auto unit, lost $1.6 billion in the first three months of 2005, plunging the company into the largest quarterly loss since a 1992 collapse that cost then-CEO Robert Stemple his job. With credit agencies preparing to downgrade GM debt to near-junk status and investors driving its stock price to a ten-year low, Wagoner reassigned the North American auto unit's chairman and president to other duties, and on April 4 took over the operation himself.

"Given the challenges we face in North America," he explained at the time, "it makes sense for me to assume control of GM North America's day-to-day operations and shorten the lines of communication and decision-making." Wagoner was already familiar with the business: he had run the North American operation from 1994 to 1998, when he had returned it to profitability. Now all its day-to-day decisions would be directly in his hands, along with decisions for the entire enterprise.[19]

Retrieving devolved decision-making authority can prove extremely hard, whether you are dealing with a division president, a field commander, or a teenager at home. Few of those who have accepted authority are ready to return it, but when the stakes are high or threats large, recalling decision authority can be the most essential decision of all.

Taking Decisions Up

The net includes those above, not just those below and around, but deciding which decisions to send up the chain of command can be particularly delicate. As much as some decisions cry out for review from on high, no one wants to appear weak or indecisive to the boss or the board. Referring a decision upward runs the risk of having your superiors think you are not ready to exercise the assigned responsibilities of your own level, let alone the next one up.

To smooth the path to the top and to prevent it from becoming clogged with less-than-vital matters, many companies have created a decision protocol to provide formal guidance by itemizing decisions that executives must take up to the board or resolve themselves. HBOS, one of Britain's largest financial services companies, requires that final decisions be made by its directors on top executive pay, transactions exceeding £50 million, and new lines of business that constitute more than 1 percent of a division's gross income.[20]

Beyond the written guidelines, directors and executives at many firms have established a norm on what should go up to the board or remain within management. The norm is an informal prescription that material issues be resolved by the directors: issues with the potential for substantial gains or losses for the company, ones that lie outside the company's normal business operations, and ones likely to affect the company's strategy or reputation.[21]

Betting the Company

At Boeing, one of the thousands of normal decisions of its engineers would be whether to include "gaspers," those little round overhead nozzles that blow cool air toward your seat, on a new aircraft. The decision would seem to be a no-brainer. Who wants *less* air on a plane stuck on some runway? Yet in designing its new 787, once dubbed the Dreamliner, Boeing engineers found themselves debating seriously whether to include the gaspers. The engineers' goal was to make the 787 a quieter, simpler, roomier, and more efficient aircraft than anything Boeing or archrival Airbus had ever produced. Without gaspers, ductwork would be easier and reconfiguring seats faster. That was the upside. The downside would come if customers started complaining that the cabin was stuffy or that they felt a draft from a centralized air system.

Before reaching a final decision on the gasper, chief architect Walter Gillette referred the question to his own net. He asked his fluid dynamics specialists to model the airflow within the fuselage with and without the gaspers. He also asked the airlines that he hoped would one day purchase the aircraft if the gaspers were needed or not. Gaspers were just one of dozens upon dozens of calls Gillette had to make, but the cost of getting all those decisions right was estimated to run in the billions of dollars, an expensive process with a potentially huge penalty for error. If the design features ultimately proved unappealing, the Dreamliner might prove Boeing's first-ever commercial aircraft fiasco.

With his own due diligence completed, Gillette carried the overall design up the ladder to Boeing's executive team, first led by CEO Philip M. Condit and then by successor CEO Harry C. Stonecipher. As much as both men might have liked to stop the buck there, they knew that with billions of dollars potentially on the line, they also had to carry the decision up to the board. The company norm—and common sense—called for directors to make calls of that scale. As nonexecutive chairman Lewis Platt recalled, it was a "bet-the-company decision."

Boeing's board ultimately made three critical strategic decisions on the 787. The first was to approve a budget and timeline for the aircraft's development. Next, board members authorized the company's sales managers to discuss specifications, cost, and delivery date of the aircraft with the airlines. Finally, the board gave the go-ahead to launch the program of actually building the aircraft.

The first decision involved placing a bet on the future of airline travel. Airbus had already cast its lot with the double-decker A380 on the premise that crowded hub-and-spoke airports would make this "superjumbo" with its 840 potential seats more appealing since it could carry nearly twice the load for the same number of gates, pilots, and takeoffs. Boeing, by contrast, came to believe that the hub-and-spoke system was breaking down. Passengers, so this theory went, would far prefer faster direct service between two points if it could be made feasible in distance and economical in price. The 787 promised long-haul service for 20 percent less cost because of its new technologies.

The second decision required that the board be confident that the company could manufacture the 787 with its promised specifications, cost, and delivery date. The aircraft was to be built with a higher percentage of lightweight, high-strength composite materials that Boeing had pioneered on earlier commercial jet programs, such as the 737 and the 777. The composites would allow for lower costs and creature comforts ranging from bigger windows to higher humidity. With decisions one and two made, the board finally had to commit the billions of dollars needed to put the aircraft into production well before its customers had given it the billions to do so.

In the end, after extensive discussions with company executives at a number of board meetings, the directors voted unanimously to go ahead on all three decisions. None of the decisions was easily arrived at, and one or more of them might still prove costly in the extreme. But all three calls were finally made where they had to be. When putting the company on the line, the bet is best placed at the very top, and taking it to the top was essential.[22]

THE DECISION TEMPLATE
FOR USING THE NET

How strong are the circles in your nets, both those close-in and those on the perimeter? Is there an oracle or expert you can count on at crunch time? Are you ready to let a decision go, or retrieve it, or carry it to the top? Think back to Paul Grangaard, the Dalai Lama, Arlene Blum, and the others you have just read about; draw out the enduring lessons from their experiences by imagining you are in their shoes, facing the same go points; then compare your own principles and tools with the ones I have extracted in the template below.

Principle	Tool	Illustration
1. Construct a net.	Turn to others and bring in still more upon whom you will depend when making decisions.	In making the jump to new, high-pressure jobs, Paul Grangaard and Mark Hurd worked to build a net above and below them before they acted.

Principle	Tool	Illustration
2. Consult the inner circle.	Identify several informed and unbiased insiders for informal advice.	Cisco's CEO John Chambers turned to board chair John Morgridge and CFO Larry Carter.
3. Consult an oracle or expert.	Seek out wise associates who are exceptionally clear-minded about what the future may hold.	The Dalai Lama asked the state oracle if it was the right moment to flee Tibet.
4. Consult the outer circle.	Pursue advice and guidance from those with whom you have only weak ties.	Investment bankers who reached beyond their inner circle within the firm were more likely to complete a deal.
5. Devolve and retain decisions.	Make intent clear, then let those close to the front line decide for you or with you.	Haier's CEO Zhang Ruimin created mini-mini corporations and invested decision authority in them.
6. Retrieve decisions.	Pull back decisions from others when the consequences become more critical.	Time's CEO Norman Pearlstine and GM's CEO Richard Wagoner retook control over legal strategy and a losing operation.
7. Take decisions up.	When the impact is potentially great, escalate the decision to a higher level.	Boeing executives carried the decision to design, sell, and launch the 787 up to the directors.
8. Decide on which decisions to take.	Prepare a decision protocol that makes explicit which decisions are retained, delegated, retrieved, or taken up.	British bank HBOS followed its written "Matters Reserved for the Board" protocol.

4

Seeing Ahead

We were standing on the left flank of Pickett's Charge, the open field where on July 3, 1863, Confederate General George Pickett led 13,000 troops—some say 15,000—into an attack on a well-fortified Union line at Gettysburg, Pennsylvania. Pickett's men walked into cannon bursts, then musket volleys, and finally fixed bayonets. It would prove a disastrous charge, a stunning defeat for Robert E. Lee's Army of Northern Virginia, one of the great turning points of the Civil War.

We all tried to visualize Pickett's soldiers, arrayed in disciplined lines stretching a full mile along Seminary Ridge, drums rolling, as they commenced their valiant march forward. We then turned our gaze toward Cemetery Ridge, imagining the massed federal defenders crouched in wait behind a stone wall. And we wondered how Robert E.

Lee could have decided to order his infantry to attack with no cover against what certainly looked to us now—and to many then—to be a nearly impregnable line of defense.

A group of thirty-three midcareer managers had come here to study decision making during the Battle of Gettysburg, July 1–3, 1863. With us were managers from Bristol-Myers Squibb, Deutsche Bank, NASA, and a diverse array of other organizations. Some had come from as far away as Australia and India. Few knew much about the Civil War, and none had mastery of the events at Gettysburg. Collectively, we had little interest in history for its own sake, but we all had a deep interest in how the history in front of us might instruct us as we made our own.

Just months earlier I had stood on the same ground with a group of MBA students. Accompanying us that time was Grant Behrman, managing partner of Behrman Capital, a private equity firm based in New York and San Francisco. In helping our students see the implications of the battlefield decisions for their own future choices, Behrman observed that in his own line of work, tactical errors can often be rectified, but strategic blunders usually cannot. Thus, he said, it is especially important to get the big decisions right. Robert E. Lee could make up for many of the small miscalculations that come with any great engagement, Behrman said, but Lee's decision to attack the center of the Union line on the third day of the battle proved irretrievably disastrous.

As they gazed across the now sacred ground of the battlefield, our midcareer managers and MBA students were reminded of the importance of seeing ahead, of thinking strategically, of appreciating the full picture before reaching big decisions.

Some institutions explicitly demand forethought. Under the operating principles of the U.S. Navy, for instance, an officer on a ship's bridge is obligated to think ahead and thus anticipate the most unlikely contingencies. "The single most important attribute for boat-ing," one naval manual says, is "forehandedness," a capacity that al-lows a captain to "avoid surprises," since they are "almost universally unwelcome at sea." The Navy, though is the exception. Most of us are left to acquire this vital skill on our own.[1]

Seeing ahead in decision making entails an ability to anticipate future developments, foresee how others will decide, and consider all the critical factors and forces that can impinge on the outcome. It re-quires transcending one's own perspective, ensuring that the decision is driven by the mission and situation of the enterprise rather than by personal interest or individual bias. Seeing ahead involves a combina-tion of intuition, analysis, and creativity to arrive at a broad and inte-grated assessment of what decision course to follow. It is a matter of thinking strategically.[2]

Few better venues exist for identifying the key components of see-ing and thinking ahead than the Gettysburg battlefield. Here, the commanders' decisions and their consequences are not only well de-fined and very tangible, but also vested with historic consequences. What is more, virtually every significant decision has been the subject of exhaustive study. One online bookseller lists more than 1,500 titles on Gettysburg, another more than 3,000. It is thus an exceptionally well-informed ground for extracting lessons on the value of seeing ahead and the tragic downsides of failing to do so.[3]

Pickett's Charge was—and remains—the most spectacular mo-ment of the Gettysburg battle, at once both transfixing and horrifying. But the historic attack and its appalling losses were not the product of a single decision. Five major decisions brought George Pickett's men to that open field and propelled them across it in the face of withering fire. The first came on May 15, 1863, in the War Department of the Confederacy; the last was made on the evening of July 2 in the field headquarters of Robert E. Lee. Had a different go point been reached at any of these junctures, the charge likely never would have been launched. Instead, the five decisions constituted a chain, each contingent upon the former, all collectively leading to a turning point in the American Civil War.

Forces far larger than any military commander brought the two armies together at Gettysburg. Yet it was the discrete decisions of individual commanders in the field and their ability to anticipate the future that determined how the armies would finally part.[4]

Go Point 1:
Taking the War North

Though regional conflicts over industrialization, slavery, and states' rights had been simmering for decades, the first real shots of the Civil War did not come until the spring of 1861. South Carolina had seceded from the Union the prior December, but federal troops remained ensconced in Fort Sumter in Charleston's harbor. Secessionist forces commanded by General P. G. T. Beauregard opened fire on the fort at 4:30 a.m. on April 12, and after thirty-six hours of bombardment, the United States surrendered its enclave. Nobody on either side had been killed or seriously wounded, but arms had been fired and the war was on.

Rapid military mobilization followed on both sides. On the eve of the Union's breakup, 16,000 soldiers were in uniform. Four years later, their ranks had risen a hundredfold, with 1 million Yankees in blue and 600,000 rebels in gray. What many observers had expected to be a six-week tempest after Fort Sumter had morphed into a seemingly endless storm. By the time it all ended four years later,

Confederate president Jefferson Davis.

more than 620,000 had perished in some 10,000 military engagements.

During the spring and summer of 1862, the Union launched its Peninsula Campaign under the generalship of George B. McClellan to capture the Confederate capital at Richmond and end the secession. Coming within 6 miles of Richmond, the offensive nearly succeeded, but on June 1, Robert E. Lee rallied the defending forces and pushed McClellan back

Confederate general
Robert E. Lee.

off the peninsula. In the months that followed, Lee led his Army of Northern Virginia through four of the greatest engagements of the entire Civil War. After successfully defending Richmond, he subsequently defeated the Union army in August at Second Manassas, engaged the same army in September at Antietam, and won decisively in December at Fredericksburg and in May at Chancellorsville.

Yet the string of Southern successes came as Pyrrhic victories, nominal triumphs but each more costly to the South than the North. The Confederacy numbered just 9 million residents—with more than a third still in slavery—while the Union counted 22 million. With the war turning from a contest over controlling territories to one of destroying armies, the escalating body count did not favor the South. The Confederacy could not field armies the size of the Union's, and replacements were even scarcer. Lee's second in command, James Longstreet, had come to characterize their winning record as one of "fruitless victories" that "would eventually destroy us." Lee himself had become despondent after his dramatic upset victory at Chancellorsville against a Union force twice as large. His army suffered 13,500 casualties in triumph, more than a fifth of its ranks, compared with just 13 percent for the army he had defeated. "Our loss was severe," he complained.[5]

Strategic Thinking

To reverse the Confederacy's declining fortunes, Lee proposed after his Chancellorsville victory of May 1863 that he march his army out of Virginia and into Pennsylvania. It would be the first time a Southern army had invaded the true North, not just a border state such as Maryland, where the battle of Antietam had been fought the prior September. In Pennsylvania, Lee argued, he could exercise an offensive upper hand and define where and how he would engage the enemy. Defeating a Union army on Northern soil, as he fully expected to do, would stir political pressures that could force President Abraham Lincoln to do what military defeats had so far failed to achieve: permit the Confederacy to endure, to stand secure.

That, in fact, would require enormous pressure. Lincoln had repeatedly asserted that there was no room for compromise with the secessionists, nothing to negotiate. But with a national election looming in 1864 and with opposition Democrats talking of a presidential platform and candidate committed to ending the war soon, Lee anticipated that the defeat of a Union army on home ground would surely intensify the peace-now drumbeat. Either Lincoln would be forced into a more conciliatory stance before the election or he and the Republicans would find themselves on the outside looking in after the election.

"If successful," wrote Lee, "next fall there will be a great change in public opinion in the North. The Republicans will be destroyed & I think the friends of peace will become so strong as that the next administration will go in on that basis."[6]

Robert E. Lee was seeing well ahead, sensing that his war-as-usual victories would ultimately spell Confederate defeat. "We should assume the aggressive," Lee wrote Confederate president Jefferson Davis, contending that the South ought to take a dramatic initiative if it was to overcome a strategic decline that had been masked so far by its tactical victories. He was also looking far afield, appreciating that his objectives might be furthered by not just armed warfare but also political dynamics.[7]

Lee carried this thinking into a meeting on May 15 with Davis and war secretary James A. Seddon in Richmond. In Lee's view, the choice was stark. His army could fall back in defense of the Confederate capital, and there "stand a siege, which must ultimately have ended in surrender." Or, he said, the army could "invade Pennsylvania" and thereby seize the strategic initiative. Davis and his war council had come to a moment of decision, one of those go points when everyone recognizes the magnitude of the stakes, and they resolved to adopt Lee's bold plan of marching his army into the Union heartland. The war secretary declared that the go-north strategy was "indispensable to our safety and independence."[8]

On May 17, Lee began to ready his troops for their northward push. Six weeks later, on June 30, 1863, not far into Pennsylvania, his army stumbled onto Yankee cavalry that had been searching for it. The next morning, the two war machines locked in mortal combat near the town of Gettysburg.

GO POINT 2:
REPLACING THE UNION COMMANDER

Although he was uncertain about Lee's precise target, Abraham Lincoln recognized the strategic import of the South's march northward and instructed General Joseph Hooker to take his Army of the Potomac in hot pursuit. Hooker's force of 95,000 substantially outnumbered Lee's 75,000 troops, but Hooker himself was increasingly a problem.[9]

On May 13, just ten days after his stunning defeat at Chancellorsville, Lincoln summoned Hooker to Washington to say that his own officers were not giving him "their entire confidence." The humiliating loss was an obvious factor, but also stoking the revolt was Hooker's poor behavior after the battle. He had held himself blameless while publicly pinning the defeat on his cavalry commander and two corps commanders.[10]

Union president Abraham Lincoln.

To be sure, several of Hooker's generals had committed errors at Chancellorsville worthy of criticism, but the public finger-pointing by the commanding general led nearly all of his own generals to close ranks against him. One of his top subordinates, George Meade, offered that the Chancellorsville "operations have shaken the confidence of the army in Hooker's judgment, particularly among the superior officers." Another officer wrote that "no one whose opinion is worth anything has now any confidence in General Hooker."[11]

Union general Joseph Hooker.

With the upper ranks of the Army of the Potomac severely demoralized, Lincoln worried that his biggest army was ill-prepared for the momentous task of finding and destroying Lee's army as it marched northward. After meeting with Hooker on May 25, Lincoln evidently reached the decision that the time had come for Hooker to go.

A week later Lincoln approached one of Hooker's most respected corps commanders, John Reynolds. General Reynolds set as his precondition for taking command the end of administration interference in military field decisions, but Lincoln was unwilling to grant such independence. Earlier informal soundings with three other senior commanders had proved equally unproductive, each declining to be considered. Now Reynolds did the same. Faced with subordinates who were in open revolt yet unwilling to assume responsibility, Lincoln opted to stay with Hooker, but only for the moment and only as the lesser of several evils.

Acting Decisively

As Hooker led his army up through northwest Maryland in late June, General Henry W. Halleck ordered him to secure the nearby army stronghold at Harpers Ferry. Hooker viewed the garrison as worthless, and at 1 p.m. on June 27 he wired Halleck to say that he was unable to comply with the order and asking to be relieved of his position. Although two great field armies were clearly on a collision course, Lincoln accepted the eleventh-hour resignation and promoted George Meade in Hooker's place. His decision was not a difficult move by now. Meade had already been recommended to Lincoln by other corps commanders, four of whom had previously said they would not accept the command themselves. That evening, the War Department issued General Order No. 194, formally replacing Hooker with Meade as commanding general of the Army of the Potomac.[12]

In retrospect, Lincoln's decision seems all but inevitable. A showdown was coming, and the president had run out of other options. Indeed, Meade appears to have been the only one surprised by his elevation.

A courier traveled through the night with the order to Meade's corps headquarters near Frederick, Maryland, arriving at 3 a.m. on June 28. Meade later reported that when he saw the courier approaching,

Union general George Meade.

"I thought that it was either to relieve or arrest me," and he preemptively told the messenger that "my conscience is clear." Unlike the other corps commanders Lincoln had unsuccessfully sounded out, Meade was given no choice. Lincoln simply ordered him to take command at once. Relieved that he was neither dismissed nor detained, Meade quickly and fully embraced his promotion into a far larger game, a game whose most historic and deadly round was just three days away.[13]

Abraham Lincoln was no stranger to acting decisively when his generals fell short of expectations. He had already relieved four army commanders: Irvin McDowell after First Manassas, George McClellan after the Peninsula Campaign, John Pope after Second Manassas, George McClellan again after Antietam when he hesitated to take advantage of his weakened opponent, and finally Ambrose Burnside after Fredericksburg. Each successor had failed to think strategically in the big battle, and each was gone before the next chance arrived. Now Lincoln had acted again, but this time he finally found the right executive. Meade was normally cautious in style, but the anticipated collision of the armies in Pennsylvania called for foresight and decisiveness, and he readily embraced a strategic and aggressive style in the days that followed.

GO POINT 3:
TAKING CEMETERY HILL AND CULP'S HILL

The two armies first spotted each other on the afternoon of June 30 several miles west of Gettysburg, then a town of 2,400 residents, but neither fired a shot. The following morning advance units of Confederate infantry reapproached the town. On its western outskirts, they encountered nearly 3,000 dismounted Union cavalry blocking the way. Each side quickly formed into battle lines, and both sides rushed troops from miles around toward the emerging battle.

Robert E. Lee had not intended to fight at Gettysburg, but he now committed much of his army to attacking the enemy that was in and around the town. Lee concentrated his forces on the western and northern perimeter, and with their superior numbers giving them an upper hand, the rebels pushed Yankee soldiers back through Gettysburg onto a long, curved ridgeline on the other side of town known locally as Cemetery Ridge. One of its high points, Cemetery Hill, crested near the edge of town some 80 vertical feet above the town center. To the east, the ridge rose to Culp's Hill, another 100 feet higher, and to the south it stretched toward a third hill called Little Round Top, which enjoyed an equally commanding height above the surrounding countryside. In all, the ridge and culminating hills were some 3 miles in length.

Since the ridge and hills provided good defensive ground for Meade's 95,000 troops, both sides quickly recognized their strategic value. The ridge's convexity allowed for rapid communication and quick repositioning of defending units. Both flanks—the most vulnerable points of a defensive line—would be anchored on high points. For the Union, the terrain offered a textbook defense if troops could dig in before the Confederate advance reached the ridge and its hills.

The retreating Union soldiers backed onto Cemetery Ridge and there re-formed and began to erect a defensive line to repulse the Confederate advance. Strategically, it was the right move, but the Union force was not yet of sufficient strength to spread onto either Little Round Top or Culp's Hill. Much of Meade's army was still rushing toward Gettysburg from the south. Until additional units arrived, the manpower was simply insufficient to secure those hills as well.

Lee sensed that Cemetery Hill would prove particularly critical. If Northern forces secured it first, they would have guaranteed their center-right flank. If Southern forces forced them off, they would have positioned themselves for a downhill assault on the Union forces arrayed along Cemetery Ridge.

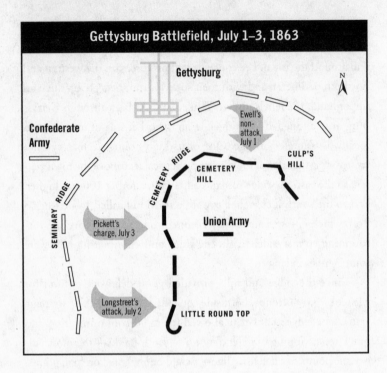

Gettysburg Battlefield, July 1–3, 1863

Gettysburg

N

Confederate
Army

Ewell's
non-
attack,
July 1

CULP'S
HILL

CEMETERY RIDGE

CEMETERY
HILL

SEMINARY RIDGE

Pickett's
charge, July 3

Union Army

Longstreet's
attack, July 2

LITTLE ROUND TOP

Ambiguous Phrasing

Near 5 p.m. on July 1, Lee dispatched his personal aide, Major Walter H. Taylor, to deliver an order to the corps commander nearest
Cemetery Hill, Richard Ewell. The order instructed Ewell, with some
20,500 troops at his disposal, "to carry the hill occupied by the enemy, if
he found it practicable," but the order also warned Ewell "to avoid a general engagement until the arrival of the other divisions of the army."[14]

Richard Ewell had only recently come to command, having served
under Thomas J. "Stonewall" Jackson. On the evening of May 2, 1863,
Jackson had ridden too far forward during the Chancellorsville battle
in an effort to reconnoiter the Union position. Reentering Confederate lines, he was shot by one of his own soldiers. Stonewall Jackson lin-
gered until May 10. On his deathbed, he informed Lee that Ewell

should be his replacement, a request that
Lee honored after reorganizing his army
from two corps into three.

As great an honor as Jackson conferred on Ewell with his deathbed request,
Jackson had done little in life to prepare
his ranking subordinate for command.
Jackson had a habit of keeping his officers
in the dark, fearing that the more people
who knew his plans, the more likely it was
that the plans would leak to the enemy. In

**Confederate general
Richard Ewell.**

battle, too, he granted little discretion to his officers in the field, prefer-
ring to give them authoritative and unambiguous instructions.

Jackson's poor mentoring had left Ewell ill-prepared to work with
Lee's ambiguous phrase: "if he found it practicable." A reconnaissance
team dispatched by Ewell had reported back that the nearby Culp's
Hill was not yet occupied by the enemy—a powerful incentive to
move forward quickly on Culp's, if not Cemetery Hill. The team also
reported that Culp's height would enable Confederate occupiers to
shell the massing Union troops just then entrenching themselves along
Cemetery Ridge. On the downside, Ewell's troops were exhausted
from the day's fighting and preoccupied with managing Union POWs.
He also did not know if he could count on the support of nearby Confederate units.

Unknown Quantities

Within the discretion that Lee's order seemed to allow, Ewell chose to
interpret seizure of Cemetery Hill and then Culp's Hill as impractical,
a decision with momentous consequences for the battle itself and for
the future of the Confederacy. As "some of the most fateful seconds in
American history ticked past," in the words of one historian, Ewell

chose not to attack, and Yankee troops soon moved onto both hills in large numbers, allowing them to establish a defensive perimeter on the center and right of the Union line that would not be broken or flanked during the two days of pitched battle to follow. The Yankees' overnight entrenchment on Cemetery Hill and occupation of Culp's Hill would become a major factor in Lee's decision a day later to mount Pickett's Charge on the center of the Union line.[15]

Stonewall Jackson was well known by Lee to be aggressive and decisive. Had he received Lee's order to take Cemetery Hill "if practicable," Jackson most likely would have found it so. But Richard Ewell was no Stonewall Jackson; his training and temperament called for more authoritative guidance. Ewell was much criticized after the war for his decision not to take Cemetery Hill and Culp's Hill. He himself said that "it took a dozen blunders to lose Gettysburg, and I committed a good many of them." Yet behind Ewell's decision was Lee's decision to use language that could be misinterpreted by a subordinate not yet schooled in Lee's more discretionary methods.[16]

Would Lee have acted differently if he had known Ewell better? Probably, but in fact he had had almost no chance to familiarize himself with Ewell's decision style. Ewell, too, might have reached a different go point if he had been better prepared for command. But seeing ahead in decision making requires you to ensure that those around you are capable of making the right moves when they are called upon to do so. Robert E. Lee's record of picking and commanding subordinates had been strong, but in this instance Lee fell short at the worst possible time for his army and his fledgling nation.

GO POINT 4:
DEFENDING LITTLE ROUND TOP

By the end of July 1, the Army of the Potomac was well dug into Culp's Hill, Cemetery Hill, and Cemetery Ridge. Anticipating a continuation of Lee's attack the following day, George Meade now extended his defensive line south, ordering corps commander Daniel E. Sickles to move his 10,000 soldiers onto Cemetery Ridge and thence to Little Round Top at the tip of the line. From Little Round Top's commanding heights, Sickles' corps would constitute an unassailable left anchor.

Meade's forecast of Lee's intentions proved prescient. Lee had decided overnight to make an assault on the Union's left flank the centerpiece of his July 2 effort to break and destroy the Union army, the very reason he had entered Pennsylvania. If his troops could sweep around the Union left, they could grievously damage the undefended backside of Meade's army. Panic, collapse, and rout should follow. Soon Lincoln would be ready to negotiate an end to the war and accept the Confederacy's existence. With so much at stake, Lee assigned 20,000 infantry to the task, more than a quarter of his ranks, and instructed his top commander, James Longstreet, to lead the charge. Launched at 4 p.m., it would be one of the largest single attacks of the entire Civil War. In Dan Sickles, Longstreet would also find an unintentional ally.

Of all the eleven corps commanders engaged at Gettysburg, Sickles was the sole nonprofessional. The others had graduated from the Military Academy at West Point and in many cases had been in uniform for years, while Sickles was a career politician who had persuaded well-placed friends in Washington to commission him a general. Now, with so much in the balance, Sickles' lack of training asserted itself in the worst way. Contrary to Meade's instructions, Sickles decided to move his corps at 2 p.m. on July 2 to well in front of Cemetery Ridge and Little Round Top. He formed a triangular defensive line a half mile to three-quarters of a mile forward toward the Confederate position on Seminary Ridge. The relatively flat area between Cemetery and Seminary Ridges offered scant natural protection, with predictable results when Longstreet launched his attack. Confederate forces readily sliced through Sickles' weak position, and Lee's objective of routing the

Yankee army on the afternoon of July 2 looked like it might come to pass.

The only obstacle still in the way was Little Round Top, the high point and left anchor of the Union line, but Sickles' earlier advance from his assigned position had left that promontory virtually devoid of defenders. Like Cemetery Hill and Culp's Hill, it offered superb overviews of the surrounding countryside. If Lee's forces could capture the hill and roll cannons onto it, the Union defenders on the lower heights would find themselves utterly exposed. Confederate infantry could then flank their line and swarm into a defenseless rear.

Acting on Necessity, Not Command

Not long before Longstreet's forward unit was to reach the foot of Little Round Top, Union general Gouverneur K. Warren had climbed the hill to have a look. Appalled to discover no one there to prevent its imminent fall, the general sent word to the nearest corps commander, who in turn dispatched a messenger to order a division commander to rush his troops onto the hill. In the enveloping chaos, the courier could not find the division commander, but he did happen upon Strong Vincent, a subordinate officer responsible for a brigade of 1,500 infantry.

A lawyer by profession, Vincent sensed that the messenger carried a vital instruction and ordered him to reveal its contents. Thus apprised of the situation, Vincent decided to rush his brigade onto Little Round Top. He had no order to do so, and his action was a violation of military protocol that might have exposed him to personal repercussions. But to Vincent,

**Union commander
Strong Vincent.**

the need was clear and the time to act nearly gone. With just minutes to spare, he positioned his troops along the crest of the hill, and though vastly outnumbered, they and another brigade that later arrived were able to hold the hill against Longstreet's determined assault. The day ended with the Union still in secure possession of the hill—and the Confederacy no better positioned than when the day began.

Lee's failure to break Vincent's defense of Little Round Top factored prominently into his decision later that evening to launch Pickett's Charge the following afternoon. If the two anchoring hills could not be taken, Lee reasoned, the weakest point of the enemy line must be its center.

Strong Vincent's decision on July 2 to take his brigade onto Little Round Top proved vital for the defense of the Union's left flank. Although he acted without formal authority, Vincent had made his decision in accord with the Union's strategy and situation of the day. Appreciating how important Little Round Top was to the defense of the entire army, he brought his own judgment to bear in rushing his brigade into the breach. In doing so, he saved the day and perhaps far more.

Dan Sickles also exercised his own judgment in moving his unit to an unauthorized location, but unlike Vincent, Sickles' actions were inconsistent with the day's conditions and larger goals. Indeed, Vincent's right call proved critical in making up for Sickles' flawed actions, reminding us that seeing ahead requires a thorough appreciation for the strategy and situation of the moment if decisions are to be taken on behalf of the mission.

GO POINT 5: PLAN OF ATTACK

The first day of the Gettysburg battle, Wednesday, July 1, had proven a tactical victory for Lee's army, as it forced Meade's men to retreat through the town. The second day was a tactical draw, a stalemate, with Lee's soldiers unable to overrun the Union's left flank. On the evening of Thursday, July 2, Meade and Lee both faced perhaps the biggest decisions of their military careers: whether to attack the opposing army, wait for an attack by the enemy, or withdraw from the battlefield to fight another day.

Take a moment now and put yourself in both men's shoes. Consider what you have learned about the battle thus far and the larger issues—political and military—that surround it. Think, too, about the chapters that have preceded this one and the decision templates that have been derived from them. Then reach your own decision on what to do next. The hopes of two nations are riding on your shoulders. July 3, 1863, would be a day that would live in history. In preparing for it, in formulating your plans for the next day's fighting and reaching this critical go point of the war, what would be the optimal approach for each commanding officer? And what would be suboptimal and perhaps least optimal? Move on from there to the plan itself. From what you have learned, what would be the best approach for each side to take?

Collecting Wisdom

On the evening of July 2, George Meade called a council of war with his nine top generals to convene in a small house not far from the center of the Union's defensive line. There, without reporting his own views on which decision was best, he had his chief of staff put three questions in front of his inner circle:

1. Under existing circumstances, is it advisable for this army to remain in its present position or to retire to another nearer its base of supplies?

2. It being determined to remain in the present position, should the army attack or wait the attack of the enemy?

3. If we wait attack, how long?[17]

General Meade asked the least senior officer to respond first, and then the others, moving up the hierarchy. The first general responded to the first question with "not retreat," and the others echoed his choice. On the second question, the nine again voted in unison—against attacking. On the third question, opinion varied from waiting for one day to attacking only when Lee attempted to move his army, but here too the commanders all agreed on attacking Lee at some point if Lee did not attack them first.

The least senior commander, John Gibbon, observed that "there was great good feeling amongst the Corps Commanders at their agreeing so unanimously," and that Meade had declared, "Such then is the decision." Gibbon also reported that Meade told him later that evening that if Lee attacked, it would be on the center of the Union line—precisely where Gibbon's corps was located—since Lee had failed to take the two flanks. Meade again had presciently seen ahead and correctly anticipated the future.[18]

Deciding Alone

Robert E. Lee was facing much the same moment of decision: to attack or not, and if so, what to attack. Retiring from the battlefield was not an option in his mind, but unlike Meade, Lee conferred with none of his officers. Taking his own counsel, he reached precisely the conclusion that Meade had anticipated. Since the two ends of the Union line were now anchored on well-defended hills, Lee reasoned the center of the Union line to be the most vulnerable point.

General Lee did not meet with his second in command, James Longstreet, to convey his intent but instead sent a courier with the order, evidently delivered orally since no written order is on record. The messenger likely reached Longstreet around 10 p.m. on Thursday, July 2. Lee instructed Longstreet through the messenger to use the division commanded by George Pickett to attack the center of the Union line on Cemetery Ridge. Lee also sent an order to Richard Ewell, instructing him to attack Culp's Hill the next day as a diversionary measure to assist Pickett's assault. Both Longstreet and Ewell thought the attack on the Union center would be ill-fated or worse. A brigade commander in Ewell's corps said it would be "nothing else than horrible slaughter," and Longstreet later said, "I could see the desperate and hopeless nature of the charge." But in choosing not to meet directly with his corps commanders, Lee heard no push back of his plan to attack the Union center.[19]

In what amounted to silent resistance to the received order, Longstreet sent scouts out to study the possibility of moving around the Union's left flank, finding a good hill of their own to take a stand, and then letting Meade be pulled into making an attack. But when Longstreet met Lee early on Friday, July 3, Lee waived off the counterproposal without discussion. This time face-to-face, Longstreet bluntly responded: "General, I have been a soldier all my life. I have been with soldiers engaged in fights by couples, squads, companies, regiments, divisions, and armies, and should know, as well as any one, what soldiers can do. It is my opinion that no fifteen thousand men ever arrayed for battle can take that position."[20]

Longstreet's words, so close to insubordination, reveal the depth of his opposition to Lee's decision, but they were being heard hours after Lee had already made up his mind, issued his commands, and set his army in motion around the decision to attack. Unlike Meade, Lee had not sought the opinion of his key commanders the previous evening. Nor had he even given Longstreet and Ewell a chance to report in person on the battered conditions of their troops after a day of brutal fighting. Now that he was finally getting a response from the front-line commanders—and a vehement one at that—Lee would have found it all but impossible to reverse his course even had he wanted to.

The absence of collective input was partly a matter of style. Lee preferred to meet with his senior officers individually when he sought their counsel at all. But Lee also had become supremely confident—arguably overconfident—in his own command abilities after a string of victories over the opposing army. After all, Lee's Army of Northern Virginia had fought Union armies five times over the past year with four different Union commanders, and the record stood at 4–0–1.

New to command, George Meade had no won-lost record of his own. He was junior even to two of the corps commanders who now reported to him. Meade was known to be decisive, but the humbling expansion of his responsibilities—from commanding 10,000 troops to leading 95,000 soldiers at a moment when the country's future hung on his decisions—might well have brought with it a willingness to take the pulse of his inner circle and not just his own counsel before deciding.

"General Lee, I Have No Division!"

One thing was certain as the sun rose over Gettysburg on July 3, 1863: this would be *the* day.

George Pickett needed hours to assemble and position his thousands of soldiers along the less imposing Seminary Ridge, opposite the enemy stronghold. When he was through, the troops were arrayed in straight-line formations that stretched for a mile. As Pickett prepared, more than 150 Confederate cannons pounded the center of the Union line on Cemetery Ridge for well over an hour. Now they were running low on ammunition. The time had come.

Waiting to give the command to attack until the moment was just right,
James Longstreet asked the Confederate
artillery commander if he had been able to
open up the center of the Union line.
With smoke hanging in the still, hot air
of July, the artillerist said he could only
guess at success. The answer unsettled
Longstreet. He was still hesitating, standing motionless near the center of the
Rebel line poised for attack, when George

**Confederate general
George Pickett.**

Pickett approached him for the final go-ahead. Paralyzed by the disaster he foresaw, Longstreet could utter no words and simply nodded as
an approving gesture. Receiving his "silent order," Pickett saluted and
declared, "I shall lead my division forward sir." With drums rolling,
Picket shouted, "Up, men, and to your posts! Don't forget today that
you are from old Virginia."[21]

Pickett's Charge would prove to be one of the greatest Southern
blunders of the entire Civil War, a metaphor for bloody futility. It was
repulsed within an hour, more that half its infantry wounded, cap-
tured, or killed. When Lee instructed Pickett during the retreat to rally
his division for an anticipated Yankee countercharge, Pickett is famously said to have responded, "General Lee, I have no division." The
next day, Lee began a retreat toward Virginia, ending his Pennsylvania
campaign defeated and with his army drastically depleted. His casualties totaled 28,000 for the three days, while Meade lost 23,000. The
most forward point of Pickett's advance near what became known as
the "bloody angle" is sometime referred to as the high-water mark of
the Confederacy.[22]

The South had come to the North to end the war on its terms,
but now the tide began to run the other way. Lincoln would be re-
elected by a decisive margin in 1864, defeating the Democratic can-

didate, George McClellan, the general Lincoln had twice dismissed. The North would end the war on its own terms twenty-one months later at Appomattox, Virginia. There, on April 9, 1865, Lee surrendered his Army of Northern Virginia. The final surrender may well have been inevitable, but the course of the war after Gettysburg had been decisively shaped by the decisions that Meade and Lee had reached on the evening of July 2, 1863.

FACTORING IN THE FUTURE

Taken together, the critical decisions of Robert E. Lee, Jefferson Davis, Abraham Lincoln, George Meade, Richard Ewell, Daniel Sickles, and Strong Vincent are a haunting reminder of how important it is to make decisions that take the future into account. "For General Lee, Gettysburg was a defining defeat," concluded historian Stephen Sears. And Pickett's attack was the reversal that defined the disastrous defeat.[23]

Looked at from the vantage of nearly a century and a half later, many of the decisions that shaped the outcome at Gettysburg seem predictable, almost foreordained, as if the commanders there had been little more than agents for great impersonal forces sweeping around them and manifest through them. Yet none of the decisions chronicled here can be reduced to the inevitable. Lee's decision to campaign in Pennsylvania was innovative and by no means obvious. Similarly, his decision to attack the Union center on July 3 was bold but hardly predictable. Had Lee been taken out of action on July 2, Longstreet by seniority would have taken command of the Army of Northern Virginia. Given his bitter opposition to the plan of attack, it is doubtful if he ever would have considered it. Longstreet could not even verbalize the final command to start the attack.

The many decisions of the period became part of a complex tapestry, each influencing the others. When asked why his charge against the Union line on July 3 did not succeed, George Pickett shot back, "I think the Union Army had something to do with it." Lee's decision to attack failed in part because Lincoln had decided to replace Hooker with Meade, Ewell had decided to take a pass on Cemetery Hill and Culp's Hill, and Strong Vincent had decided to rush his brigade onto Little Round Top.[24]

Pull the camera back further, and we can see that Lee's Pennsylvania campaign was the key element in regaining the upper hand in a war whose evolving strategy would likely lead to the defeat of the Confederacy despite its continuing success on the battlefield. To reach that decision, Lee brought an appreciation for anticipated developments far beyond the battlefield, an arena in which military and political strategy could work together for Southern ends. He was, in short, looking far ahead in making his decisions.

Seeing the Entire Field

Abraham Lincoln viewed the future decisions of Lee's counterparts, Joseph Hooker and then George Meade, as critical to stopping Lee's initiative to force Lincoln to the bargaining table or out of office. Prior army commanders from McDowell to Burnside had made a series of inept decisions that helped defeat their armies in battle after battle. In elevating Meade to army command, Lincoln banked on the reputation that Meade had developed among his peers for solid, forward-looking decisions, and that is exactly what he got from him at Gettysburg.

Not long before Lincoln promoted Meade to army command, Lee had promoted Richard Ewell to corps command. Going into the Gettysburg battle, Ewell brought an established reputation for sturdy performance, but it came under the tutelage of Stonewall Jackson, who tended to make clear what he required of subordinates and to allow them less field discretion than was Lee's wont. Lee evidently did not fully appreciate Ewell's heritage, and thus in looking forward to good decisions from this new direct report, Lee effectively allowed Ewell to falter on the afternoon of July 1 in a way that proved very costly during the two days that followed. Seeing ahead in decision making includes anticipating how associates will make their own decisions.

George Meade had deployed his forces along a line from Culp's Hill to Little Round Top to defend against Lee's anticipated attack on July 2. Field discretion is essential if front-line commanders are to make good decisions in fast-moving circumstances, but the discretion is only as good as the associates' understanding of the strategy and situation. Corps commander Daniel Sickles failed dramatically to appreciate what Meade had in mind when Sickles decided to move his 10,000 men a mile forward of where Meade had intended. Conversely, brigade commander Strong Vincent did appreciate the strategy and situation of the day when he rushed his unit onto Little Round Top to make up for Sickles' error. Looking ahead to decisions not yet made, then, requires that the strategy and situation be well understood by associates whose good independent decisions will be essential for execution of the mission.

Given the battlefield array and experience that these and hundreds of other decisions had created by the evening of July 2, Meade and Lee both faced one of the greatest decisions of their careers, if not *the* greatest: what action to take the following day. Meade sought collective guidance from all of his direct reports; Lee sought none individually nor any jointly. Other factors contributed to Meade's successful decision to wait for Lee to attack and Lee's faulty decision to launch the attack—history is rarely reducible to single factors—but the quality of the decisions on the two sides reflected their divergent uses of their battlefield nets for forecasting the future. In seeing ahead, many eyes are almost always better than a single pair.

THE DECISION TEMPLATE
FOR SEEING AHEAD

Once again, readers should draw their own lessons from the experience of the commanders and their decisions portrayed here. What follows are my own principles and tools for seeing ahead. This is also a good time to review the decision templates that have emerged from the heat of the moment, getting into the game, and using a net. Together with the template for seeing ahead, they will provide useful guidance for the following chapter, in which we will seek to make four difficult decisions. It is an opportune moment to test what we have mastered so far and thereby strengthen our capacity to apply go point principles and tools to decisions yet to be made.

Principle	Tool	Illustration
1. Take the strategic initiative.	Ask if current strategy will still prove winning in the days or months ahead, and if not, look to succeed by alternative means.	Faced with a string of Pyrrhic victories, Robert E. Lee and Jefferson Davis decided on May 15, 1863, to take the war into the North to create political pressure to end the war in the South's favor.
2. Ensure that key decision makers can see well ahead.	Train associates and subordinates to think clearly about what lies ahead and to base their own decisions upon that foresight.	Abraham Lincoln fired five commanding generals before appointing George Meade on June 28.
3. Appreciate the capabilities of others for making decisions.	The same command can be interpreted differently by two subordinates, and thus customized to the individual.	Lee instructed Richard Ewell to attack "if practicable" on July 1, but Ewell demurred, allowing the Union Army to entrench on Cemetery Hill and Culp's Hill.
4. Build a capacity in others to make discretionary decisions consistent with mission and situation.	Keep associates and subordinates informed about the objectives of the moment and the situation facing the enterprise.	Daniel Sickles' decision to move his unit forward on July 2 proved nearly disastrous for the Union's defense, while Strong Vincent's decision to move his unit onto Little Round Top proved lifesaving for the North's security.
5. In making large decisions that depend upon seeing ahead, consult those most familiar with the context and situation.	Ask associates and subordinates for their collective input on a decision before it is taken.	Meade sought advice from his nine top officers before reaching his decision for what to do on July 3; Lee apparently sought little from his officers before launching Pickett's Charge.

5

Making Decisions

Now is the time to strengthen your hold on the decision templates by direct application. This is a well-worn path for transforming ideas into action, theory into practice, concepts into behavior. It is akin to action learning projects in which people come to more fully embrace concepts through personal use of them.

Businesses, of course, are well aware of this. The best of them work hard to feed the minds of their management team and then to pragmatically transform that learning into the bottom line. When Coca-Cola brought together thirty-five promising managers from around the world for a week's leadership development program, organizers divided the group into six teams and asked each to identify a company problem or opportunity on which they would work to create a solution or a strategy over the ensuing six months. Abbott Laboratories assembled similar groups of managers in its leadership development program near Chicago, assigning teams to work with nonprofit organizations on intractable social problems. At both venues, managers were pressed to transform their program's concepts into real action.[1]

The same principle guides a program that we have developed at the Wharton School to strengthen decision making among our own students. In our version of action learning, we transport ninety MBA candidates twice a year to Quantico, Virginia, for a brief but intensive immersion in the training programs of the U.S. Marine Corps Officer Candidates School. For decisive decision making, few better programs on earth can be found than the one that prepares future combat officers.[2]

At Quantico, our students are handed off immediately to drill instructors, who impose iron discipline and intense stress through hours of harsh orders and merciless harassment. For the students, the effect is often shocking, but the experience subjects them to an extreme analog of the business battlefield. Officer candidates spend ten weeks in this environment. We do not ask that of our students—they are there for only two days—but even from this far more modest exposure, MBA candidates come away more appreciative of the need to remain disciplined and decisive in making decisions during corporate combat.

To further test our students' mettle, the Marine Corps divides them into four- or five-person "fire teams" to confront a series of problems in its Leadership Reaction Course. One Marine instructed his team that it had just fifteen minutes to solve the seemingly unsolvable problem of moving a 50-pound steel drum over a near-vertical 10-foot barrier with no evident tools for doing so. The team devoted more than half its allotted time to studying the situation, then found itself without sufficient time to execute the task. The Marine instructor complimented them on their analytic study of the problem but bluntly panned them for devoting too little time to active decision making.

You cannot fully understand the problem you face until you swing into action to test your assumptions about how to best solve it, the officer told them, in words not quite so civil. I doubt the students, now managers themselves, will ever forget the lesson. Nor, having gone through the same exercise, will I. The students arrived at the next challenge on the course eager to solve the problem and far more ready to indulge in active decision making.

MBA student fire teams preparing to solve problems in Marine course.

ANALYSIS TO ACTION

Intellectually, our students know long before they arrive at Quantico that fast-changing markets place a premium on decisive decision making, but by its very nature, academia tends to create a bias for analysis over action. Under the Marines' tutelage, the students find themselves failing and learning in a way that they could never experience in the classroom. Maybe most essential, they come to realize that readiness for action can be critical, especially in a fast-changing and uncertain environment that can render a plan faulty almost as soon as it is conceived.

I will not attempt to re-create conditions at Quantico here. As Marine officers and now hundreds of Wharton MBA students know, you have to undergo it to appreciate it. But in presenting four difficult decision challenges in the pages ahead, I will try to make the experience as hands-on as possible. As you proceed, keep in mind the standards by which wildland firefighters judge the quality of their field decisions: suppression, speed, and safety. In that same spirit, you should strive for decisions that are not just good—the analog of the firefighter's suppression—but also timely and consistent with the values of the enterprise. If it helps, imagine a drill instructor standing just over your shoulder, ready to offer a special form of encouragement if you show any signs of faltering.

One more note before we proceed. The four decisions you are asked to make here might seem distant from your own world. Yet by undergoing experiences far away, we often acquire a sharpened appreciation for what is particularly important nearby. As Dorothy said upon returning to Kansas from her bewildering visit to the Land of Oz, "Oh, Auntie Em—there's no place like home!"

Necklace Trading

This first decision—Necklace Trading—looks on the surface straightforward and simple, yet it can prove surprisingly difficult to reach the right choice in a timely fashion. The objective is to use your decision template to make a good and fast decision.

Take just a single minute to read the Necklace Trading problem below and then decide on the correct answer. The one-minute limitation is a way of introducing timeliness. After reaching your decision in no more than sixty seconds, go on record by writing the answer on this page—unless you plan to loan this book to a friend. (A better decision would be to buy another copy of the book for your friend!) The very act of writing it down meets one of the earliest principles in this book: Getting into the game.

Necklace Trading

A man buys a $78 necklace at a jewelry store, and he gives the jeweler a check for $100. Because the jeweler does not have the $22 change on hand, she goes to another merchant next door. There she exchanges the man's check for $100 in cash. She returns to her store and gives the man the necklace and the change.

Later the check is returned by the bank due to insufficient funds in the buyer's account, and the jeweler must then give the other merchant $100. The jeweler originally paid $39 for the necklace.

Decision: What is the jeweler's total loss? $_____

I have presented this problem to hundreds of MBA student and management groups in the United States and more than a dozen other countries—Argentina and Brazil to China, Denmark, Japan, India, and Thailand. Every now and then, a participant will be reluctant to record an answer, probably because of a wariness of being wrong, but with modest prodding, virtually everyone writes one down and, like you, gets into the game. But recording an answer is just the beginning of the exercise.

For phase two, let me use an actual venue: the resort town of Cha-Am, Thailand—a two-hour drive southwest of Bangkok—where on August 19, 2005, I asked forty-three people in a management development program to do just what you are doing now. After the one-minute time restriction had passed, I instructed everyone to walk to one of five locations in the room corresponding to the array below. Thus, for example, those with an answer of $39 would head to the front left corner of the room. Take another moment now, and decide in which location you belong according to the answer you wrote down.[3]

Jeweler's Total Loss		
$0–50	$51–75	$76–100
$101–150	Back of Room	$151–200

In the Cha-Am venue, as the next chart shows, the greatest number of participants gathered in the back left-hand corner ($101–$150), while the fewest met in the front left corner ($50 or less). The rest were arrayed as follows:

Number of Individuals Deciding on a Specific Total Loss by the Jeweler		
$0–50	$51–75	$76–100
N = 2	N = 9	N = 4
$101–150		$151–200
N = 21	Back of Room	N = 7

As we can see from the array, a rapid decision—nobody in this instance took more than a minute to decide—did not yield a correct answer for at least half of the people involved. Since only one answer is right, if the correct answer lies between $101 and $150, twenty-two of forty-three people must be wrong. If the actual loss is between $51 and $75, then thirty-four of forty-three are wrong. Indeed, the remarkable dispersion of people around the room points to just how difficult this seemingly simple decision is. Everyone got to a go point in a hurry, but whatever the correct answer, more than half the players are wrong.

Inner and Outer Circles

Thailand yielded typical results, but wherever I am conducting the exercise, I inform participants that they now can take a little more time to be sure they have the right answer. After all, we had already established that both speed *and* accuracy are criteria for judging the quality of any decision, and in the interest of improving accuracy we should be prepared to sacrifice some speed since at least half of the room is currently incorrect. Many participants at this moment implicitly seize upon a principle from our net template: they turn to those standing closest to them to discuss their answer, in effect consulting their inner circle. Virtually nobody, however, walks over to those in other parts of the room where people stand with different answers.

Next, I remind all the players that they are more likely to have the right answer at the end if they move beyond those who most agree with them to test their thinking against an outer circle. I find that this rarely happens without prompting. Once encouraged, though, most participants take this template principle to heart, and the room erupts in animated movement and debate as participants rove from answer group to answer group. Many seek to change the minds of those in what has become their outer circle, and we see some conversions at this point, but I have found that the initial changes generally are random, with people migrating across the room in no particular pattern.

Consult an Oracle

As the cross talk intensifies, though, the net flow always begins converging on a single location. If the group includes financial specialists—the Thai group had five commercial bankers and even a central bank official—a few participants draw upon another template principle in reaching their final decision. They consult an oracle or expert, in this instance seeking out the financial expertise of one of the bankers. The number of participants who take this route is never large; for some it can be hard to admit publicly that someone else knows more. But those who do seek out and heed the advice of an expert often move toward the right go point.

After several more minutes, I make two more announcements that have the effect of moving almost all those still locked into a wrong decision into the right camp. First, I clarify an issue that I had kept intentionally vague at the start of the exercise: the matter of opportunity costs. In reaching a final answer, I now instruct participants, opportunity costs should not be considered. The particulars of the situation that they face are now clearer.

Second, I announce that the mission of the exercise is for everyone in the room to reach the correct answer in a timely fashion. Until this point, virtually everybody assumes that the objective is to come out personally right. Now they embrace a different strategy embedded in another of the template principles: seeking to ensure that all participants understand the objective and situation of the moment so everybody can reach the right outcome. With that, the tenor of the room changes radically. Conversation becomes far more animated, the mood far more urgent, the engagement far more collective.

Several people typically step forward to ask everybody in the room to terminate their private conversations and focus on one or two discussion leaders for the entire group. With the help of a flip chart or blackboard, the several temporary leaders argue why their reasoning is superior and should be accepted by all. Private dialogue gives way to the public conversation of a Vermont-style town meeting. Those convinced that they had indeed reached the correct conclusion zealously proselytize others, knowing that time is running out.

Clarify Objectives

Like Union commander George Meade at Gettysburg, I have communicated the day's objectives and situation to all involved. Unlike Meade, however, I have done so midway through the exercise rather than on the eve of the battle. My decision to delay the communication was deliberate, intended to bring out this very point: those who carry overall responsibility cannot expect good and timely decisions from their associates unless the objective and situation are well communicated ahead of time. Strong Vincent, for one, never would have rushed his brigade onto Little Round Top if he had not known in advance what his commanders wanted and how the Union forces were arrayed.

Armed now with the right objective and more keenly aware of the situation—opportunity costs are not to be considered—the management participants almost invariably move quickly and efficiently to the correct place in the room. Among the forty-three managers in the Thai program, only five were still stuck with wrong decisions by the end. Among the several hundred groups in a dozen countries where I have conducted the exercise, in only two instances has the majority failed to reach the correct solution, and in almost all cases it is not just the majority that comes out on the right side but the *vast* majority, many having migrated all the way across the room. Among a group of forty health care managers who went through the exercise in September 2005, only two people had initially embraced the right answer; by the end, only two had *not* embraced it.[4]

Necklace Trading participants find that talking to the inner circle comes easily, but consulting with the outer circle does not. They also discover that they have implicitly assumed an incorrect strategy and situation. But through active dialogue with the outer circle once the objective and situation are clarified, majorities convert from the wrong decision to the right one. The value of the template principles and tools that we have unearthed comes first from articulating them—and then from applying them to a real go point.

As for the answer you presumably wrote down at the start of this section, go back and take a look at it. Are you still convinced of its accuracy, now that objective and situation have been clarified? Do you need to consult an inner or outer circle? An oracle or expert? Once you are sure you have reached the decision, e-mail your response and an explanation for it to TheGoPoint@wharton.upenn.edu, and I will provide a password and Web page location to obtain the correct answer.

CARTER RACING

Our second decision is both more complex and more fraught with pitfalls, including the ancient one of hubris. This will be particularly true if, as highly likely, you successfully completed the Necklace Trading exercise. People are more prone to commit decision errors after an affirmative experience. When self-assurance is soaring, when things are going well, when an organization has had a successful year, personal pride and overconfidence spring up like mushrooms. At the very outset, then, you would do well to remind yourself of the increased likelihood of falling into an unforced error the next time around.[5]

The issue at stake, prepared by authors Jack W. Brittain of the University of Utah and Sim B. Sitkin of Duke University, is whether a race car company should compete in or withdraw from a major race at a track located in the Pocono Mountains of Pennsylvania. Compete and do well, and the company is certain to nail down a major source of advertising support for the following season—critical money since this is a start-up outfit that has already run up significant debt. Based on the race team's overall performance, the prospects look good, but the team has been plagued by occasional engine blowouts. If this should happen in today's nationally televised race, the company can say goodbye to the big sponsor. One more thing: there is no time to lose, as the race starts in a little more than one hour.

The initial challenge is to quickly reach the correct decision on whether to race the car or not. Before you make up your mind, read the scenario in the box below, then check "Yes, race" or "No, do not race" at the end. When I present this to management groups, I limit them to six minutes. You should limit yourself to the same.[6]

Carter Racing

BJ Carter was not sure. Chris Carter (a sibling and business partner) was on the phone and needed a decision. Should they run in the race or not? It had been a successful season so far, but the Pocono race was important because of the prize money and TV exposure it promised. This first year was hard because the team was trying to make a name for itself. They had run in a lot of small races to get this shot at "the big time." A successful outing could mean more sponsors, a chance to start making some profit for a change, and the luxury of racing only the major events. But if they suffered another engine failure on national television . . .

"These engine failures are exasperating," thought BJ. The team's car had failed seven times in twenty-four outings this season, with various degrees of damage to the engine and car. No one could figure out why. It took a lot of sponsor money to replace a $50,000 racing engine, and the wasted entry fees were no small matter either. BJ and Chris had everything they owned riding on Carter Racing. This season had to be a success.

Pat Edwards, the engine mechanic, was guessing the engine problem was related to ambient air temperature. When it was cold, the different expansion rates for the head and block seemed to be damaging the head gasket and causing the engine failures. It was below freezing last night, which meant a cold morning for starting the race.

Robin Burns, the chief mechanic, did not agree with Pat's "gut feeling." The data seemed to support Robin's position (see Exhibit 1) in that the gasket failures had occurred over the entire temperature range. This suggested that temperature was not the issue. Robin had been racing for twenty years and believed that luck was an important element in success. "In racing, you are pushing the limits of what is known," Robin argued, "and that means some things are not going to be under control. If you want to win, you have to take risks. Everybody in racing knows it. The drivers have their lives on the line, I have a career that hangs on every race, and you have every dime tied up in the business. That's the thrill: beating the odds and winning." Last night over dinner Robin had added to this argument forcefully with *Burns' First Law of Racing:* "Nobody ever won a race sitting in the pits."

BJ, Chris, and Robin had discussed Carter Racing's situation the previous evening. This first season was a success from a racing standpoint, with the team's car finishing "in the money" (one of the top five) in 12 of the 15 races it completed. As a result, the sponsorship offers critical to the team's business success were starting to come in. A big break had come two weeks ago after the Dunham race, where the team scored its fourth first-place finish. Goodstone Tire had finally decided Carter Racing deserved its sponsorship at Pocono—worth a much needed $40,000—and was considering a full season contract for next year if the team's car finished in the top five in this race. The Goodstone sponsorship was two million a year, plus incentives. BJ and Chris had gotten a favorable response from Goodstone's Racing Program Director last week when they presented their plans for next season, but it was clear that Goodstone's support depended on the visibility they generated in this race.

"BJ, we only have another hour to decide," Chris said over the phone. "At the end of the Dunham race, we were $80,000 in the hole. Since Dunham, we got the $40,000 from Goodstone and paid the $30,000 Pocono entry fee. If we withdraw now, we can get back half the $30,000 entry. We'll lose Goodstone, they'll want $25,000 of their money back, and we'll end the season $80,000 in the hole. If we run and finish in the top five, we have Goodstone in our pocket and can add another car next season. You know as well as I do, though, that if we run and lose another engine, we're back at square one next season. We'll lose the tire sponsorship, and a blown engine is going to lose us the new $800,000 oil contract. No oil company wants a national TV audience to see a smoker being dragged off the track with their name plastered all over it. We can't live without the oil sponsorship. Think about it—call Pat and Robin if you want—but I need a decision in an hour."

BJ hung up the phone and looked out the window at the crisp, fall sky. The cars were already on the grid, spectators admiring the gaudy paint, excitement mounting in anticipation of the start. This was what made racing at this level special, the cars on display with crowds mingling around and waiting for the engines to roar to life. In an hour, the spectators would retreat to the stands and the cars would circle the track in anticipation of the start. The temperature sign across the street flashed "40 DEGREES 8:23 A.M."

Exhibit 1: Note from Robin Burns

BJ,

I got the data on the gasket failure problem from Pat. We've run 24 races this season, with temperatures at race time ranging from 53 to 82 degrees. Pat had a good idea in suggesting we look into this, but as you can see, this is not our problem. I tested the data for a correlation between temperature and gasket failures, and found no relationship.

In comparison with some of the other teams, we have done extremely well this season. We've finished 62.5% of the races, and when we finished, we were in the top five 80% of the time. Our rate of blown engines is 29%, but we are running fast, so we have to expect

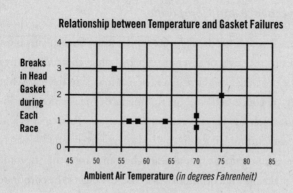

some difficulties. I'm not happy with the engine problems, but I will take the four first-place finishes and 50% rate of finishing "in the money" over seven engines any day. If we continue to run like this, we will have our pick of sponsors.

Robin

Now that you have digested all the data, imagine you are in a room with about forty others who have been asked to make the same decision within six minutes. For some of your fellow participants, the decision is a slam dunk: "If we're running a race company, let's race!" someone inevitably declares. But others are more ambivalent or unsure.

If you were BJ or Chris Carter, you could simply impose your initial decision. Ownership has its privileges. But as we have seen several times, both in this chapter and before, you are more apt to hit the right go button if you consult with both inner and outer circles. To this end, I ask participants after they have studied the scenario and made their initial choice to design a decision-making team that will optimize their chances of reaching the best decision, again in a timely fashion.

Good Governance and Composition

A first issue is deciding on the right size for the team. Participants most often suggest three, five, or seven members—an even number, they warn, risks a tie vote. They have barely begun to design the team, but already they are concerned with the rudiments of governance, specifically, how to reach a collective and timely decision. Participants also suggest almost without fail that teams be kept relatively small—wisely so, since research confirms that as teams become large, they become less able to make optimal decisions. As a rule, the bigger the corporate board of directors, the smaller the performance. It was on this principle that Sony decided in 1998 to shrink its board of directors from thirty-five members to just seven—part of a constellation of related changes designed to yield "quicker decision making and execution in a rapidly changing environment."[7]

A related issue is the composition of the decision-making team. Suggestions vary, but participants generally agree that it should include some combination of the inner and outer circles. The former—the driver, say, and the engine mechanic, chief mechanic, and largest sponsor—have the greatest stake in the outcome. From the outer circle, though, comes relevant expertise not otherwise available from the inner circle: finance, for example, as well as accounting, statistics, marketing, engineering, metallurgy, and meteorology.

Far less frequently called for but often equally important is a third criterion for choosing team members. The team should include some who favor racing today and some who are against it. Whatever direction the owners are leaning in—to race or not to race—they need to hear from at least one person who is leaning toward the opposite conclusion, as Robert E. Lee did not on the eve of Pickett's Charge, and preferably more than one opponent.

With all these considerations in mind, I ask the forty people in the room to organize themselves into optimal decision-making teams.

Obviously, they have to scramble a bit at this point. The room is often top-heavy with finance and accounting experts, and rarely does the group include an actual metallurgist or meteorologist. To compensate, I tell participants that a metallurgist for our purposes is anyone who has repaired anything metallic in the household during the past month; meteorologists are those who have watched the Weather Channel or visited weather.com at least once during the past week. Once the teams are ready—and the process rarely requires more than a minute or two—I ask the teams to reach their go points in just eight minutes.

The teams most frequently devote the opening minute to how they will make their decisions. Some groups opt to follow a democratic protocol: one person, one vote. Others say they need to reach a consensus, while still others adopt the corporate practice of giving only one person—a CEO—the final say. But whatever the governance model adopted, several teams will typically raise two matters that rarely emerge when individuals alone face the Carter Racing decision.

Asking the Right Questions

The first matter is whether all competitors at the race track are equally subject to concerns about their potential for engine failure on this cold racing day. If that is the case—if the threat is universally shared—then the company will not necessarily put itself at a disadvantage if it decides to race. But if some of the competitors have no history of gasket problems at low temperatures, the Carters have cause for alarm. Competitor performance is potentially vital information, but it is also unobtainable at this late hour. Perhaps a consulting firm might have been able to extract the data from the other race car companies, but that analysis should have been launched months ago—a reminder once again of the need to see ahead.

The second matter raised by the decision teams is the prior record of the company itself. During team discussions, several people almost always suggest examining the temperature data for days when Carter Racing competed without gasket problems. They reason that if the company had previously raced on cold days without gasket failures, then it would heighten the probability of a successful race today because of the morning's very low temperature. By contrast, if the company had previously raced without gasket failures only on warm days, then it would point to the opposite conclusion, namely, that the company should not race given today's record lows.

One or two participants often ask me at this point if those data are available. Since temperature points are in the company's files, they can be immediately extracted and analyzed, and here they are:

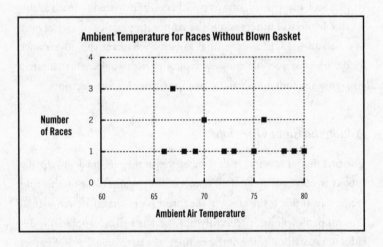

Prior to the introduction of this new data, a majority of participants is almost certain to be leaning toward the wrong go point. Individually, they simply did not think to ask for the data. Not until they have pooled their thinking and created a network of inside-the-circle and outside-the-circle advisors does the idea emerge and the need for these data suddenly become obvious. Now, with this new racing information added to the prior racing data, many people change their decision. When I call for a final vote from the entire room, a majority of participants opt for the correct decision in better than 80 percent of the cases.

I will not divulge the answer here to protect the integrity of the problem, but again, if you will e-mail your answer and the rationale behind it to TheGoPoint@wharton.upenn.edu, I will send a password and Web page location to check your answer against the correct one and the rationale for it.

Explicit Values

For almost everyone and every team that takes part in the Carter Racing exercise, the criterion for reaching the right decision is obvious: will the company gain or lose more money if it races? But it is not the only metric of success, and indeed, some teams will add the additional criterion of the safety of the driver. That leads them to consider whether racing with the gasket problem is likely to result in injury or worse, but because I have not specified that this should be a consideration when I launched the exercise, safety is rarely incorporated into the final decision.

Should it be? Well, that takes us back to individual and organizational values. If those values are made explicit and clear before a decision is taken, they may be well taken into account during the decision. If they are left unacknowledged, then they are less likely to play a role in reaching a go point. In the particular case of Carter Racing, including the driver in the decision-making team would have brought safety to the forefront since the driver had the most to lose if a gasket blew at high speeds. This is one reason why the Rogers Commission that investigated the 1986 *Challenger* disaster recommended that astronauts be incorporated into NASA management since they would bring an especially keen appreciation for flight safety. It is also a reminder that we should not assume organizational values such as safety will be factored into decisions unless they are a specific part of the charge or unless a representative of those values is included on the team.[8]

MOUNTAIN CLIMBING

For our third decision, a study in extreme situational complexity, we head for the world's second-highest mountain peak and one of nature's most inhospitable environments: the 28,250-foot monster known as K2. Our focus this time is on a summit expedition organized by veteran Chilean mountaineer Rodrigo Jordan.[9]

Rodrigo Jordan.

Approaching K2.

The situation is this: At 9:30 a.m. on August 13, 1996, four members of Jordan's Chilean expedition reached the summit of K2 after a grueling, sixteen-hour ascent. Mountaineers the world over recognize K2 as significantly more challenging than Mount Everest, even though Everest tops K2 by 785 feet. Often called "the savage mountain," K2 features sheer slopes and severe weather conditions that combine to produce one of the highest climbing fatality rates of any major mountain in the world. Add to that the fact that any environment above 26,000 feet—and K2 is one of just fourteen peaks that rise higher—is so inhospitable that the human body begins to physically deteriorate from dehydration and shortage of oxygen. No wonder climbers know these upper reaches as the "death zone."

In mountaineering, the "crux" refers to the single most difficult point on the climb. Successfully negotiating the crux move on a climbing route requires great physical strength, technical agility, and emotional resolve. It also requires good and timely

Nearing the summit of K2.

decisions, especially on mountains such as K2, where the margin of survival is so slim. Indeed, the difference between coming home alive and not coming home at all is often the decisions taken at the crux as well as ones taken in anticipation of it.

On K2, on that triumphant August day in 1996, the climbers toasted one another with a precious glass of Chilean wine carried to the summit for that very purpose. Treated to a rare display of sunny and windless conditions, they spent more than two hours savoring their victory over the mountain and, undoubtedly, thinking they had surmounted their crux—but it still lay ahead.

Up or Down? Oxygen or Water?

The four mountaineers finally began their treacherous descent at 12:30 p.m., roped together in two pairs. They departed at different times and moved at distinct paces, so the two teams soon separated on their way down the mountain. Ninety minutes after the second pair had left the summit, one of its members—Cristián García-Huidobro—placed an urgent radio call to Base Camp, the expedition's control center, located more than two vertical miles below, near the bottom of the mountain at 16,400 feet. The condition of ropemate Miguel Purcell had suddenly become dire. "Miguel is exhausted," warned García-Huidobro. "He sat down and he does not want to continue walking!"

The rope team of García-Huidobro and Purcell was still at 27,600 feet, on the side of a mountain whose apex is known for ghastly weather that predictably arrives by midafternoon. The stricken Purcell was reporting that he had lost feeling in his hands and could no longer stand.

Miguel Purcell.

"My head was clear," he recalled, "and I wasn't scared, but I didn't know how I was going to get out of there." Purcell urged García-Huidobro to continue down without him, but García-Huidobro refused. "I got you into this," he told his companion, "and we'll both walk out of it."

In an effort to lighten their loads on the way up, the two teams had stashed fuel, pots, and a stove for melting water. Additionally, Purcell had deposited a partially filled oxygen cylinder on the ascent when it had become too cumbersome to carry. Unfortunately, though, he had collapsed 650 feet above the equipment cache and 200 feet below the oxygen cylinder. Whether dehydration or oxygen starvation had caused Purcell to stumble into the snow, he was still at least 200 grueling feet from replenishment of either. Purcell could not move, and García-Huidobro himself was utterly exhausted.

Nor was immediate help available from the support team down

the mountain. Several intermediate camps had been established during the ascent to move gear up for the final push: Camp 1 at 20,500 feet, Camp 2 at 23,000 feet, and Camp 3 at 25,600 feet. But only Camp 1, where two expedition members waited to assist the summit team with the descent, was occupied, and that was some 7,000 feet below Purcell and García-Huidobro. Otherwise, the closest help was more than 11,000 feet down the mountain at Base Camp, where an expedition doctor and several other climbers waited. Two-way radios connected the various climbers on the mountain to the two summit rope teams.

The choices, then, were stark. Given the high altitude, precipitous terrain, and distances involved, García-Huidobro could not carry Purcell down, not even with the help of the other rope team. Unless he could find some way to help restore Purcell's physical capacity and will to descend, he would have to abandon him. And he had to act quickly. If García-Huidobro did not resume his own descent within the hour, he risked being caught on the open slopes overnight. To be stranded near the summit of K2 at night without a tent, water, or oxygen would almost surely prove fatal to both climbers.

Situational Awareness

Faced with a crux moment, where on the mountain as expedition leader would you have earlier decided to position yourself at this point? With the summit team itself? At Camp 1? Or at Base Camp? Try to imagine yourself in Jordan's boots, and think back to the various decision principles we have looked at so far. What would your choice have been? And whatever the location decision, when García-Huidobro asked you what he should do, would you send him up for oxygen, down for water, or take still other measures?

Over the last half decade, I have asked many groups of students and managers to form into teams and consider those questions.

Mountain Climbing

Location Decision: Summit team ___   Camp 1 ___   Base Camp ___

Resource Decision: Oxygen ___   Water ___   Other measures ___

Discussion is always lively, but as an indicator of how complex the situation is, a final vote always results in considerable dispersion, with a quarter to a third of the teams typically opting for each of the three locations. Dispersion is great as well on whether to go for the oxygen or water or take other steps.

I have also asked the questions of Rodrigo Jordan himself. Here is his reasoning in his own words (Jordan can be seen as well in a short video clip of the crisis on K2 at the book's Web page):

The conditions faced by men and women who climb summits over 8,000 meters [26,247 feet] are extremely demanding and intensely draining. Consequently, we have always considered having someone with experience in base camp to guide the climb. We consider this as an indispensable necessity. Only from this vantage is it possible to remain sufficiently calm to visualize with clarity the environment in which these men risk their lives.

My climbing mentor, Claudio Lucero, had taken the base-camp position on our prior expedition to Mt. Everest, but he was not with us this time. I was the veteran and organizer, and I thought I was the most suitable candidate for the assignment. So I stayed in Base Camp to assist the climbers above in their decision making. This decision to remain in Base Camp was possible because of the complete trust I had in my colleagues, in their technical skills and their decision-making ability and judgment. Having worked with them in similar situations, I knew what they were experiencing, and I had a good understanding of their capabilities. I also was in a good place to offer clear-headed and sound counsel when they needed it most.

Keeping a Clear Mind

After receiving the SOS radio message from García-Huidobro high up on K2, Jordan consulted with the most relevant expert, trip physician Alfonso Díaz, whom Jordan had also positioned at Base Camp. Diaz's conclusion: rehydration was the first priority. But diagnosis, in a sense, only added to the complexity. Since Purcell was immobile, García-Huidobro would have to descend 650 feet, then climb back up with a stove to melt ice into water—a Herculean effort. Instead, Jordan suggested that García-Huidobro first climb back up 200 feet to retrieve the oxygen cylinder, in the hope that the extra oxygen would revive Purcell enough so he could make the descent with García-Huidobro to reach the stove for water.

García-Huidobro did as requested, but the plan only half worked. When García-Huidobro radioed Base Camp again, he reported that although Purcell looked better with the oxygen, he still couldn't decide about going down. Purcell, he said, had stood, then stumbled, staggered, and finally sat down again.

By now, the other summit rope team had reached the equipment cache 650 feet below, where they were monitoring the life-and-death drama above them via the two-way radios. With plan A unsuccessful, Jordan now decided the second team would have to melt snow at the cache, then carry the fresh water back up to Purcell. One of the team members—Misael Alvial—immediately volunteered to carry it up. Fortified by the oxygen García-Huidobro had brought down from above and now by the water and hydrating salts hauled up by Alvial from below—in both cases by dint of superhuman effort—Purcell abruptly revived and then slowly but deliberately began to move down the mountain.

At the equipment cache, the two rope teams joined to descend in tandem. Finally, at 11:30 p.m.—after more than twenty-four hours of climbing in the death zone—they all reached Camp 3 at 25,600 feet. Although they were utterly exhausted, Jordan insisted they stay awake through most of the night so they could drink massive amounts of water and otherwise focus on overcoming the accumulated effects of hypothermia and hypoxia. Then with dawn's early light, he pressed them to descend as fast as possible to Base Camp, where they could more fully recover from their ordeal. The four summit climbers reached the base of the mountain at 9 p.m. on August 14, forty-eight hours after starting for the summit from the high camp.

Close Is Not Always Best

The three options that Rodrigo Jordan had considered—the summit team, Camp 1, or Base Camp—each brought distinct advantages. If Jordan had placed himself with the summit team, he would have been able to deal directly with Purcell's collapse; optimal situational awareness comes from direct witnessing. On the other hand, awareness without clear-mindedness is not a prescription for great decisions, and above 26,000 feet few climbers remain fully sharp-witted. If Jordan had opted for Camp 1, he would have been able to climb up to render direct personal assistance to the descending climbers once they were substantially below the summit, but that might have distracted him from a detailed appraisal of the entire array of resources on the mountain, including the oxygen bottle, water-making equipment, and medical expertise. Opting for Base Camp left him distant from the scene of the action but far better prepared to appreciate what would be needed at the crux moment.

Five days before summit day, García-Huidobro had in fact pleaded with Jordan to join the summit team with him. Jordan's health remained robust, and he was one of the strongest and most experienced climbers on the mountain. Reaching the summit of K2 is a dream of any Himalayan mountaineer, but Jordan had refused, saying his own leadership would best be exercised at Base Camp. "I truly believed that this was essential for the expedition," explained Jordan. "The role of leadership had to be taken by somebody, and it had to be me."

In deciding on Base Camp, Jordan had opted for the best of the three alternatives given the particular problem that emerged near the K2 summit. The other choices might have been preferable in another crux moment, but given what did occur, his being at Base Camp combined maximal situational awareness with optimal clear-mindedness for making good and timely choices when they counted most. As we have earlier seen, the absence of full awareness of the situation proved fatal on Storm King Mountain and vital on Gettysburg's Little Round Top. Deciding on the right location can be as important as deciding on the right team members in reaching the optimal go point. Just ask Miguel Purcell.

AIRLINE BUILDING

Last in this chapter on hands-on decision making is a challenge that is probably far closer to the experience of most readers than necklace trading, auto racing, or Himalayan summiting: a chance to start and grow a new business in a computer-based simulation developed by John Sterman of MIT.

The model here is People Express, an airline carrier launched in 1980. The United States had deregulated the airline industry in 1978, allowing airlines to compete on service and price. People Express joined the fray a scant two years later, offering bare-bones service—no baggage check, no food service—at bargain-basement price. By mid-1981, a People Express passenger could fly from Newark, New Jersey, to Boston for $23, a little over $50 in 2005 dollars, cheaper than any other means of transport between the two cities.

Entrepreneur Donald Burr created the airline around six management principles: (1) good service and commitment to people, (2) being the best provider of air transportation, (3) highest-quality management, (4) being a model for other airlines, (5) simplicity of operations, and (6) maximization of profits. Burr's model is remarkably akin to that invented by Herb Kelleher, who at the very same time was launching Southwest Airlines. Remove the references to air travel, and Burr's and Kelleher's formulations equally echo the goals and principles so many entrepreneurs bring to their fledgling enterprise.

Both Southwest Airlines and People Express would prove explosively successful in the early 1980s, drawing thousands of backpackers and bus riders to the airways for the first time. More than three decades later, Southwest continues to prosper as one of the most successful American carriers ever. Latecomers such as JetBlue and Ryan Air are making millions with much the same model. Yet just six years after its launch, People Express had ceased to exist despite a stellar start.

Given Herb Kelleher's proven success with the same model, much of the onus for People Express's abrupt collapse can be traced to Donald Burr's ill-fated decisions at the top. As brilliant an airline visionary as he was, his executive decisions proved his undoing. In this exercise, you get a chance to step into his shoes—to build the company or to send it into a tailspin of your own making. Welcome aboard.

Starting Right

The date of your takeover as chief executive of People Express is New Year's Day, 1981, and you have plenty of reason for optimism. Although the airline is flying just three aircraft and employing only 155 people, the past year under prior management has been successful by any small business standard, with income of $2 million on revenue of $32 million. A summary of your starting position appears below, along with an actual fare card for the airline in mid-1981.

Summary of Starting Position of People Express, December 31, 1980			
Capacity growth rate (%/year)	0	Employees	165
Demand growth rate (%/year)	0	Hiring	9
Aircraft	3	Turnover	9
Aircraft acquisition	0	Marketing ($million/year)	3
Load factor	0.57	Market share	0.002
Break-even load factor	0.54	Reported service quality (index: 1981 = 1.00)	1.00
Fare ($/seat-mile)	$0.090	Revenues ($million/year)	$32
Competitor fare ($/seat-mile)	$0.160	Net income ($million)	$2

John Sterman, People Express Microworld, Global Strategy Dynamics Limited

If you possibly can, recruit four other people to run the airline with you—your top management team. In this challenge, you will be competing via the Internet against seven other similarly structured teams that met in early October 2005. And be aware that your fellow competitors are anything but slouches. The thirty-three midcareer managers that make up your opposing teams come from a host of organizations and countries, ranging from the Federal Reserve to General Mills, from Belgium to New Zealand.

Keep it Simple

The criterion by which performance will be judged has already been determined by the competition. After collective discussion, the midcareer managers agreed to compete on the basis of market capitalization, the value of the company's stock to investors. Since the challenge tests your performance over a nine-year span, the winning team thus will have achieved the greatest market capitalization by the end of 1989.

Note, too, the initial difference between this decision test and Necklace Trading. In the earlier challenge, the ambiguous criterion at the outset—was the objective for individuals to reach the right answer for themselves or for the entire group to do so?—resulted in initial wheel spinning. If such were the case this time around, you would be taking up much valuable time debating not only the means of flying high but also the very purpose of building

People Express fare card.

the airline. Is it to optimize net income, employ the most people, maximize market share, or create value? Instead, with a clear opening objective that puts everyone on the same competitive page, teams can quickly set about trying to make good and timely decisions.

For the purposes of this challenge, People Express' real-time operating experience prior to its failure has been compressed into the computer simulation that reduces each team's decisions to just five per quarter: (1) the number of aircraft to be purchased, (2) the amount to be spent on marketing the airline, (3) the number of employees to be hired, (4) the airfare to charge passengers, and (5) the scope of services, such as checked baggage and meals in flight. The five default decisions—preset in the simulation and displayed below—are to acquire no aircraft, devote 10 percent of last quarter's revenue to marketing, hire 9 new employees, keep the airfare fixed at 9 cents per seat mile (competitors are charging 16 cents), and leave the target service scope unchanged at 0.6, meaning that People Express offers only 60 percent of the amenities major carriers such as American and United Airlines provide.

The Five Default Simulation Decisions in Building People Express	
Number of aircraft purchases	0
Fraction of last quarter's revenue given to marketing	0.1
Number of people	9
People Express airfare in cents/seat-mile	0.09
Target service scope (index: competitor scope = 1.0)	0.6

Although the number of decisions that need to be made has been radically simplified, the choices are still deeply complex. In making them, your team can draw on a vast range of operating data that are updated every quarter. Two of seven data displays appear below. Go to the book's Web site and twenty-two graphs that track virtually everything over time can be called up as well.[10]

Team governance is, of course, up to you, but with five decisions to make per quarter over thirty-six quarters—a total of 180 separate

Employee and Stock Data for People Express, December 31, 1980

Employee Data	
Total employees	165
Rookie fraction	0.10
Labor flows (people/quarter)	
Hiring	9
Employee turnover	9
Net change in employees	0
Fractional turnover (fraction/quarter)	0.06
Average workweek (hours/week)	43
Reported service quality (index: 1981 = 1.00)	1.00
Average market value of employee shares (thousands/employee)	$46
Stock Data	
Share price ($/share)	$1.88
Earnings per share ($/quarter/share)	$0.10
Shares outstanding (million)	4.00
Market value of firm ($ million)	$8
Cumulative net income ($ million)	$0

decisions—and with only an hour to complete the decision-making process if you are going to maintain parity with the other teams, it behooves you to agree quickly on a process for reaching good and timely decisions. Among the seven other teams, the adopted governance model varied from team to team, but a majority opted for one of the two simplest governance models, consensus or majority rule. Several teams also established a functional division of labor, assigning one member to serve as CEO, another as CFO, a third as chief marketing officer, a fourth as human resources executive, and a fifth as chief operating manager.

Once these issues have been tackled, open the simulation by e-mailing a brief description of your team's governance model to TheGoPoint@wharton.upenn.edu. You will immediately receive a password and guidance on how to open the Web-based People Express simulation. As just noted, you will have one hour to complete the simulation. Remember to operate the airline to maximize the market value of the firm, and assume that you will be transferring the airline to family or friends after the ninth year. This is to guard against any temptation to make last-quarter decisions that will spike short-run market value but damage long-term value. At the end—when you have reached the end of the fourth quarter of 1989—record five summary pieces of information in the box below and enter them on *The Go Point* Web page as well.

Airline Building	
Results of Team Decisions	
Number of aircraft	_____
Number of employees	_____
Total revenue ($ million per year)	_____
Net income ($ million)	_____
Market value of firm ($ million)	_____

Next, review the decision strategies that guided your team over the thirty-six quarters, and record your conclusions in the box below and on the book's Web page:

Decision-Making Governance and Strategies in Building People Express

1. How did your team make its decisions during the first several quarters, and how did its decision making evolve over the remaining quarters?

_____

_____

_____

_____

2. On the basis of this experience, what advice would you have for top teams on how to make their decisions over time?

_____

_____

_____

_____

Go Point Value

Now, the results. As advertised, this was a stellar field. On most occasions when I have led the People Express challenge, at least a quarter of the teams have gone bankrupt midway through the 1980s. Not this field. All seven teams against which you were competing not only managed to avoid bankruptcy, they also grew the business.

The numeric results are displayed below. I encourage you to compare your team's results with the competition. The first column, "Start," presents five metrics for the airline at the moment that the teams took control. The second column, "Autopilot," reports the results on the assumption that the decisions listed for the first quarter of 1981 remain unchanged across all thirty-six quarters. If a team chose to run the company on autopilot—none actually did so—it would have achieved a market value of $95 million, up from $8 million at the start. Not bad, but we can see from subsequent columns that doing so would have left a lot of value on the table.

Results of Building People Express for 36 Quarters from 1981 through 1989					
Performance Metric	**Start**	**Auto-pilot**	**Team A**	**Team B**	**Team C**
Number of aircraft	3	3	4	7	20
Number of employees	155	92	381	543	894
Total revenue ($ million/year)	32	39	32	132	239
Net income ($ million)	2	17	79	44	69
Market cap of firm ($ million)	8	95	162	246	409
Performance Metric	**Team D**	**Team E**	**Team F**	**Team G**	**Your team**
Number of aircraft	32	20	23	71	
Number of employees	2,282	1,896	1,540	3,038	
Total revenue ($ million/year)	410	340	303	793	
Net income ($ million)	79	77	62	246	
Market cap of firm ($ million)	425	513	713	1,427	

When the final market capitalizations of the seven team's firms are displayed in the figure below, the impact of good and timely decisions becomes dramatic. While autopilot management grew the airline to a market value of $95 million, the active decision making of Team C generated a value four times greater, $409 million. Team G created value more than fourteen times greater, a total of $1.4 billion. During other runnings of the simulation, teams have sometimes produced market caps of $2 billion and more, powerful testimony to the dollar value of hitting the right go points.

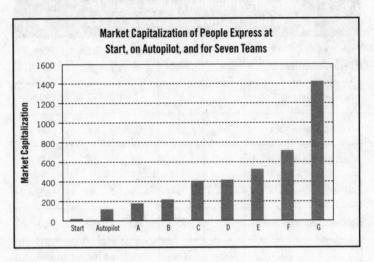

Market Capitalization of People Express at Start, on Autopilot, and for Seven Teams

After-Action Review

After the simulation, the seven teams performed just what Marine combat units undertake: an after-action review to extract lessons from the experience. In doing so, they compared their own experience with that of Donald Burr as he actually built the enterprise. Typically, three conclusions emerge from the discussion.

First, teams talk about the value of learning quickly from past decisions—exactly what after-action reviews are designed for. By rigorously analyzing the results from every quarter's decisions, the teams built an understanding of what drove their airline's market value. Several teams learned, for example, that they produced the best growth in market capitalization if they kept employee turnover to a minimum. When fewer employees quit, passengers experienced higher service quality, and that proved critical for attracting and retaining customers. By tracking these trends and seeing which decisions worked and which failed quarter after quarter, teams became better masters of their decision-making universe.

Second, teams reported that they worked best when they worked together. The more collaborative and mutually respectful the team was, the better the results their decisions achieved over time. By actively discussing their early results and collectively identifying the lessons to draw from them, the teams evolved a decision-making strategy in which they became increasingly confident.

Third, teams said that they came to think more strategically over time. They learned to keep an eye on not only their own results but also those of their competitors, which began to lower their own airfares as People Express rose in market share. The teams appreciated that they had to grow by buying airplanes and hiring staff, but also that an overly aggressive growth strategy resulted in an inexperienced workforce, which so tarnished the flying experience that increasing numbers of customers refused to return. Their business success, they came to understand, was only as good as their human resources decisions.

All of these lessons, it should be noted, stand in sharp contrast to the actual decisions of founder Donald Burr. Burr never came to fully appreciate that high rates of employee turnover would soon result in a dreadful reputation among flyers. He rejected the advice of some of his top lieutenants to slow People Express' sizzling growth to allow greater seasoning of the workforce. And when the competitors responded to the newcomer's rapid ascent by cutting their own airfares, Burr found he was presiding over an airline whose organization was too inexperienced and poorly organized to withstand aggressive competition.[11]

To share your own conclusions and results from the simulation experience, return to the Web page where you ran the airline, and post your responses to the questions listed above under "Decision-Making Governance and Strategies in Building People Express Airline." Also enter the five results that you achieved by the end of the thirty-sixth quarter: the number of aircraft and employees, and the revenue, income, and market value. Once you have done that, the Web page will report the percentile ranking of your market value compared with other teams that have run the simulation and posted their results.

Finally, let me encourage you to undertake the simulation a second time with your same team. By drawing upon your first experience, you are likely to achieve a market capitalization that is at least half again as high as on the first run, and sometimes even double or more.

THE DECISION TEMPLATE
FOR MAKING DECISIONS

In this chapter, we have freely applied decision principles and tools from the previous templates to the varied worlds of necklace trading, auto racing, an assault on K2, and an attempt to build value in an airline that in reality went down in flames. In doing so, we have also discovered additional principles, a reminder that a decision template can always be strengthened by learning from new experience. Building and mastering the decision-making template is an extended enterprise. Below are additional principles with tools and illustrations that I have drawn from these four challenges:

Principle	Tool	Illustration
1. Make clear what the decision entails before trying to make it.	Request clarification of the underlying assumptions and the purpose of a decision.	In Necklace Trading, decision making suffered because no one knew for certain if opportunity costs were to be considered or whether the objective was to reach the right answer individually or embrace the correct outcome collectively.
2. Emphasize underlying values and ideals.	Before focusing upon a decision, review the enterprise's ethics and principles.	Including the driver on the Carter Racing decision-making team would have ensured that safety was part of the risk calculation.
3. Position yourself for optimal situational awareness and clear-mindedness.	Identify where you will be able to both appreciate the context of a decision and reason through good and timely choices.	In Mountain Climbing, Rodrigo Jordan remained at the K2 Base Camp on summit day to ensure he could both appraise emergent problems and devise solutions for them.
4. New decisions should be self-consciously informed by prior decisions.	As with after-action combat reviews, routine after-decision reviews help refine what should go into the next set of choices.	In Airline Building, careful tracking of the results of early decisions enhanced the quality of subsequent decisions.

6

Transcending Personal Profit

For American business, 2002 was the year when ethics seemed to take a walk out the door. The parade got under way in January with top executives of Enron taking the Fifth Amendment before congressional committees looking into the energy trading giant's bankruptcy filing. By spring, a jury was on its way to convicting the old-line accounting firm of Arthur Andersen of obstructing justice, and WorldCom was veering toward bankruptcy.

Then, on June 3, Tyco International fell headlong into the abyss when chief executive L. Dennis Kozlowski suddenly resigned. The next day came the public announcement that Kozlowski had been indicted on charges that he evaded paying a million dollars in sales tax on art purchases totaling $13 million, including paintings by Renoir and Monet. As Tyco directors peered under the tent to see what their disgraced CEO had left behind, they found he had also misused $600 million in company funds. Eventually, Kozlowski would be convicted and sentenced to a New York maximum-security prison for eight to twenty-five years.[1]

Dennis Kozlowski had made hundreds of major decisions during his time at the Tyco helm. He had jumped into the game, consulted his inner circle, taken timely actions, and otherwise followed many of the precepts for properly reaching his go points. Collectively, those decisions had proven a roaring success by most measures. Tyco was a Wall Street high flyer. But on one vital dimen-

sion, Kozlowski had come up grievously short: many of his decisions had placed private welfare ahead of company well-being. As a result, he not only ended his career in prison but also gravely damaged thousands of investors, customers, and employees who had looked to him for responsible behavior when he sat in the privacy of his office with their fate in

Dennis Kozlowski.

his hands.

A final principle for reaching the go point is the imperative of being clear-minded about going beyond self-interest in forging decisions that affect others. Doing so is not easy—maximizing personal gain can be instinctual. Even when we want to, it is hard to separate responsible interests from parochial ones. Wall Street has its own agenda. Employees have theirs. Lawyers and auditors are not always disinterested parties. And rarely are we, even when our decisions are supposed to transcend private objectives. Nor do American values, especially business culture, actively promote self-sacrifice in the interest of the common good.

Yet no capacity is more essential for attaining the right go point.

By way of illustration, we start with the stark contrast between the decisions of Dennis Kozlowski and those of an outside director recruited by Tyco to help clean up his mess.

RECRUITING A LEAD DIRECTOR

To fill the vacuum and begin the restructuring after Kozlowski's abrupt exit, the Tyco board temporarily installed one of its own as CEO, then set out to find both a permanent CEO and a lead director who would take the company out of its misery. On July 25, the board tapped Edward D. Breen, who had been number two at Motorola, as its new chief executive. Next, it went after John (Jack) A. Krol for the lead directorship. This newly created position would require a strong, experienced, independent outsider who could work hand in hand with Breen to restructure a management team and board equally discredited by Kozlowski's malfeasance. Krol fit the bill.

A chemist by early profession and a nuclear engineer during his years of military service, Jack Krol had joined DuPont in 1963, reached its corner office by 1995, and retired as chairman three years later. He was enjoying golf at his Florida retirement home when the Tyco board called. Krol told the directors that they might regret inviting him inside the company since he thought a quick and complete shake-up of management and the board was inevitable. With 240,000 employees and $35 billion in revenue, Tyco was a supertanker that would have to be turned like a tugboat; otherwise it could follow Enron and WorldCom into bankruptcy court.

Even though the Tyco directors reiterated their support for him, Jack Krol was still reluctant to join the board of the badly damaged company. His first fear

John A. Krol.

was that Tyco could yet implode if Kozlowski's sins ran deeper than first thought. When a team of sixty forensic investigators led by prominent attorney David Boise tentatively concluded that there were plenty of knives at Tyco but no smoking guns, Krol became convinced that the company would not go under, at least not immediately, but there was still the fear that he might get caught up in personal liability issues as shareholder lawsuits came piling in. Just as important, his wife was adamantly opposed to having their agreeable retirement put on hold to save a company Krol had never worked for.

"I was on the fence," he told me when we talked about the Tyco offer, "but this challenging thing kept on gnawing at me. It would be *something* to turn this around."

When Jack Krol met new CEO Breen for lunch on August 2 he intended to listen politely to the pitch, then decline the offer. Instead, he walked away from the meal as Tyco's new lead director. "I'll tell you what happened," Krol said. "There were two salesmen sitting together at lunch, and he outsold me."

MORE THAN MONEY

It was not cash that got Jack Krol to his go point. Krol had retired from DuPont with all the wealth he and his wife would ever need, and he was already serving on the board of three other companies: ACE Limited, MeadWestvaco, and Milliken. At Tyco, Krol would receive an annual retainer of $100,000 and another $120,000 annually in stock set-asides until retirement. Not a pittance, but hardly the lottery either, and only a modest increment to his DuPont wealth and the compensation from his other director posts. Just as Tour de France winner Lance Armstrong entitled one of his books *It's Not About the Bike,* for Krol it wasn't about the money.[2]

Instead, it was the challenge, Krol explained—the chance to play a leading part with the CEO "to make this thing turn around" and to have "fun," by which he meant winning, getting the job done against difficult odds. He had concluded that many of Tyco's businesses were solid, a good base to build upon. Above all, though, Krol said, the prospect of serving is what brought him on board. "When you're doing that kind of job, you're here to serve, not to be served. We're here to help and to lead, and we're not here to have company airplanes, the highest pay, and chauffeured cars."

With neither aircraft nor limo, Jack Krol retired from retirement by joining the Tyco board as lead director on August 6, 2002. In the year that followed, he would devote more than half his time to turning the ship around, even working full time during the more turbulent moments. He and CEO Ed Breen worked in concert to replace their entire board, a step almost without precedent for a major company short of bankruptcy. They spun off more than four dozen business units even as they dug through massive accounting irregularities and repaid a huge loan that came due in 2003. They also removed a staggering 290 of Tyco's top 300 executives. And in the process, they transformed the company culture from building by acquiring to prospering by operating. By 2005, the company had been stabilized, restructured, and restored. With the worst behind him, Krol finally managed to reduce his engagement to just one-third of the time.[3]

In deciding to join the Tyco board, Jack Krol had transcended personal profit in favor of larger purpose. During the several times I talked with him during the fall of 2002 and again in 2005, he consistently mentioned the satisfaction he found in being part of a high-octane team with a compelling mission that carried the hopes of tens of thousands of the company's stakeholders. As the lead director, his specific challenge was to take the Tyco governing board from worst to first, and that he did. In less than three years under Krol's prodding, the Tyco board became one of the best in the business, with ten new, strong-willed, independent directors and far-reaching governance rules in place that should never again allow a CEO to ransack the firm.

COLLECTIVE INTEREST,
NOT SELF-INTEREST

What a contrast Dennis Kozlowski provides. The former CEO had built Tyco from $3 billion in annual revenue in 1992 when he took the helm to $35 billion at the point of his ouster. He had assembled a mammoth conglomerate through acquisition after acquisition, shelling out $62 billion for some nine hundred companies. By 2001, Tyco's market value exceeded that of Ford, General Motors, and Sears combined. So successful had been his management decisions that Kozlowski found himself being mentioned in the same breath with the most celebrated executive of the era. Kozlowski's "Midas touch in deal after deal has transformed Tyco from an obscure manufacturer into a powerhouse worth 50 times more than when he took over," exclaimed *Business Week* in 2001. "It's an achievement that has led some to compare Kozlowski with General Electric Co.'s Jack Welch. But unlike Welch, Kozlowski shows no signs of slowing down anytime soon."[4]

The problem was, too much of what came in Tyco's front door quickly went out the CEO's back door. In an era of corporate wrongdoing, Kozlowski's trail laid bare an unmatched record of personal excess. Kozlowski had used Tyco funds to pay for a $2,200 wastebasket, a $6,000 shower curtain, a $15,000 umbrella stand, a $2 million birthday party, $12 million in paintings, a $31 million apartment, and, just for good measure, a $58 million bonus. In all, it added up to a $600 million heist, and the theft did not stop with the number one felon.[5]

Kozlowski had persuaded his own aides to cross the same line. Chief financial officer Mark Swartz was sentenced along with his boss to eight to twenty-five years. The CEO had similarly encouraged a board member to put his own interests above those of Tyco's shareholders. In 2001, nonexecutive director Frank E. Walsh facilitated Tyco's $9.2 billion acquisition of a large commercial finance firm, the

CIT Group. Kozlowski rewarded Walsh with $20 million for his "service" but never reported the payment to the other directors or to the stockholders. In later barring Walsh from ever serving again as a director or officer of a publicly traded company, a Securities and Exchange Commission enforcement director cut to the chase: "Shareholders entrusted him with the responsibility of watching out for their interests in Tyco's boardroom and executive suite. Instead, Mr. Walsh himself took secret compensation and kept those same shareholders in the dark."[6]

As a director and an officer of a public corporation, Jack Krol and Dennis Kozlowski carried similar responsibilities for making wise business decisions on behalf of their shareholders. Their responsibility was to honor a norm of reciprocity that is enshrined in securities regulations and business understandings: investors lend directors and executives their money with the expectation that the directors and executives will wisely decide how to use it. Their responsibility was also to serve as fiduciaries for the company's investors, requiring that investors' interests trump their own in all decisions. Yet although Krol and Kozlowski worked for the same company and shared the same responsibilities, their decisions on how to employ the investors' money could not have been more opposite. One used his go points for his own well-being. The other used the collective good as his personal touchstone, and that made all the difference, for him and for Tyco's stakeholders.

CHARACTER COUNTS

The same contrast between personal and public interest is readily found in politics. Some political figures are consumed with self-promotion, others with national purpose. And the difference can have profound consequences.

Consider two towering figures of the mid-twentieth century: Lyndon B. Johnson and George C. Marshall. Johnson was one of the most effective Senate leaders ever, and his first years as president following

John F. Kennedy's assassination in 1963 were equally consequential. He pushed sweeping civil rights legislation through Congress, yet his presidency ultimately became so mired in the Vietnam conflict that, in 1968, he declined to seek a second full term and left office under a cloud. Many factors impaired his presidential decisions during the war, but among them was a self-centeredness that stood out even in a profession not known for self-effacement. "Johnson was a narcissistic character," offered presidential historian Robert Dallek. Whatever the comparison, Johnson always "had to be the best, the greatest."

Like Johnson, George Marshall found himself thrust into a critical moment in American and world history. Unlike Johnson, Marshall made the most of the opportunity and secured for himself one of the most revered reputations of the modern era. Promoted by President Franklin Delano Roosevelt ahead of thirty-three more senior generals, Marshall became Army chief of staff in 1939 and led the nation's armed forces during the Second World War. He later served as secretary of state and secretary of defense, authored the U.S. plan to assist Europe's economic recovery, and won the Nobel Peace Prize in 1953 for what became known as the "Marshall Plan."

Many differences distinguished Johnson and Marshall, but character played a role in their varying responses to the challenges they were called to face. Marshall "put honor, duty and service to others ahead of self promotion or aggrandizement," wrote Dallek. "He was willing to sacrifice himself and his career when he spoke out to" his superiors. Marshall radiated "integrity and selflessness," had "no agenda of his own, only the agenda of his leader and his country," and "exuded sacrificial leadership born out of servant leadership." The world recognized it, too. At Dwight D. Eisenhower's request, George Marshall represented the nation at the coronation of Queen Elizabeth on June 2, 1953. As Marshall entered Westminster Abbey, the great assemblage of luminaries from across the British Commonwealth, led by prime minister Winston Churchill, rose to honor his appearance.[7]

PERSONAL PROFIT AND PUBLIC GAIN

Alexis de Tocqueville, the nineteenth-century French chronicler of U.S. mores, observed in *Democracy in America* that Americans "are fond of explaining almost all the actions of their lives by the principle of self-interest rightly understood"—what we think of today as "enlightened self-interest." This accent on self-interest, even if enlightened, was notable for its contrast with the sensibilities of the European aristocracies, where those who ruled, according to de Tocqueville, "were fond of professing that it is praiseworthy to forget oneself and that good should be done without hope of reward, as it is by the Deity himself."[8]

In fact, many personal decisions are rightly framed around *not* forgetting oneself. What are the private gains and losses, it is fair to ask, associated with pursuing one career option or another? Would obtaining a college education result in greater lifetime earnings than directly entering the workforce? Is there better value in attending Colorado College or the University of Colorado? Would accepting an entry-level offer from ABC lead to brighter career prospects than one at CNN?

Predisposition, anxiety, and naiveté cloud that calculus, and pure utility is rarely maximized in practice. Still, personal calculations provide a benchmark for framing and judging such decisions. Moreover, American culture and the ideology of capitalism have long placed a premium on being clear-minded about one's self-interest. "Insofar as there is a dominant belief in our society today," observed hedge fund manager and social critic George Soros, "it is a belief in the magic of the marketplace. The doctrine of laissez-faire capitalism holds that the common good is best served by the uninhibited pursuit of self-interest."[9]

Economist Milton Friedman maintains that it should not be otherwise. Because self-interest is good for commerce, Friedman contends, business executives should rivet on maximizing their return on investment. Business leaders who "speak eloquently about the 'social responsibilities of business in a free-enterprise system' " are "the unwitting puppets of the intellectual forces that have been undermining the basis of a free society these past decades." Instead of seeking to serve society, firms should stick to their own knitting: there "is one and only social responsibility of business," Friedman argues, and that is "to use its resources and engage in activities designed to increase its profits."[10]

ALIGNING PERFORMANCE AND PAY

The pursuit of personal profit has become institutionalized in the way publicly traded companies have come to pay their executives. To ensure that management decisions are consistently disciplined by stockholder requirements—and to meet the demands of large institutional investors such as Fidelity, Vanguard, and the California Public Employees Retirement System—corporate boards over the past two decades have transformed executive pay from largely fixed to widely variable. And they have directly linked the variable component to investor value through the remarkable invention of the stock option. Though not a perfect gearing, when stockholders see their company holdings rise in value, executives' stock options rise in lockstep.[11]

The increasing alignment of executive gain with shareholder performance is shown in the chart below for the top seven to eight managers of forty-five large U.S. firms from 1982 to 2005. As long as top executives in 1982 arrived at their office by 9 a.m. and turned out the lights by 5 p.m., they would receive at least two-thirds of their expected pay package. By 2004, however, their base pay had dropped to a third, with well over half now coming in stock-based pay. In other words, for self-interested reasons, their discretion in decision making had narrowed. If they failed to focus their decisions on increasing stockholder wealth between 9 and 5, they felt it in their own paychecks.[12]

Compensation of Top 7–8 Managers at
45 U.S. Manufacturing Firms, 1982–2005

■ Base (salary and benefits)   ■ Short-term incentives   ■ Long-term incentives

To Harvard Business School professor Michael Jensen, it all makes perfect sense. "Who can argue," he writes, against an enterprise that "aligns the interests of owners and managers" and thereby "unlocks hundreds of billions of dollars of shareholder value?" That alignment, Jensen contends, will come when "directors recognize the importance of incentives—and adopt compensation systems that truly link pay and performance."[13]

WHEN PERSONAL AND PUBLIC DIVERGE

Linking executive pay to shareholder value is one of the grand innovations of contemporary business, a powerful tool for forcing executives to focus on investors when reaching decisions, but tying pay to profit has also reinforced the premium in American culture on self-interest as the proper criterion for framing and reaching responsible decisions. To be sure, when personal profit and public gain are well aligned, the criterion works: what is good for each is good for all. When they are not—and that is the rule rather than the exception for those with responsibilities for others—the unbridled creed of personal advantage can get in the way of reaching the right go point.

Recall for a moment Don Mackey's last decision on Storm King Mountain during the South Canyon fire of July 6, 1994. Mackey could have decided at 4 p.m. to run up Lunchspot Ridge to the comparative safety of the previously burned area, where eight other firefighters found protection from the engulfing flames. Doing so certainly would have been in his self-interest. Instead, Mackey dashed back across the fire line to hasten the retreat of those under his command—a decision that helped save the lives of six other firefighters while sacrificing his own. Had Mackey's decision been driven by the principle "every man for himself," those firefighters most likely would not be alive today and he might well have survived.

Or think about Enron, where shareholder value—and thus the value of the executive stock options tied to it—was created through accounting sleights-of-hand that ultimately brought the company down. To borrow from Lord Acton, the absolute pursuit of profits can corrupt responsible decisions absolutely.

Unless self-interest "is tempered by the recognition of a common interest that ought to take precedence over particular interests," George Soros warns, our society "is liable to break down." Enron, WorldCom, Tyco—the corporate woods are full of examples: when key decision makers give primacy to their own self-interest, the result is collective irresponsibility.[14]

Decision making that affects others demands a different computation than decisions made solely for the advancement of personal welfare. It requires a capacity to transcend private agendas and parochial objectives, a willingness to swim against the normative tide. Self-effacement comes naturally to some, a product of upbringing, schooling, or temperament. Nelson Mandela and Mother Teresa are exemplars; we have all known local ones, the private saints. For many of us, though, transcending the lure of personal profit is at least partially an acquired taste. The principles and devices that follow are guides for getting beyond yourself.

LOOKING AT THE PHOTO

As vice chairman of the U.S. Joint Chiefs of Staff since October 2001, and chairman since September 2005, General Peter Pace has played a key role in every major decision on the U.S. military involvement in Afghanistan and Iraq. His actions have impacted literally millions in uniform and well beyond—an enormous responsibility. To keep his job in perspective and to make certain that his commitment to the military personnel under him supersedes all other agendas, Pace keeps a photo of Lance Corporal Guido Farinaro tucked under the glass on his desktop.[15]

General Peter Pace.

On July 30, 1968, twenty-two-year-old Peter Pace and nineteen-year-old Guido Farinaro were approaching one of the many hamlets that dotted the rice fields near Danang, South Vietnam, when an enemy bullet tore through Farinaro's chest. Other Marines in Pace's unit would fall during the months ahead. One even took a fatal shot in the side when by a quirk of timing he happened to stand up between Pace and a sniper at the wrong moment, but Farinaro was the first Marine lost in battle under Pace's command.

The Vietnam experience left an indelible mark on almost everyone who served there. For some it resulted in stress disorders; for others, permanent disabilities; for still others, prideful or poignant memories. For Peter Pace, the war in Vietnam has shaped how he has approached most major decisions in the more than three decades since. "I felt that I really owed those men who didn't come home a debt that

I could never pay," he said. That hasn't stopped him from trying, though. Pace vowed to himself to remain in the Corps as long as the Marines would have him and to always keep in mind the men lost in battle when he was deciding on the fate of today's servicemen and servicewomen.

Every day when he walks into the chairman's office, Pace says, "I know it's not about me. It's about the exercise of my authority; my responsibility is to do the right thing for the country." As an enduring reminder, Guido Farinaro waits under that desktop glass, ready to catch the chairman's eye as he nears a moment of decision.

General Peter Pace with photo of Guido Farinaro.

A photo, of course, is only one such reminder. The voice of a parent, the words of a mentor, a flashback to a traumatic moment—they all can serve as useful touchstones for keeping self-interest at bay when it threatens to intrude on a go point.

Another useful device is to personalize the institutional. If Sara Lee were an experienced baker, General Electric a retired Army officer, or the Red Cross a blood distributor, what decision would he or she make? Like most people, organizations want to live long and prosper. They want security, growth, respect, and a sense of purpose. Since they cannot decide for themselves, their people can do it for them, and in doing so do the best by them.

Sometimes a remembered maxim can achieve much the same. Peter Pace's Marine Corps has long instructed its leaders that the "officer eats last"—a catchphrase meant to capture the essence of a culture in which mission comes first, front-line welfare second, and officer well-being last. A similar Civil War dictum was "Feed your horses, feed your men, then feed yourself." On Christmas Day 2001 at a makeshift Marine camp inside Afghanistan, commissioned officers served the enlisted Marines who had spearheaded the invasion there two months earlier, then ate their own Christmas dinner only after everyone else had been served. It was an unspoken reminder of what is valued most.

GAZING FROM THE APEX

We cannot all get to the mountaintop, but we can all stand there metaphorically when we are called upon to make decisions that affect not just our own well-being but the fortunes of those around us. Imagine you are the coach, not the player; the teacher, not the student; the provost, not the assistant professor; the CEO, not the assistant to the vice president. Imagine, in short, that you can see the whole picture, the big terrain, not just your own, inevitably blinkered portion of it. From that mountaintop, how would you decide?

Enron vice president Sherron Watkins was shocked when she learned on August 14, 2001, that chief executive Jeffrey Skilling had abruptly resigned for "personal reasons." Her immediate thought was there must be far more to the story, and she had a fair inkling of what the larger story might be. The company's chief financial officer, Andrew Fastow, had hired Watkins earlier that summer to review his "special-purpose entities," an arcane contrivance used to mask Enron's massive indebtedness from public scrutiny. As a professional accountant, Wat-

Sherron Watkins.

kins was so appalled by what she discovered that she had begun to cast around for a new employer, a self-interested move that made good sense. Now, with Skilling's unexpected resignation, she began to feel responsible for more than her own future.

Rather than quitting, as pure self-interest might have dictated, Watkins decided to alert the person most responsible for the company. She knew that going over Fastow's head to report his suspected malfeasance to chairman Kenneth Lay might well constitute a career-ending move, but she also knew that if she were in Lay's position, she would surely want to know what the vice president had discovered. Standing on her imagined apex, her decision to reach up from below seemed natural.

Watkins itemized her discoveries in a memo to the chairman and conveyed them again in a personal briefing on August 22, warning that his company was about to "implode in a wave of accounting scandals." Lay, of course, brushed her warnings aside, and less than four months later Enron did implode, just as Watkins had forecast, in one of the greatest accounting scandals of all time. The accountant, though, had looked at the whole picture and risked her career to save the company. The chairman—the one who actually stood on the mountaintop—evidently could see little beyond his own self-interest, and hundreds of thousands of employees and investors suffered dearly for his myopic view.[16]

Viktor Yushchenko pursued a similar course in his 2004 bid to become president of the Ukraine. After Yushchenko lost a rigged election in November, he and tens of thousands of protesters took to the streets, demanding a new, fair election. During the tumultuous days that followed, in what came to be called the "Orange Revolution," Yushchenko was harassed, threatened, even poisoned by his powerful opponents. But he refused to pull back from his democratic course, even though armed suppression looked possible and even as elements within his own movement demanded more radical actions. When the country's incumbent president finally relented and allowed a fair rematch on December 26, Yushchenko emerged the unequivocal winner, a democratic victor for a new nation that had demanded democratic processes.

"Yushchenko has become an authentic statesman precisely because he has not sought power for himself but has instead sought truth and integrity for his fellow citizens." So observed Polish president Aleksander Kwasjniewski. Put differently, Yushchenko became one of Europe's democratic heroes by deciding to act as a president should well before he had achieved the office. "That success would have been impossible," concluded Kwasjniewski, "if Yushchenko has not put the public good above his own sense of personal wrong."[17]

Like Sherron Watkins, Viktor Yushchenko found his go point by standing above himself, by viewing his nation from its summit more than from its angry streets. In both cases, it was the imagined heights that made the difference.

WHAT WOULD YOU DO?

Now, an opportunity to stand at the apex yourself, at one of the pivotal moments in American history. First, though, some background that should be at least partially familiar to many readers.

The Union Army of the Potomac under the command of Ulysses S. Grant finally cornered Robert E. Lee's Army of Northern Virginia on Sunday, April 9, 1865, near Appomattox, Virginia. Outnumbered six to one, the Confederates tried a final, desperate breakout at 5 a.m. When it sputtered, Lee called together his top aides, including his artillery chief, twenty-nine-year-old E. Porter Alexander, for an urgent council. Alexander argued for what Lee's superior, Confederate president Jefferson Davis, had already been calling for: a protracted guerrilla struggle to be waged from the South's hills, forests, and swamps.

Without decisive resolution, the war could sputter along indefinitely, draining the North of what men and materiel remained in an endless pursuit of an evanescent enemy. Federal garrisons would be required throughout the South for years to come; casualties could soar and morale would sink. Lee knew as well as anyone that a guerrilla strategy would be a pragmatic way for the weak to long persist, and he wanted nothing to do with it.

The Confederate general explained to his artillery chief that it would take years for the country to recover if the rebel army melted into the bush, adding that they "had no right to consider only how this would affect us." It was essential, declared Lee, to "consider its effects on the country as a whole." Accordingly, Lee sent a letter across the lines to Grant, saying he would like to meet "to discuss the terms of surrender of this army."

At one o'clock that afternoon, dressed in ceremonial uniform with sword and sash, Lee entered the home of Wilmer McLean, one of twenty or so dwellings nestled around the tiny way station of Appomattox Court House. Grant arrived thirty minutes later and wrote out the terms of surrender. It required that Confederate soldiers relinquish their muskets, but officers could retain their small arms and horses. The two generals signed the document, and three hours after arriving, Lee shook hands with Grant and walked out the door.

In effect, Lee had agreed to an unconditional surrender, precisely what his commander in chief and some of his top aides did not want. Grant, for his part, had proposed terms wholly in keeping with Abraham Lincoln's desire to "let 'em up easy." Both leaders had gazed down from the apex and done what was best for the collective whole, but more work remained.

Lee's formal surrender of April 9 was followed by a ceremonial surrender on Wednesday, April 12. Grant had instructed Lee's infantry, under the command of General George B. Gordon, to march onto a field where they were to be met by a line of three Union brigades, some 5,000 soldiers, under the command of Joshua Lawrence Chamberlain, whose regiment had helped defend Little Round Top during the battle of Gettysburg some twenty-one months earlier. Twice wounded and now a brigadier general, Chamberlain was an unlikely choice since he was neither a West Pointer nor a ranking officer, yet Chamberlain embraced the assignment and took his own counsel in scripting it.

Before reading on, place yourself in Chamberlain's shoes. Grant has required that the Confederate infantry yield its firearms and regimental flags to you; otherwise, he has given you a free hand to orchestrate the surrender. Keep the ceremony simple, your commanding general advises, and don't "humiliate the manhood" of the vanquished soldiers. Stand on the mountaintop now. See the big picture from above. Remember that your decisions are likely to affect the tenor of the peace to come, after four terrible years of war. How would you arrange the formal surrender?

Once you have designed your plans, go once again to the book's Web page and click on the "Apex Principle at Appomattox" to enter your plans and your rationale for them. Your response and justification will be posted for others to see, and you can read what others have proposed as well. What follows is what Joshua Lawrence Chamberlain actually did on April 12, 1865.

Respect Meets Respect

When the first Confederate infantry under General Gordon approached the field, Chamberlain ordered his officers to bring the Union line to a posture of "carry arms," a respectful marching salute just a notch below "present arms." With a bugle call, unit after unit of federal soldiers smartly raised their muskets to the vertical on their right side and placed their left hands across the stocks. In military terms, this constituted an unambiguous display of honor, wholly unanticipated by both sides. Part of the same military heritage, Gordon immediately appreciated the gesture's significance. In response, he tipped his sword toward Chamberlain and ordered his marching column to carry arms as well, salute answering salute, respect meeting respect. Both sides had been shooting at each other just seventy-two hours earlier.

"Before us in proud humiliation," Chamberlain later wrote, were those "whom neither toils and sufferings, nor the fact of death, nor disaster, nor hopelessness could bend from their resolve." With no order from above but appreciating what Lincoln would have valued under the circumstance, he explained the carry arms gesture: "Was not such manhood to be welcomed back into a Union so tested and assured?"

Chamberlain could not help but share the pain as the front-line Confederate commanders laid their colors, their near-sacred regimental flags, at his feet. As the last color-bearer came forward in tears, Chamberlain told him, "I admire your noble spirit and only regret that I have not the authority to bid you keep your flag, and carry it home as a precious loom." His words were repeated through the Confederate ranks and would soon become part of the South's lore. The war had begun exactly four years earlier, with the Confederate shelling of Fort Sumter. Now, although 175,000 rebels still remained in uniform, it was finally ending with Chamberlain's help in a spirit of reconciliation and reunification that Lincoln had expressed so powerfully in his second inaugural address: "With malice toward none, with charity for all."[18]

Union general Joshua Lawrence Chamberlain receives Confederate army surrender at Appomattox.

In the years ahead, William Tecumseh Sherman and other Union generals would remain widely despised throughout the South, but for what he did at Appomattox, Chamberlain became one of the few Northern officers respected in the South. By viewing his world from the apex above, he had established a first but important bridge across a great divide.

In Their Own Words

Whatever the words or metaphors used to describe the apex principle, it was a recurrent theme among the many people I interviewed and observed for this book. Here is how they expressed it:

From Todd S. Thomson, chief financial officer of Citigroup, with more than $100 billion in annual revenue and $1 trillion under management:

> My view of the CFO job is that you must be the conscience of the organization. That requires making sure that you are the one who thinks about the shareholder.

From Daniel Cooper, chief operating officer for the Department of Surgery of the Hospital of the University of Pennsylvania and former senior manager for the European operations of chemical maker Monsanto Company:

> What you learn in a corporation is to be absolutely right on in terms of the focus of the decision and in doing what is right. It sounds a bit corny, but at Monsanto, those of us in a leadership position had a great deal of trust and responsibility that the shareholders had given us, and I took that very seriously.
>
> In making decisions, you're "messing" with people's careers here, and you cannot take that lightly.

From Lieutenant Colonel Joseph Bernard, second in command of the U.S. Marine Corps Officer Candidates School based in Quantico, Virginia, and a Marine since 1982:

I am a Marine Corps officer, and my allegiance is to the institution of the Marine Corps and its mission accomplishment. For me, that's always at the top of the list of priorities when I am making a decision.

From Thomas W. Jones, chief executive of Global Investment Management at Citigroup:

I have little tolerance for people who measure success in terms of money. I'm attracted by people who go for extraordinary accomplishments and pull others into that vision, people who want to achieve something special.

From David Pottruck, former chief executive of Charles Schwab Corporation, the retail brokerage firm with 14,000 employees and 7 million customers:

You have to find your passion by reminding yourself that your job is not to do what you like to do, but to do what's critical for the company.

From John J. Brennan, Vanguard Group chief executive, with 10,000 "crew members" (as Brennan calls his employees) managing $850 million on behalf of 18 million clients:

If you're a careerist, you're not going to succeed here. If you want to be a rock star, this is not the place for you. The first time you break out the guitar, we are going to take it and break it over your head.

The greater good of the client comes first, the crew member comes next, and you're last. The day any one of us thinks it's about *us,* it's time to go!

I never wanted to make a decision that was good for me and bad for business.

And finally, an observation from the ancient Chinese philosopher Lao-tzu:

He who loves the world as his body may be entrusted with the empire.[19]

THE GO POINT IS
NOT ABOUT YOURSELF

At the bottom of the food chain or the work ladder, the opportunities to make far-reaching decisions are few and far between. Selfless go points are hypothetical; putting food on the table is the reality. As we move up the ranks, though, the chances for self-serving decision making grow ever greater, as does the temptation to yield to the self-maximizing precepts that run so deeply in American values and the culture of capitalism.

Yet the evidence suggests that even capitalist enterprise is best driven by decision makers who consistently transcend their own self-interest. In his study of how eleven U.S. firms elevated their performance from "good to great" and sustained the change over a decade, author and researcher Jim Collins found that the great performers had executives at the helm who consistently placed the enterprises interest ahead of their own.[20]

In fact, the research and anecdotal evidence is so overwhelming that selflessness constitutes a go point principle of its own: the more privileged your position, the less self-serving your decisions must be. The go point can never be about you alone. That is why the ability to surmount personal agendas in favor of collective goals is one of the defining qualifiers for reaching the top in the first place.

THE DECISION TEMPLATE FOR TRANSCENDING PERSONAL PROFIT

"We've got some difficult days ahead," Martin Luther King Jr. told striking sanitation workers in Memphis, Tennessee, on April 3, 1968, the night before he was gunned down by an assassin. "But it doesn't matter with me now. Because I've been to the mountaintop. And I don't mind. Like anybody, I would like to live a long life. Longevity has its place. But I'm not concerned about that now. I just want to do God's will." A deeply religious man, King had gone to the highest authority he knew for direction and was acting now in concert with what he understood the common good to be, whatever the danger to himself.[21]

Do the same: imagine yourself on that mountaintop, consult the touchstones that help you balance the equation between personal profit and public benefit. Even if events do not turn out as you might hope, you will know you acted as if you were at the apex. Speaking to several thousand business and political leaders in 2006, President Bill Clinton offered kindred advice. As a measure of one's achievements in office, he urged, "Make sure that people are better off when you're done," and whatever the setbacks from the decisions taken, as he should know, "you just have to keep going."[22]

Principle	Tool	Illustration
1. A touchstone or lodestar, some object or memory can serve as a powerful reminder of the need to transcend personal gain for public purpose when making responsible decisions.	Look at a telling image or recall the example of a parent, the advice of a mentor, or their equivalent.	General Peter Pace keeps a photo of Lance Corporal Guido Farinaro under the glass on his Pentagon desk.
2. Asking yourself what the top person in your enterprise *should* do helps to ensure that your decisions will serve multiple needs of the enterprise, not just your own.	Before you get to the go point, imagine that you are gazing down from the apex, perfectly positioned to appreciate the entire enterprise and its situation.	Enron vice president Sherron Watkins risked her job and Ukrainian presidential candidate Viktor Yushchenko risked his life in acting as they felt their ultimate authority should; Joshua Lawrence Chamberlain scripted a Confederate surrender as he believed the nation needed.
3. The more responsible the position, the less self-serving must be its decisions.	Remind yourself of whom you are working for aside from yourself and who stands to benefit and suffer most from the decisions you make.	With little thought of personal gain, Jack Krol gave up a comfortable retirement to help turn Tyco around for its employees, customers, and investors.

7

Unforced Errors

Edward D. Breen Jr. was enjoying his last afternoon as chief operating officer at Motorola when a message began scrolling across the bottom of his CNBC desk monitor: Tyco International was about to declare bankruptcy. The day before, the company's stock had climbed to $11.58. Now as Breen looked on, it went into free fall, bottoming out at under $7 a share. The date was July 25, 2002, a Thursday. As soon as the market closed that day, Tyco would announce that Ed Breen was going to be its next CEO, charged with the Herculean task of cleaning up Dennis Kozlowski's mess.

The bankruptcy claim proved bogus, but Tyco was every bit the cauldron it appeared to be. Breen's new job was no assignment for the faint-hearted. "You need to be willing to stand up and make the tough decisions," he says. "It is not always pleasant, it is not always easy, but at the end of the day we're paid to fix problems." With the help and backing of new lead board member Jack Krol, Breen did just that, dismissing virtually the entire senior staff and forcing the resignation of all the directors who had just hired him. Not every decision was the right one, Breen acknowledges, but inaction would have been a far

Edward D. Breen Jr.

worse route. "It is more important to make ten decisions and get eight right than to sit around and *not* make any at all."

Ed Breen has a decision-making rule of thumb that he applies to people and the companies they run. "When a company CEO says he has only 80 percent of the information and 'can't make that decision yet,' I tell myself the company contains a fatal flaw. . . . A lot of people are petrified about making mistakes, but that's not the way the business world works. I love people who analyze and make a decision and move on."[1]

That same message emerged time and again among the more than one hundred decision makers that I interviewed and observed for this book: good decision making is a decision itself—an act of will, a personal resolution. It requires an eagerness to face, embrace, and make choice after choice, even when the going gets rough. Mark Crisson, who oversees power, water, and rail utilities for the city of Tacoma, Washington, estimates that he reaches dozens of thorny decisions weekly, hundreds annually, many of them with large economic and political consequences for Tacoma's citizens and leaders. Yet, he says, he never flinches in the face of a crisis. Rather than witnessing history, the go point requires a penchant for repeatedly writing it in small and large ways.[2]

Lou Gerstner decided to move from advising clients such as IBM at McKinsey to running companies such as IBM because "I wanted to be the person making the decisions," he explained, "not just consulting on them." Former secretary of state and chairman of the Joint Chiefs of Staff Colin Powell warned, "You can't make someone else's choices," and "You shouldn't let someone else make yours." Robert Druskin, president of Citigroup's Corporate and Investment Bank and the key player in Citigroup's recovery from the 9/11 attacks, said much the same thing in an interview: "It is good to get opinions. It is good to go out to talk to a lot of smart, experienced people. But at the end of the day you cannot let other people make decisions for you. . . . You have got to make your own calls, and you have to be willing to live with them."[3]

Thoracic surgeon Larry Kaiser oversees seventy-five physicians who annually perform more than ten thousand surgical procedures at the Hospital of the University of Pennsylvania. As chair of the Department of Surgery and surgeon-in-chief of the University of Pennsylvania Health System, Kaiser makes hundreds of personnel and operating decisions that affect the lives of thousands of patients. Yet he leaves the office without a trace of decider's regret. "I never have trouble making decisions," he told me, "and I don't ever leave here at the end of the day agonizing." Mogens Lykketoft, leader of Denmark's Social Democratic Party and its former minister of finance and foreign affairs, was of the same mind: "I've never had problems with taking actions or decisions."[4]

Still, virtually everyone has been pained from time to time by having to make a difficult choice. Thomas Jefferson once referred to his presidency as a "splendid misery."[5] Not every decision, however confidently taken, thoroughly researched, and well intended, turns out right. But the Inverse Rule of Go Point Misery should be a comforting one: the more decisions you make, the fewer regrets you are likely to have about making the next one.

SMART PEOPLE SOMETIMES MAKE DUMB CHOICES

Good decisions lead to satisfaction, prosperity, and advancement. Really bad ones—the Edsel usually comes to mind—are the stuff of terminal embarrassment.

Some decision errors are largely personal, of little consequence except for the individuals involved. Consider British broadcaster David Frost's compilation of some of the worst such blunders:

- South African prospector Sors Hariezon's decision to sell his gold claim in 1886 for $20. During the next century, the mines on or near his claim produced more than half of the gold sold in the Western world.

- The Munich Technical Institute's 1889 decision not to accept an applicant by the name of Albert Einstein. Einstein, the institute determined, "showed no promise."

- The 1977 decision by a glider pilot to make an obscene gesture to a woman sunbathing on a rooftop. Her husband responded with a submachine gun.[6]

Fortune magazine writer Jerry Useem (the name is no coincidence; Jerry is my son) and his staff compiled their own list of some of the best and worst decisions in business history. Among the best business go points of all time, they concluded, were Boeing's decision to build the 707, IBM's to build the 360, and Intel's to make the microprocessor. But their compilation also included such "appallingly stupid" and very consequential decisions as:

- Western Union's decision in 1876 not to purchase the rights to Alexander Graham Bell's telephone, believing that its own network of telegraph lines would better define the future of national communication.

- Ford Motor Company's 1972 decision not to correct the gas tank on its Pinto even after it learned that the tank was prone to explode when the car was rear-ended, incinerating drivers and passengers. Ford's astounding logic: Defending against wrongful-death litigation would be less expensive than investing the $11 per tank to fix the problem.

- AT&T's 1982 decision to break itself up by spinning off its seven local phone companies while hanging on to its equipment-making and long-distance services. The upside-down logic in this case: the convergence of computing and communications eventually would make equipment and long-distance service the most profitable divisions.[7]

This intersection of high success quotients and low go points might have found its apogee in Enron. Its spectacular rise during the 1990s brought it a year 2000 ranking as America's most admired company for innovativeness. Yet when faced with critical decisions, Enron's directors repeatedly opted for paths that led directly to the firm's demise. Similarly confronted, the energy giant's chief officers did the same, from Andrew Fastow's accountant-dodging "special-purpose entities" to the sustained dissembling by chair Kenneth Lay and CEO Jeff Skilling. From the boardroom to its executive suite, Enron directors and executives faced go points critical to thousands of shareholders and employees, and they frequently chose the wrong way.[8]

THE GO POINTER'S GUIDE TO UNFORCED ERRORS

While decisions by Enron directors and executives were central to its downfall, the application of a few template principles and tools might have saved the empire. Their absence and the terrible consequences that followed should stand as enduring reminders to build and absorb the decision templates before they are needed. Otherwise we may see yet again the "horrendous miscalculations of people," in the phrasing of writer Jonathan V. Last, "who get paid a lot of money for making decisions." He was referencing filmmakers of such Hollywood flops as *Ishtar* and *Waterworld,* but his warning would apply to virtually any realm whose denizens make consequential decisions without an adequate set of guiding templates.[9]

What follows is a final set of guidelines to help you avoid what in tennis are called "unforced errors," those smallish glitches that in the end can help spell the difference between victory and defeat.[10]

Problem: AUTHORITY IS NOT BESTOWED
Tool: PURSUE RESPONSIBILITY

For some, responsibility is simply bestowed: a princess is handed the kingdom upon the passing of the monarch; a favorite son inherits the family business. For most, however, the authority to make decisions must be actively sought.

Born in the Bronx of an interracial marriage, Jaime Irick thrived from his earliest days by tackling new challenges. In high school, he jumped into sports; at college, he took on social service projects. After graduation, Irick joined the military, qualified as an airborne Ranger, and found himself promoted up the officer ranks. Back in civilian life, he repeatedly asked for larger and stretch assignments. "I've never been fully qualified on paper for a job that I've had," he told me, yet he so readily embraced his duties that ever more responsibility came naturally his way. With a new MBA degree in hand, Irick brashly contacted GE's chief executive, Jeffrey R. Immelt, with a simple message: "I always wanted to run something." The personal appeal to the CEO worked. Today, as director of sales in General Electric's

Homeland Protection division, Jaime Irick plays a significant role in one of Immelt's growth businesses.[11]

Jaime Irick.

Madhabi Puri Buch did much the same at ICICI, one of India's premier banks, which she joined in 1997. With little experience in fairly specialized fields, she tackled a succession of responsibilities, ranging from Internet trading to mortgage financing. Finally, she asked chief executive K. V. Kamath to give her a crack at running the "boiler room" of the bank, the back office that handles the enormous volume of paper, telephone, and electronic data that surges through the bank every day. "In the past," she explained, "I had been given assignments where I had no experience. Yet they worked well!" Now she upped the stakes by taking on one of the bank's least glamorous but most critical operations. Her friends thought she had been "sidelined." Instead, Buch mastered the essence of still another banking function by taking responsibility for deciding how to remake it.[12]

Madhabi Puri Buch.

Problem: UNFAMILIAR RESPONSIBILITIES
Tool: APPRAISE THE PAST

In embracing new responsibilities, past decisions can serve as a natural curriculum for avoiding future mistakes.

Liu Chuanzhi was working at the Chinese Academy of Sciences in 1984 when his country commenced its momentous liberalization.

Inspired, Liu formed what would become Legend Group, at first distributing
a few foreign personal computers and
eventually morphing into China's largest
PC producer. In 2005, rechristened as
Lenovo, the company acquired IBM's
personal computer line, making it the
number three PC producer globally. As
a young man, Liu had wanted to become
a fighter pilot with the People's Liberation Army. Instead, he became one of
the world's most successful entrepreneurs.

Liu Chuanzhi.

When Liu left the state-sponsored research laboratory in 1984, he
knew nothing about how to build an enterprise, so he set about learning to do so by studying his own go points in minute detail. At the end
of every week, Liu and his top aides met to review major decisions of
the past five days. Many errors were committed, he told me, but the
weekly debrief helped "to ensure that we don't make [the same] mistakes in the future." Thanks to the reviews and lessons drawn from
them, Lenovo was able to weather China's economic gyrations while
others faltered. By routinely looking back on his decision processes,
Liu Chuanzhi constructed his own decision template for going
forward.[13]

The after-action review can be monthly, quarterly, yearly, or even
daily, depending on the decision-making tempo. In July 2004, I
watched a wildland fire crew in action against a raging blaze in
Yosemite National Park. Every afternoon without fail, the incident
commander, operations director, planning chief, and a dozen responsible firefighters gathered to review the present day's decisions and decide on the next day's actions. At the end of each of the fact-drenched,
disciplined reviews, one of the participants would pose four questions:
What had been planned for the day? What actually happened during

the day? Why did that happen? And what should be done next time? Round-robin style, each crew member addressed each of the topics. Only in that way could firefighters stay on top of a situation that changed constantly with the fire's ever-changing momentum. The principle: study the past, even if it is only yesterday, and heed its continuing lessons.[14]

Problem: INEXPERIENCED GUT
Tool: EDUCATE YOUR INSTINCTS

"Go with your gut." "Follow your intuition." "Trust your feelings." The sayings are commonplace, but do our instincts make good decisions? In fact, blind instinct cannot be trusted, but it can be educated. The main purpose of flight simulators, for example, is to allow pilots to experience unlikely surprises so many times that, should one actually occur, their response will be reflexive. "Train like you fly and fly like you train" is how they put it at NASA's astronaut training program at the Johnson Space Center in Houston. Consistent with that dictum, astronauts undergo an exhaustive curriculum that includes some five hundred simulated landings of the shuttle before flying it. No wonder so many of the space travelers are apt to say upon returning to Earth, "When something went wrong, I went into my training mode."[15]

Practice does not always make perfect, but it certainly helps. When he was named Episcopal bishop for the diocese of Pennsylvania in 1998, Charles E. Bennison drew on the three decades of experience since his ordination to tackle a succession of touchy issues. Despite widespread opposition from priests and laity, he pushed through plans to hire a full-time fund-raiser to shore up finances for the 162-parish diocese. Later, again knowing he would encounter protests, he suspended a church rector who opposed the ordination of women and gays. "Day by day I don't have too much doubt because I trust my intuitions," he said. "I may be making big mistakes, but I feel fairly confident on an incremental daily basis that I am in touch and that I am making the right decisions." That doesn't mean Bennison jumps to the go point. Far from it. "I'll stew and waver and listen and take in data and talk to all kinds of people before I feel comfortable with something," he said. But it does mean, that in getting to go, he consults a well-educated gut.

"If you get educated about something and then you live that, the line blurs between what your instincts used to be and what they are now," General Peter Pace explains. "Your mind touches on resources it's not even conscious of touching on." In the words of *Blink* author Malcolm Gladwell, that is the "power of thinking without thinking."[16]

Problem: ANALYSIS PARALYSIS
Tool: THE 70 PERCENT SOLUTION

Only professors and journalists get paid to say, "On the one hand . . ." When the rest of us continue to mine and massage the data in pursuit of perfect knowledge—and thus perfect certainty—we are edging toward that clinical condition of decidophobia, fear of facing a go point.

The Marine Corps battles this syndrome with the "70 percent solution." If you have 70 percent of the information, have done 70 percent of the analysis, and feel 70 percent confident, then move. The logic is simple: a less than ideal action, swiftly executed, stands a chance of success, whereas no action stands no chance. The worst decision is no decision at all.[17]

Analyze, but not overanalyze: that is the message Hewlett-Packard executive vice president Ann Livermore sends to HP's Technology Solutions Group, a $30-billion-plus business that encompasses enterprise storage and systems, software and services, and employs 95,000 IT professionals. She places a primacy on "fast enough"—decision making based on sufficient information, not perfect data. GE teaches the same at its retreats. By requiring ranking managers to vote up or down, individually and publicly, on a variety of proposed changes, GE avoids the endless analysis that compromises decision tempo.[18]

Drawing upon his own tumultuous experience as president of Pakistan since 1999, Pervez Musharraf says that while a leader must hear opposing views and engage people in the deliberations, he or she "must never suffer from paralysis." More-

Ann Livermore.

over, in reaching a decision, rarely are all the data available to be sure of its outcome. "Decisions are two-thirds facts and figures," Musharraf contends, and "one-third a leap in the dark where you don't have all the facts." If you increase the short side of the equation, you're too impulsive, but if you increase the other side, you're not a leader.[19]

Problem: MISTAKES HAPPEN
Tool: TOLERATE THEM—ONCE

Short of perfect information and analysis, mistakes are sure to happen. The secret, says Peter Pace, is: "Don't beat yourself up. If you're not making mistakes, I don't need you in my organization," which in his case includes some 2.4 million uniformed troops. "I want you doing 90 percent right in a big universe rather than 100 percent right in a small universe."[20]

Charles Elachi directs the Jet Propulsion Laboratory, NASA's contract agency for unmanned space missions, including the 2004 *Spirit* and *Opportunity* Mars landings that found evidence of water between layers of volcanic rock. Given the technical complexity of space flight, Elachi insists that every significant pre-mission decision at JPL receive intense peer appraisal and even outsider review. To ensure disciplined decision making during a mission, he also insists on resilience. "We operate under very heavy pressure," he says. "Many critical things are riding on our decisions. You have to have nerves of steel. Everyone involved in the project has to keep calm and composed so that we can think clearly about what is happening. Anyone who panics under pressure is just in the wrong business." To instill those steel-like nerves among his 5,500 employees, Elachi requires less experienced workers to witness JPL veterans making decisions.

Charles Elachi.

Predictably, though, some of JPL's decisions do go wrong. A mission to Mars in 1998 ended in such a high-profile, costly failure that the mission's top two managers were ready to resign. Elachi would not let them. "Normally, when a project fails, people look around for someone to blame," he says, "but if you hang the person who made the mistake, you've also lost a lot of experience." Instead, Elachi told the two managers, "We have spent $400 million training you. You have to learn from those mistakes, and I'm sure you will not repeat them." Six years later one of the managers was serving as a mission director and the other as a deputy manager for the highly successful *Spirit* and *Opportunity* trips to Mars.[21]

Problem: RUSH TO JUDGMENT
Tool: PRESERVE OPTIONALITY

Many decisions come with looming deadlines: the battle is lost, the market opportunity gone if you do not act in timely fashion. Even without a deadline it can still be tempting to get the hard business of choice making over with. The more one can tamp down the uncertainties and let the pieces fall in place before deciding, however, the more likely one will reach the right go point.

As U.S. treasury secretary from 1995 to 1999, Robert Rubin faced a string of momentous decisions ranging from the bailout of the Mexican peso to China's application to join the World Trade Organization. Time and again, Rubin elected to keep his "choices open for as long as possible," a proclivity that his then-deputy Lawrence Summers calls "preserving optionality."[22]

As CEO of Scottish Power, an energy producer with major operations in the United States and United Kingdom including extensive wind farms, Ian Russell makes investment decisions entailing hundreds of millions of dollars at a shot. One of his new power plants alone can guzzle $350 million; wind farms have consumed $3 billion. With so much riding on each go point, a rush to judgment on any one decision could result in a strategic error from which recovery would be extremely costly.

Not surprisingly, Russell takes his time in making such choices. "Let's be careful," he warns, and to that end he works to ensure that his team understands the decision options, appreciates their upsides and downsides, and knows what might go wrong with each so that the company does not look "foolish in a year's time." For decisions of such scope, Russell counsels waiting three, six, or even twelve months to diminish complexity and reduce uncertainty as much as possible before pulling the trigger.[23]

Problem: ANXIETY OVERLOAD
Tool: LOOK AT THE CLOCK

Low levels of anxiety are productive: they concentrate the mind. High levels can be counterproductive. A panicked mind stops processing new information, as JPL's Charles Elachi warned, reverting to tried-and-true responses and giving way to snap decisions that can make things worse.

What one needs is a circuit breaker to snap the anxiety loop.

Steering a faltering F/A-18 toward a carrier deck, some Navy pilots steady themselves by studying the clock. Other gauges may be spinning alarmingly, but the clock is not. Emergency-room physicians check their own pulse. Firefighters touch the shoulder of an anxious colleague. Zen breathing, sacred texts, private retreats—they all can help restore our own equanimity.

Problem: SUNK-COST SYNDROME
Tool: BURN THE BOAT

Seymour Cray built two things: sailboats and supercomputers. Each new Cray supercomputer—he produced his first in 1963—was its own masterpiece, crafted with the care and brilliance of a Stradivarius. One even had a decorative fountain in its coolant system. But in computing, Cray knew, there is no such thing as timeless perfection, only obsolescence. To drive the point home, legend goes, he would build a beautiful sailboat each spring, then burn it in the fall.[24]

It is always painful to destroy something we have built, be it a machine, an organization, an idea, or even a paragraph. Our investment is both psychic and economic, but it often can be a shackle. "My advice to young men," Henry Ford warned in the 1920s, "is to be ready to revise any system, scrap any methods, abandon any theory if the success of the job demands it." Ford did just that—until the systems and theories in question were his own. Presented with a prototype to succeed the Model T, one story goes, Ford literally took an axe to the effrontery.

In fact, by refusing to abandon his own psychic ties to the obsolescent Model T,

Seymour Cray.

Henry Ford was axing his own company's future. By the time he introduced the Model A in 1928, General Motors had stolen his lead. Seymour Cray, by contrast, annually sank his sunk costs.

Problem: Yes-Man Echoes
Tool: Voice Questions, Not Opinions

"I don't want any yes-men around me," movie mogul Samuel Goldwyn once declared. "I want them to tell me the truth, even if it costs them their jobs." We laugh because we recognize the moment. Organizations are not in the habit of rewarding people who speak uncomfortable truths. Yet they deservedly need to hear them.

"If you walk into a room as a senior person and innocently say, 'Here's what I'm thinking about this,' you've already skewed people's thinking," says General Peter Pace. His approach: "Start out with a question and don't voice an opinion." Why? Because people cannot line up behind you if they do not know where you stand. If you present subordinates with an intellectual challenge, they feel freer to offer their opinions without fear of giving offense. As for the old bromide of announcing at the start of a meeting that all the stars are off, that we are all equals here, forget about it, Pace says. People know the stars will be back on; they know at the end of the meeting who will still be in charge. Besides, Pace adds, "I like my stars."[25]

Problem: Warring Camps
Tool: Let the Battle Rage

In the early 1980s, Gillette had an internal war on its hands. After years of losing market share to Bic's throwaway razors, the venerable shaving giant had split into two camps: steel and plastic. One camp wanted to meet the price competition head-on by pushing Gillette's own plastic disposables. The other said to cede the low ground to Bic and invest millions in creating better metal razors. Many CEOs would have stepped in to quell the strife, but Colman Mockler could not afford to get to the wrong go point, so he let the divisions slug it out.

Political infighting can be destructive, but battles over substance, managed well, can be just the opposite. A furious volley of fact is met with a fierce counterattack of analysis, and the battlefield ends up littered with useful information. The self-interest on both sides tends to cancel out as long as the boss stays neutral. For nearly two years Mockler played a perfect Switzerland. Then one day he walked in and sided with the steel camp. Its argument—which would lead to "shaving systems" such as the spring-mounted Sensor, the Mach 3, and razors marketed like jet fighters—had carried the day.[26]

Problem: A Wily Adversary
Tool: Clone Your Opponent

In January 2004 football's New England Patriots found themselves about to face a uniquely dangerous opponent. Peyton Manning, quarterback of the Indianapolis Colts, could not be contained by conventional means. His arm was too accurate, his feet too quick, his style too different. So a week before their big game, Patriots coach Bill Belichick gave his backup quarterback, Damon Huard, a challenge: become Peyton Manning.

Huard did more than study a few game films; he threw himself into the role. "I read about him," he told a reporter. "I tried to duplicate his mannerisms as he got to the line, how he called his audibles, how he handles the ball, all the little things I could come up with." Huard's performance, teammates said, was Oscar-worthy, and the real Peyton Manning suffered for it. Given a week to scrimmage against Manning's doppelgänger and to adjust their tactics accordingly, the Patriots intercepted Manning four times to advance to the Super Bowl. After the game, Belichick singled out Huard, who had not set foot on

the field that day, as a key contribu-
tor to the win.[27]

Cloning translates easily to
other competitive situations. Since
nobody is better at spotting holes in
a plan than an opponent, assigning
a person or even a team to think like
your competitor can often expose
flaws that, identified early, are less
likely to be fatal. By making it their
job to stress-test a plan—much as
new products are dropped from
heights and set afire—in-house
clones can guard against excessive
optimism without damping the energy needed to carry out a strategy.
Nobody wants to be tagged a nay-
sayer, but imitation is more than
flattery. It can be a high kind of
heroism. It worked for Bill Belichick.

**New England Patriots backup
quarterback Damon Huard (left)
and starting quarterback Tom
Brady.**

Problem: **CONSTRICTED THINKING**
Tool: **WRITE POETRY**

Sometimes our thinking cannot escape the walls we get caught within.
To get out of the box, Bill Gates retreats alone twice a year for a week
in a remote cabin. With stacks of planning papers and no interrup-
tions, Gates ponders what Microsoft should be thinking but is not.[28]

John Barr—managing director and chairman of SG Barr Devlin,
a unit of the French banking giant Société Générale, and an investment
banker for more than two decades—has a different solution. When he is
not dispensing strategic and financial advice to Fortune 500 companies,

Barr writes poetry and even serves as president of the Poetry Foundation, following in the honored heritage of such businessmen-poets as publishing executive T. S. Eliot and insurance executives Wallace Stevens and Ted Kooser, the latter also the U.S. poet laureate.

"I think that a life of poetry—as a reader or a writer—gives one an appreciation of the fullness and complexity of things," Barr says. "The process of writing a poem is really one of synthesis and inclusion. . . . You basically find a group of words in a certain sequence that have the magic within them of capturing and containing a moment of external reality. There's a mystery to that, and there's also an inclusion that goes beyond anything that we might be able to simply put in a rational sentence.

"That sense of art expanding to the limits of the human experience makes for a better decision maker in the business world because it tends to offset the tendency to reduce every business question to a simple algorithm or a simple proposition that we can boil down and make a decision about." In serving investment clients, Barr concludes, "I've done a better job because I've appreciated that there's more in the room than just a voice on the telephone."[29]

Problem: REPEATED FAILURE
Tool: RESTRATEGIZE AND RESTAFF

Some plans and products were not meant to be. Some, like Henry Ford's Model T, were perfect for an earlier age but have outlived their time. If you find your enterprise pounding futilely against the door of success, it is probably time for new leadership and a new strategy for getting where you want to be.

Consider the moment in 1953 when Edmund Hillary and Tenzing Norgay first summitted Mount Everest, the world's loftiest peak. Everybody has heard the story of how they did it. Hillary and Tenzing confronted the mountain, braved its dangers, and made it to the top through sheer talent and determination. It is an inspiring tale, yet it obscures a deeper one, a less visible story about an unassuming manager and an anonymous committee without which the famous duo never would have made it to the top. Here is the story behind the story.[30]

Eric Shipton, not Edmund Hillary and Tenzing Norgay, had been picked by the Royal Geographical Society's Himalayan Committee to lead England's 1953 attempt on Everest. A romantic adventurer and the country's leading climber of the day, Shipton had been central to four of England's seven Everest expeditions and knew the mountain better than anyone. His latest expedition had discovered a new, more promising route to the top.

He seemed the natural choice, yet almost immediately committee members had second thoughts. Shipton's lightly equipped, improvisational climbs had shown entrepreneurial flair, but his

Eric Shipton.

inattention to detail and planning was notorious. On one trip, he even forgot his backpack. The committee worried that his style might not be up to the task.

Foreign competition also figured into the committee's buyer's remorse. Ever since the legendary British attempt on Mt. Everest in 1924 when George Mallory and Sandy Irvine mysteriously disappeared near the summit, the British had viewed the world's highest mountain as a national challenge. Yet just the year before, a Swiss team had come within several hundred vertical feet of Everest's 29,035-foot summit. Should the British fail this time out, both the Germans and the French would have a crack at reaching the summit first.

The Himalayan Committee did not want another romantic

failure, something gentlemen adventurers excelled at, so just six weeks after choosing Shipton, it turned around and fired him, replacing him with John Hunt, a career military man and a virtual unknown in mountaineering. Hunt, in turn, brought a new strategy to the old dream of conquering Everest.

A demon for logistics, Hunt applied the principles of modern industry to the Everest expedition, specifying for example that each box of rations contain exactly twenty-nine tins of sardines. His strategy—soon to become standard in expedition mountaineering—called for an army of climbers, Sherpas, porters, and yaks that would methodically move up the mountain, shuttling supplies to ever higher camps. Hunt gave the human element systematic attention as well. Everest demanded an "unusual degree of selflessness and patience," he later wrote. "Failure—moral or physical—by even one or two [people] would add immensely to its difficulties." The desire to reach the top, he added, "must be both individual and collective." That last point was important: The goal of his human engineering was to deliver just two climbers to the summit.[31]

Who would the two climbers be? Had Shipton been in charge, it seems likely he would have included himself. What daring adventurer would leave the final ascent to underlings? In Hunt's hands, though, no fewer than ten climbers—including a thirty-three-year-old New Zealand beekeeper's son named Ed Hillary—were in the running. The final choice, Hunt declared, would hinge on impersonal factors: who was climbing well, and who was in high camp when the weather broke. The others would go into support.

On May 26, 1953, Tom Bourdillon and Charles Evans were selected for immortality and came within 300 vertical feet of it, thwarted finally by waning stamina, oxygen, and daylight. Yet in retreat Bourdillon and Evans laid an invaluable platform, stashing oxygen canisters and returning from their failed assault with a trove of useful intelligence. True to his methodical approach, John Hunt himself had ferried supplies to within 2,000 vertical feet of the summit and had a second team ready to go.

Tenzing Norgay and Ed Hillary moved out swiftly on the morning of May 28, reaching Hunt's supply cache, which made a miserable night at least survivable. At 4 a.m. they arose, five miles in the sky. The frozen air had turned Hillary's boots to steel, but a stove was on hand to thaw them, as was a breakfast for nourishment: crackers, lemonade, and, most satisfying of all, the final tin of Hunt's sardines. Restored, the two set out to bring thirty years of frustration to an end. Seven hours later, at 11:30 a.m. on May 29, Hillary snapped the famous photo that marked their victory: Norgay, ice axe raised aloft, left foot planted atop the highest point on the planet.

Their extraordinary feat of mountaineering rightly made them instant legends. Tenzing Norgay became a national hero in India and Nepal, both of which laid claim to him. Edmund Hillary was knighted by

Tenzing Norgay on summit of Mt. Everest.

Summit ridge of Mt. Everest with Edmund Hillary's and Tenzing Norgay's footsteps visible in the snow.

the queen and had his image added to New Zealand's five-dollar bill. For his part, John Hunt would enter the House of Lords. Still, to say that Hillary and Tenzing "conquered" Everest is a bit like saying that Neil Armstrong and Buzz Aldrin conquered the moon. Like those *Apollo 11* astronauts, the two mountain-

Edmund Hillary, John Hunt, and Tenzing Norgay looking at Mt. Everest after its summiting.

eers stood atop a pyramid of people and supplies, in this case erected by John Hunt. But the unsung hero of mountaineering's most celebrated moment was not even in Nepal.

By redefining the expedition as a methodical effort—and having the backbone to take the criticism that followed Shipton's dismissal— the Himalayan Committee built the ultimate platform for success. Talent and determination, it proved, will get you a long way up the mountain, but crackers and sardines take you to the summit. The mountain was too big for the most gifted climber of the day, so the committee fired him, changed the game, and attained the top. Their go point in a London meeting room placed two climbers on Everest's summit for the first time ever.

THE DECISION TEMPLATE FOR PREVENTING UNFORCED ERRORS

In previous matrices, I have concentrated on principles and tools to help you get to the right go point. In this final one, I focus in on the tools for when you are facing some of the most commonly encountered problems in reaching a decision.

Problem	Tool	Illustration
1. Decision authority is not bestowed.	Pursue responsibility for decision making.	Jaime Irick and Madhabi Puri Buch repeatedly sought more responsibility than was otherwise given to them.
2. Unfamiliar responsibilities.	Appraise the past.	Liu Chuanzhi built a leading global computer maker by recurrently reviewing the past week's major decisions.
3. Inexperienced gut.	Educate your instincts.	Flight simulators help NASA astronauts train their intuition so they can decide instinctively.
4. Analysis paralysis.	The 70 percent solution.	The Marine Corps trains officers to make decisions when they are 70 percent confident of the outcome.
5. Mistakes happen.	Tolerate them—once.	Jet Propulsion Lab director Charles Elachi insists that space-mission decisions be well taken but treats onetime errors as a learning laboratory.
6. Rush to judgment.	Preserve optionality.	U.S. treasury secretary Robert Rubin and Scottish Power CEO Ian Russell both delayed major decisions as long as possible to reduce complexity and uncertainty.
7. Anxiety overload.	Look at the clock.	When other dials are whirling on their instrument panels, Navy pilots control themselves by studying the steady hands of the clock.

Problem	Tool	Illustration
8. Sunk-cost syndrome.	Burn the boat.	Supercomputer innovator Seymour Cray annually built and burned a sailboat, a reminder to routinely abandon last year's model.
9. Yes-man echoes.	Voice questions, not opinions.	General Peter Pace queries his subordinates before tipping his own hand.
10. Warring camps.	Let the battle rage.	Gillette CEO Colman Mockler pitted "steel" and "plastic" camps against each other to see which had the best strategy.
11. Wily adversary.	Clone your opponent.	New England Patriots coach Bill Belichick assigned a backup quarterback to mimic the Colts' Peyton Manning.
12. Constricted thinking.	Write poetry.	Investment banker John Barr uses a "sense of art" to make better decisions in business.
13. Repeated failure.	Restrategize and restaff.	The Royal Geographic Society's Himalayan Committee changed plans and replaced leadership for its triumphant 1953 assault on Mt. Everest.

Lifelong Learning for the Go Points Ahead

Consequential decisions require comprehensive attention if the right go point is to be reached at the right moment. To discover the principles and tools that most usefully govern decision making, I have drawn upon the interviews, observations, and studies of a wide array of contemporary and historical decision makers in fields ranging from business and politics to the military, medicine, education, religion, even firefighting and mountain climbing. Fifty distinct principles and tools have emerged from their varied experiences.

In practice, of course, fifty principles or fifty tools or fifty anything is more than most decision makers can keep actively in mind when getting to their own go points. My advice is to identify the five or ten that are most salient for the decisions that you most frequently face and then concentrate on just those. If your position entails rapid decision making—with a touch of the urgency found on the trading floor at Lehman Brothers, say, or the fire zone on Storm King Mountain—you will find cautions against rushing to judgments of scant value. Those with the luxury or necessity of pondering their decisions—with parallels to the big investment decisions at Boeing and Scottish Power—will have less reason to draw upon intuition or omen in reaching their go points. It is good not to be too parochial, though: next year's decisions may be very different from this year's, and a passing familiarity with all the principles and tools gathered here should help make for stronger decision making across a range of venues in the future.

Since this book is intended to facilitate our collective understanding of the art and science of decision making with consequences, I and other readers would value knowing which principles and tools seem most useful to you. By posting your top five to ten choices on our book Web site along with a brief description of the decision world you inhabit, that will help guide all of us. I also encourage you, while visiting the site, to add additional principles, tools, and illustrations. In that way, the ideas developed here will evolve into a collective product built around the living experience of its readers. Our go point templates should be viewed as an open-source initiative, a collectively generated product.

Finally, three suggestions for turning these principles and tools into lifelong initiatives: First, continue to read about responsible decision making and decision makers. To that end, I have included a further reading list below. Second, identify the decision makers you admire—people who are making a difference in your workplace, community, and beyond—and then witness and learn from how they arrive at their go points. Finally, do the same with your own decisions. That requires getting into the game, testing the templates with tangible decisions, and revising and building them around the principles and tools that work best for you. All that should give you an enduring foundation for reaching the many go points that lie ahead.

Further Reading on Decision Making and Responsibility

Graham T. Allison and Philip Zelikow, *Essence of Decision: Explaining the Cuban Missile Crisis,* second edition, Longman, 1999.

Max Bazerman, *Judgment in Managerial Decision Making,* sixth edition, Wiley, 2005.

Arlene Blum, *Breaking Trail: A Climbing Life,* Scribner, 2005.

Fortune magazine, special issue on decision making, June 27, 2005.

David H. Freedman, *Corps Business: The 30 Management Principles of the U.S. Marines,* HarperBusiness, 2000.

Malcolm Gladwell, *Blink: The Power of Thinking Without Thinking,* Little, Brown, 2005.

John Hammond, Ralph L. Keeney, and Howard Raiffa, *Smart Choices: A Practical Guide to Making Better Decisions,* Broadway Books, 1999.

Kenneth R. Hammond, *Judgment Under Stress,* Oxford University Press, 2000.

Harvard Business Review, special issue on decision making, January 2006.

Reid Hastie and Robyn M. Dawes, *Rational Choice in an Uncertain World: The Psychology of Judgment and Decision Making,* Sage Publications, 2001.

Gary Klein, *Sources of Power: How People Make Decisions,* MIT Press, 1998.

Gary Klein, *Intuition at Work: Why Developing Your Gut Instincts Will Make You Better at What You Do,* Currency Doubleday, 2003.

Jon Krakauer, *Into Thin Air: A Personal Account of the Mt. Everest Disaster,* Villard/Random House, 1997.

J. Keith Murnighan and John C. Mowen, *The Art of High-Stakes Decision-Making: Tough Calls in a Speed-Driven World,* Wiley, 2002.

Michael A. Roberto, *Why Great Leaders Don't Take Yes for an Answer: Managing for Conflict and Consensus,* Pearson Publishing/Wharton School Publishing, 2005.

Robert E. Rubin with Jacob Weisberg, *In an Uncertain World: Tough Choices from Wall Street to Washington,* Random House, 2003.

J. Edward Russo and Paul J. H. Schoemaker, *Decision Traps: Ten Barriers to Brilliant Decision-Making and How to Overcome Them,* Simon & Schuster, 1990.

J. Edward Russo and Paul J. H. Schoemaker, *Winning Decisions: Getting It Right the First Time,* Currency Doubleday, 2002.

Stephen W. Sears, *Gettysburg,* Houghton Mifflin, 2003.

J. Frank Yates, *Decision Management: How to Assure Better Decisions in Your Company,* Jossey-Bass, 2003.

Bob Woodward, *Plan of Attack,* Simon & Schuster, 2004.

NOTES

Preface

1. Useem and Zelleke 2006.

Introduction

1. Parts of this section are adapted from Useem and Useem 2005.
2. Presidential Commission on the Space Shuttle *Challenger* Accident 1986; Vaughan 1996.
3. Marx 1852; Frost 1920.
4. Roth 2004; Harris 1993; Turtledove 1993; Cowley 1999, 2002, 2003; Crossen 2005; http://www.uchronia.net/intro.html.
5. Interviews and other data sources for this book are described in the preface.
6. EBS 2004; Scully interview 2005. Individual titles and dates for interviews are reported in the preface.
7. Weisman 2004.
8. Russo and Schoemaker 1990, 2002; Kahneman 2003; Hammond, Keeney, and Raiffa 1999.
9. Freedman 2000.
10. Sears 2003.
11. See preface; Useem, Davidson, and Wittenberg 2005; http://leadership .wharton.upenn.edu/l_change/trips/index.shtml.
12. Boatner interview 2005.

13. Pfeffer and Sutton 2000, ix–x.
14. Stein 2000.
15. Swartz and Watkins 2003; McLean and Elkind 2003; Useem 2003 *(Journal of Management and Governance)*.
16. Van Maanen 1995, 135.

Chapter 1. In the Heat of the Moment

1. Maclean 1990; Useem 1998, chapter 2. The chapter is adapted from Useem 2005 *(Fortune)* and Useem, Cook, and Sutton 2005.
2. Maclean 1999; South Canyon Fire Accident Investigation Team 1994; Butler et al 1998.
3. Incident Command System 1994, 3–4; National Wildfire Coordinating Group 2004; Maclean 2003; Pyne 1997.
4. Incident Operations Standards Working Team 2002, iv.
5. Incident Operations Standards Working Team 2002.
6. Ruggero 2001.
7. Simon and Houghton 2003; Metcalfe 1998.
8. Janis and Mann 1977; Finucane et al. 2000; Gilbert 2002.
9. Fiedler 1992; Weick and Roberts 1993; Edmondson et al. 2003; Salka 2004, 122.
10. Klein 2003.
11. Putnam 1995, 11.
12. *Columbia* Accident Investigation Board 2003.
13. In addition to an official investigation on the fire (South Canyon Fire Accident Investigation Team 1994; Butler et al. 1998), I have drawn upon direct personal inspection of the South Canyon fire zone on Storm King Mountain on May 29, 2002. I conducted the visit as a walking seminar in the company of seventeen wildland firefighters (including one of the survivors, Sarah Doehring). The walking seminar provided extended opportunities to discuss the decisions with experienced firefighters who themselves had taken thousands of decisions while leading fire teams of their own. I returned to the zone for a day with a CNN film crew on August 11, 2005, and I had previously walked the zone with one professional firefighter in 2000. For additional perspective on leadership decisions in wildland fires, I have also drawn upon secondary analysis of the Mann Gulch and South Canyon fires conducted by Maclean (1990), Maclean (1999), Putnam (1995), Weick (1993, 1996) and others. In addition, I walked the scene of the Mann Gulch fire in the company of nine professional firefighters and others on July 19, 2001, and there too we devoted more than a day of continuous dialogue to analyzing and un-

derstanding how the incident commander reached his decisions. Further information on these on-site seminars can be found at the Web site accompanying this book, http://leadership.wharton.upenn.edu/TheGoPoint.

14. Junger 2002, p. 43.
15. Cook 2002; Sutton 2002; and Wildland Fire Leadership Development Program 2004; Gladwell 2005, pp. 14–15.
16. Wildland Fire Leadership Development Values and Principles 2004.
17. Wildland Fire Leadership Development Training Courses 2004.
18. For example, see U.S. Military Academy 2004: U.S. Marine Corps University 2004.
19. Wildland Fire Leadership Development Staff Ride Library 2004.
20. Meyer 2003; Quintanar 2003.
21. Redding Interagency Hotshot Crewmember Report 2003.
22. Redding Interagency Hotshot Crewmember Report 2003; Bazerman 2002, p. 7.

Chapter 2. Getting into the Decision Game

1. Fitzgerald 1936.
2. Roper Center for Public Opinion Research 2000; Welch 2005, p. 40.
3. Interview of Hemingway by Dorothy Parker, *New Yorker,* 30 November 1929.
4. Sears 1992; Freeman 1998.
5. Freeman 1998, p. 144.
6. Unruh, interview and observe 1995, Wharton School, University of Pennsylvania.
7. Rieder, interview and observe, March 1, 2004, Lehman Brothers.
8. Thomson, interview 2004–05; Pace, observe, December 9, 2003, Wharton School, University of Pennsylvania.
9. Kamler 2004, 13.
10. Ferreras 2004.
11. Kamler 2004, 235; Weathers 2000.
12. This account draws primarily on the author's observing and interviewing of Roberto Canessa on February 10 and 11, 2005, Wharton School, University of Pennsylvania; it also draws upon Read 1974 and information available at http://www.viven.com.uy/571/eng. Quoted commentary by Canessa not otherwise cited is from the author's observing and interviewing of him.
13. Read 1974, 78.
14. Read 1974, 81.
15. Kahneman 2003; Hammond 2000; Klein 1998, 2003; Kahneman, Slovic, and

Tversky 1982; Russo and Schoemaker 1990, xviii; Russo and Schoemaker 2002.

16. Bazerman 2002, 152; Hincks 2005; www.phobialist.com.
17. Dar, Ariely, and Frenk 1995.
18. Lester interview 2005; Reilly et al. 2002; one of the paper's co-authors, Arthur T. Evans, quoted in Gladwell 2005, 139.
19. Robbins 2003, 84–87.
20. Karnazes 2005, 240–41.
21. Christensen interview 2005; the World Economic Forum's 2005 annual meeting is described at http://www.weforum.org/site/homepublic.nsf/Content/Annual+Meeting+2006%5CAnnual+Meeting+2005.
22. Useem 1993.
23. Bianco and Moore 2001.
24. Useem 2001.
25. Thamel 2005, D3.

Chapter 3. Using the Net

1. Collins 2001.
2. Grangaard interview 2004.
3. Tam 2005 ("Boss Talk") 2005 ("Rewiring Hewlett-Packard"); Hymowitz 2005; Rivlin 2005; Tam and Lublin 2005; Tam, Lublin, and Hymowitz 2005.
4. Finkelstein and Hambrick 1996; Useem 1996.
5. Eisenhardt 1990.
6. Cisco 2004; O'Reilly and Pfeffer 2000.
7. Chambers interview 2003.
8. Dalai Lama 1991, 122.
9. Dalai Lama and Cutler 1998.
10. Granovetter 1973.
11. Janis 1971; U.S. Senate Select Intelligence Committee 2004, 18.
12. Janis 1971.
13. Mizruchi and Stearns 2001.
14. Pace 2005.
15. Zhang interview 2005.
16. Blum 2005, 221.
17. Blum 2005, 229–30.
18. Manly and Kirkpatrick 2005; Manly 2005.
19. Hawkins 2005.
20. http://www.hbosplc.com/abouthbos/board_matters.asp.
21. Useem and Zelleke 2006.
22. Gillie 2003, E1; Platt interview 2005.

Chapter 4. Seeing Ahead

1. U.S. Navy 2001.
2. See, for instance, Mintzberg 1994.
3. Amazon.com; Questia.com.
4. What follows draws upon a range of published sources including Boritt 1999; Coddington 1968; Freeman 1994, 1998; Gallagher 1992, 1993, 1994; McPherson 1988, 1997, 2003; Sears 1992, 1999; Trudeau 2002; Tucker 1982, 1983; and especially Sears 2003. It also draws upon the author's more than fifty daylong visits to the Gettysburg battlefield with MBA students, executive MBA students, and management groups from 1995 to 2005. The visits included groups of twenty-five to fifty managers with Astra-Zeneca, Chubb, First USA, General Mills, InBev, Merrill Lynch, and other companies, and managers from a diverse array of companies and organizations who participated in open enrollment programs of Wharton Executive Education (http://executiveeducation.wharton.upenn.edu). Most of the visits were accompanied by U.S. National Park Service licensed battlefield guide William Bowling, and several by licensed guides Charles Fennell and Hans Henzel. The author also accompanied a daylong visit to the battlefield on April 27, 2003, arranged and conducted for Princeton University by Civil War author James M. McPherson, then professor of history at Princeton University.
5. Quoted in Sears 2003, 6.
6. Quoted in Sears 2003, 15.
7. Quoted in Sears 2003, 7.
8. Quoted in Freeman 1934, 19.
9. Quoted in Sears 1999, 161.
10. Lincoln 1863.
11. Quoted in Sears 2003, 20, 21, 23–24.
12. Quoted in Sears 2003, 121.
13. Quoted in Sears 2003, 123.
14. Quoted in Freeman 1998, 571.
15. Freeman 1998, 596.
16. Quoted in Freeman 1998, 605.
17. Quoted in Sears 2003, 344.
18. Quoted in Sears 2003, 345.
19. Quoted in McPherson 1988, 661.
20. Quoted in Freeman 1998, 588.
21. Quoted in Coddington 1968, 500; Sears 2003, 415.
22. Quoted in Tucker 1982, 111.

23. Sears 2003, xiv.
24. Boritt 1997, 122.

Chapter 5. Making Decisions

1. For the impact of action-learning projects, see Hirst et al. 2004 and Dotlich and Noel 1998.
2. Freedman 2000; Santamaria, Martino, and Clemons 2004; Useem, Davidson, and Wittenberg 2005.
3. The management development seminar Senior Executive Program is sponsored annually by Sasin Graduate Institute of Business Administration of Thailand's Chulalongkorn University in collaboration with the Wharton School, University of Pennsylvania, and Kellogg School, Northwestern University (http://www.sasin.edu/execed/sep).
4. The health care program was sponsored by the Leonard Davis Institute of Health Economics and the Wharton School of the University of Pennsylvania (http://www.upenn.edu/ldi/execed.html).
5. Russo and Schoemaker 2002, 75–85.
6. Carter Racing is authored by Brittain and Sitkin 1999 (updated in 2006).
7. Sony 1997, 1998, 1999, 4; Yermack 1996; Conyon and Peck 1998.
8. Presidential Commission on the Space Shuttle *Challenger* Accident 1986.
9. Jordan 1996, 2003; Jordan, Davidson, and Useem 2004; Purcell interview 2005; Jordan interviews 1997–2005; Boitano interviews 1997–2005.
10. The book Web site is at http://leadership.wharton.upenn.edu/TheGoPoint.
11. Whitestone 1983; Gittel 2003.

Chapter 6. Transcending Personal Profit

1. State of New York 2002.
2. Armstrong 2000.
3. Pillmore 2003.
4. *Business Week* 2001.
5. State of New York 2002; Lin 2002.
6. U.S. Securities and Exchange Commission 2002.
7. Dallek 2004, 10–11; Gardner 2003, 147–63.
8. Tocqueville 1835.
9. Bazerman 2002; Russo and Schoemaker 2002; Klein 1998; Hammond 2000; Soros 1997, 2000.
10. Friedman 1970.
11. Useem 1996, 2004 ("Corporate Governance").
12. Hewitt Associates, personal communication.
13. Jensen 1989; Jensen and Murphy 1990.

14. Soros 1997.

15. Brady 2005; Pace December 6, 2005; Useem 2001.

16. Swartz and Watkins 2003; McLean and Elkind 2003; Watkins interview and observation 2002–4, Wharton School, University of Pennsylvania.

17. Kwasjniewski 2005, 86.

18. Winik 2001; Trulock 1992; Marvel 2002; Chamberlain 1994; Freeman 1998.

19. Thomson interview 2004; Cooper interview 2004; Bernard interview 2004; Jones interview 2004; Pottruck observation, October 1 and November 3, 2005, Wharton School, University of Pennsylvania; Brennan interview and observation 2004, July 28, 2005, U.S. Naval Academy; Lao-tzu 1986.

20. Collins 2001.

21. King 1990; Garrow 1986.

22. Clinton observation, January 28, 2006, World Economic Forum, Davos, Switzerland.

Chapter 7. Unforced Errors

1. Breen interview and observation, September 29, 2005, Wharton School, University of Pennsylvania.

2. Crisson interview 2004.

3. Gerstner 2002; Gerstner observation, February 12, 2003, Wharton School, University of Pennsylvania; Purdum 2004; Druskin interview 2004.

4. Kaiser interview 2004; Lykketoft interview 2004.

5. Dallek 2004, 7.

6. Frost 1983.

7. J. Useem et al. 2005.

8. Colvin 2000; Useem 2003.

9. Last 2006.

10. Parts of the following section are drawn from Useem and Useem 2005.

11. Irick interview 2005.

12. Buch interview 2006.

13. Liu interview 2004.

14. W. Cook, King, Kurtz, Means, Rust, Wuchner, interview and observation, July 23–26, 2004, Yosemite National Park, California; observation of the fire team for the Meadow fire in Yosemite National Park, July 23–26, 2004.

15. Dillon, Petrie interview and observation 2003, 2004, Houston, Texas.

16. Pace interview by J. Useem 2005; Gladwell 2005.

17. Freedman 2000.

18. Livermore observation, February 2, 2005, Wharton School, University of Pennsylvania; Ulrich, Kerr, and Ashkenas 2002.

19. Musharraf observation, January 26, 2006, World Economic Forum, Davos, Switzerland.

20. Pace observation, December 6, 2005, Wharton School, University of Pennsylvania.

21. Elachi interview and observation, February 3 and March 23, 2004, Wharton School, University of Pennsylvania.

22. Rubin 2003, 186.

23. Russell interview 2004.

24. Aquilar 1994; Aquilar and Brainard 1986.

25. Pace interview by J. Useem 2005.

26. McKibben 1997.

27. Boling 2004.

28. Guth 2005.

29. Barr interview and observation, January 26 and February 2, 2005, Wharton School, University of Pennsylvania.

30. This section is drawn from Useem and Useem 2003; Hunt 1954; Shipton 1969; Venables 2003.

31. Hunt 1954.

REFERENCES

Abshire, David M. *The Character of George Marshall* (pamphlet). Lexington, Va.: Washington and Lee University, 2005.

Allison, Graham T., and Philip Zelikow. *Essence of Decision: Explaining the Cuban Missile Crisis.* Second edition. New York: Longman, 1999.

Anker, Conrad, and David Roberts. *The Lost Explorer: Finding Mallory on Mount Everest.* New York: Simon & Schuster, 1999.

Armstrong, Lance, with Sally Jenkins. *It's Not About the Bike: My Journey Back to Life.* New York: Penguin Putnam, 2000.

Aquilar, Francis. "Cray Research, Inc.: Preparing for the 1990s." Case 9-390-066. Boston: Harvard Business School Publishing, 1994.

Aquilar, Francis, and Caroline E. Brainard. "Cray Research, Inc." Case 3-985-011. Boston: Harvard Business School Publishing, 1986.

Baum, J. Robert, and Stefan Wally. "Strategic Decision Speed and Firm Performance." *Strategic Management Journal* 24, 11 (2003): 1107–29.

Bazerman, Max. *Judgment in Managerial Decision Making.* Sixth edition. New York: Wiley, 2002.

Bennis, Warren G., and James O'Toole. "How Business Schools Lost Their Way." *Harvard Business Review* 83, 5 (2005): 96–104.

Berman, Dennis K., Henny Sender, and Michael J. McCarthy. "China's Haier Is Said to Drop Offer for Maytag." *Wall Street Journal,* July 20, 2005.

Bianco, Anthony, and Pamela L. Moore. "Xerox: The Downfall, the Inside Story of the Management Fiasco at Xerox." *Business Week,* March 5, 2001.

Blum, Arlene. *Breaking Trail: A Climbing Life.* New York: Scribner/Lisa Drew Books, 2005.

Boling, Dave. "Patriots' Huard Has Backup Plan: QB's Preparation Pays Off Big for New England." *News Tribune* (Tacoma, Washington), January 29, 2004.

Boritt, Gabor S., ed. *The Gettysburg Nobody Knows.* New York: Oxford University Press, 1997.

Brady, James. "In Step with . . . Gen. Peter Pace." *Parade,* October 2, 2005.

Brittain, Jack W., and Sim B. Sitkin. "Carter Racing." In *Ethical and Environmental Challenges to Engineering,* edited by Michael E. Gorman, Matthew M. Mehalik, and Patricia Werhane. Upper Saddle River, N.J.: Prentice Hall, 1999.

Business Week. "The Top 25 Managers: Dennis Kozlowski, Tyco International." January 8, 2001.

Butler, Bret W., Roberta A. Bartlette, Larry S. Bradshaw, Jack D. Cohen, Patricia L. Andrews, Ted Putnam, and Richard J. Mangan. *Fire Behavior Associated with the 1994 South Canyon Fire on Storm King Mountain.* U.S. Forest Service, 1998. Available at http://www.fs.fed.us/rm/pubs/rmrs_rp009.html.

Carville, James. "Karl Rove: A Brilliant (Ouch!) Political Strategist." *Time,* April 18, 2005.

Chamberlain, Joshua Lawrence. *Bayonet! Forward: My Civil War Reminiscences.* Gettysburg, Pa.: Stan Clark Military Books, 1994.

Cisco Systems. "Cisco Systems to Acquire Growth Networks Inc.: Delivers Terabit Performance for Next-Generation Networks." Press release, February 16, 2004. Available at http://newsroom.cisco.com/dlls/fspnisapi3cd4.html.

Coddington, Edwin B. *The Gettysburg Campaign: A Study in Command.* New York: Scribner's 1968. Reissued by Touchstone, 1997.

Collins, Jim. *Good to Great: Why Some Companies Make the Leap . . . and Others Don't.* New York: HarperBusiness, 2001.

Columbia Accident Investigation Board. *Report.* Washington, D.C.: National Aeronautics and Space Administration and Government Printing Office, 2003.

Colvin, Geoffrey. "America's Most Admired Companies." *Fortune,* February 21, 2000, 108–14.

Conyon, Martin J., and Simon I. Peck. "Board Size and Corporate Performance: Evidence from European Companies." *European Journal of Finance* 4 (1998): 291–304.

Cook, Jim. "Leadership Toolbox: From Wildland Firefighters." *Wharton Leadership Digest,* October 2002. Available at http://leadership.wharton.upenn.edu/digest/10-02.shtml.

Cowell, Alan. "English Church Advances Bid for Women as Bishops." *New York Times,* July 12, 2005.

Cowley, Robert, ed. *What If? The World's Foremost Military Historians Imagine What Might Have Been.* New York: Putnam, 1999.

———. *What If? 2: Eminent Historians Imagine What Might Have Been.* New York: Berkley Trade, 2002.

———. *What Ifs? of American History: Eminent Historians Imagine What Might Have Been.* New York: G. P. Putnam's Sons, 2003.

Crossen, Cynthia. " 'What Ifs' Don't Thrill Historians, but They Raise Intriguing Issues." *Wall Street Journal,* February 2, 2005.

Dalai Lama. *Freedom in Exile: The Autobiography of the Dalai Lama.* New York: HarperCollins, 1991.

Dalai Lama and Howard C. Cutler. *The Art of Happiness: A Handbook for Living.* New York: Penguin Putnam, 1998.

Dallek, Robert. *Lessons from the Lives and Times of Presidents* (pamphlet). Richmond, Va.: Jepson School of Leadership Studies. 2004.

Dar, Reuven, Dan Ariely, and Hanan Frenk. "The Effect of Past-Injury on Pain Threshold and Tolerance." *Pain* 60, 2 (1995): 189–93.

Dotlich, David L., and James L. Noel. *Action Learning: How the World's Top Companies Are Recreating Their Leaders and Themselves.* San Francisco: Jossey-Bass, 1998.

EBS. *Annual Report.* London: EBS, 2004. Available at http://www.ebs.com.

Edmondson, Amy C., Michael A. Roberto, and Michael D. Watkins. "A Dynamic Model of Top Management Team Effectiveness: Managing Unstructured Task Streams." *Leadership Quarterly* 14, 3 (2003): 297–325.

Eisenhardt, Kathleen M. "Speed and Strategic Choice: How Managers Accelerate Decision Making." *California Management Review* 32, 3 (1990): 39–54.

Ferreras, Pipin. *The Dive: A Story of Love and Obsession.* New York: Regan Books, 2004.

Fiedler, Fred E. "Time-Based Measures of Leadership Experience and Organizational Performance: A Review of Research and a Preliminary Model." *Leadership Quarterly* 3, 1 (1992): 5–23.

———. *Leadership Experience and Leadership Performance.* Arlington, Va.: United States Army Research Institute for the Behavioral and Social Sciences, 1994.

Finkelstein, Sydney, and Donald C. Hambrick. *Strategic Leadership: Top Executives and Their Effects on Organizations.* Minneapolis: West Publishers, 1996.

Finucane, Melissa, Ali Siddiq Alhakami, Paul Slovic, and S. M. Johnson. "The Affect Heuristic in Judgments of Risks and Benefits." *Journal of Behavioral Decision Making* 13, 1 (2000): 1–17.

Fitzgerald, F. Scott. *The Crack-Up.* New York: New Directions, 1993. Originally published in 1936.

Forbes, Daniel P. "Managerial Determinants of Decision Speed in New Ventures." *Strategic Management Journal* 26, 4 (2005): 355–66.

Fortune. Special issue on decision making. June 27, 2005.

Freedman, David H. *Corps Business: The 30 Management Principles of the U.S. Marines.* New York: HarperBusiness, 2000

Freeman, Douglas Southall. *R. E. Lee: A Biography.* New York: Scribner's, 1934.

———. *Lee's Lieutenants: A Study in Command.* Abridged in one volume by Stephen W. Sears. New York: Scribner, 1998.

———, ed. *Lee's Dispatches: Unpublished Letters of General Robert E. Lee to Jefferson Davis and the War Department of the Confederate States of America.* Baton Rouge: Louisiana State University Press, 1994.

Friedman, Milton. "The Social Responsibility of Business Is to Increase its Profits." *New York Times Magazine,* September 13, 1970.

Frost, David, and Michael Deakin. *David Frost's Book of the World's Worst Decisions.* New York: Crown, 1983.

Frost, Robert. "The Road Not Taken." *Mountain Interval.* New York: Henry Holt and Company, 1920.

Gallagher, Gary W., ed. *The First Day at Gettysburg: Essays on Confederate and Union Leadership.* Kent, Ohio: Kent State University Press, 1992.

———. *The Second Day at Gettysburg: Essays on Confederate and Union Leadership.* Kent, Ohio: Kent State University Press, 1993.

———. *The Third Day at Gettysburg & Beyond.* Chapel Hill, N.C.: University of North Carolina Press, 1994.

Gardner, Howard, with Emma Laskin. *Leading Minds: An Anatomy of Leadership.* New York: Basic Books, 2003.

Garrow, David J. *Bearing the Cross: Martin Luther King, Jr., and the Southern Christian Leadership Conference.* New York: William Morrow, 1986.

Gerstner, Louis V., Jr. *Who Says Elephants Can't Dance? Inside IBM's Historic Turnaround.* New York: HarperCollins, 2002.

Gilbert, D. T. "Inferential Correction." In *Heuristics and Biases: The Psychology of Intuitive Judgment,* edited by Thomas Gilovich, Dale Griffin, and Daniel Kahneman. New York: Cambridge University Press, 2002.

Gillie, John. "Boeing's Balancing Act: For the 7E7 to Make It, the Aerospace Giant Must Find the Right Mix of Features and Value." *News Tribune,* April 27, 2003.

Gittell, Jody Hoffer. *The Southwest Airlines Way: Using the Power of Relationships to Achieve High Performance.* New York: McGraw-Hill, 2003.

Gladwell, Malcolm. *Blink: The Power of Thinking Without Thinking.* New York: Little, Brown, 2005.

Granovetter, Mark S. "The Strength of Weak Ties." *American Journal of Sociology* 78 (1973): 1360–80.

Guth, Robert A. "Think Pad: In Secret Hideaway, Bill Gates Ponders Microsoft's Future." *Wall Street Journal,* March 28, 2005.

Hammond, John S., Ralph L. Keeney, and Howard Raiffa. *Smart Choices: A Practical Guide to Making Better Decisions.* New York: Broadway Books, 1999.

Hammond, Kenneth R. *Judgment Under Stress.* New York: Oxford University Press, 2000.

Harris, Robert. *Fatherland.* New York: HarperTorch, 1993.

Hastie, Reid, and Robyn M. Dawes. *Rational Choice in an Uncertain World: The Psychology of Judgment and Decision Making.* Thousand Oaks, Calif.: Sage Publications, 2001.

Hawkins, Lee, Jr. "GM's Wagoner Takes Control of Ailing North American Unit." *Wall Street Journal,* April 5, 2005.

Heller, Frank Alexander, ed. *Decision-Making and Leadership.* New York: Cambridge University Press, 1992.

Heppenheimer, T. A. *Turbulent Skies: The History of Commercial Aviation.* New York: Wiley, 1995.

Hincks, Rob. "Positively Phobic." *Scanorama,* May 2005, 86–90.

Hirst, Giles, Leon Mann, Paul Bain, Andrew Pirola-Merlo, and Andreas Richver. "Learning to Lead: The Development and Testing of a Model of Leadership Learning." *The Leadership Quarterly* 15, 3 (2004): 311–27.

Hunt, John. *The Conquest of Everest.* New York: E. P. Dutton, 1954.

Hymowitz, Carol. "Chiefs with Skills of a COO Gain Favor as Celebrity CEOs Fade." *Wall Street Journal,* April 5, 2005.

Incident Command System. *National Training Curriculum: Organization Overview.* Boise, Id.: National Interagency Fire Center, 1994.

Incident Operations Standards Working Team, National Wildfire Coordinating Group. "Operational Leadership Guide." In *Incident Response Pocket Guide.* Boise, Id.: National Interagency Fire Center, 2002.

Jaffe, Greg. "Battle Lines: Rumsfeld's Push for Speed Fuels Pentagon Dissent." *Wall Street Journal,* May 16, 2005.

Janis, Irving L. "Groupthink." *Psychology Today,* November 1971, 43–46, 74–76.

Janis, Irving L., and Leon Mann. *Decision Making: A Psychological Analysis of Conflict, Choice, and Commitment.* New York: Free Press, 1977.

Jensen, Michael C. "Eclipse of the Public Corporation." *Harvard Business Review* 67, 5 (1989): 61–74.

Jensen, Michael C., and Kevin J. Murphy. "CEO Incentives: It's Not How Much You Pay, but How." *Harvard Business Review* 68, 3 (1990): 138–53.

Jordan, Rodrigo. *K2: The Ultimate Challenge.* Santiago, Chile: Servicio de Impresión Laser S.A., 1996.

———. "Strategy at the Crux: Life-and-Death Choices on Everest and K2." In *Upward Bound: Nine Original Accounts of How Business Leaders Reached Their Summits,* edited by Michael Useem, Paul Asel, and Jerry Useem. New York: Crown Business/Random House, 2003.

Jordan, Rodrigo, Mark Davidson, and Mike Useem. "Life and Death Decisions on 'The Savage Mountain': Leadership at 28,000 Feet." Case Study. Philadelphia: Wharton Center for Leadership and Change, University of Pennsylvania, 2004.

Judge, William Q., and Alex Miller. "Antecedents and Outcomes of Decision Speed in Different Environmental Contexts." *Academy of Management Journal* 34, 2 (1991): 449–63.

Junger, Sebastian. *Fire.* New York: Harper Perennial, 2002.

Kahneman, Daniel. "Maps of Bounded Rationality: Psychology for Behavioral Economics." *American Economic Review* 93, 5 (2003): 1449–75.

Kahneman, Daniel, Paul Slovic, and Amos Tversky, eds., *Judgment Under Uncertainty: Heuristics and Biases.* New York: Cambridge University Press, 1982.

Kamler, Kenneth. *Surviving the Extremes: A Doctor's Journey to the Limits of Human Endurance.* New York: St. Martin's Press, 2004.

Karnazes, Dean. *Ultramarathon Man: Confessions of an All-Night Runner.* New York: Penguin, 2005.

Killing, Peter, and Thomas Malnight with Tracey Keys. *Must-Win Battles: Creating the Focus You Need to Achieve Your Key Business Goals.* Upper Saddle River, N.J.: FT Prentice-Hall, 2005.

King, Martin Luther, Jr., A *Testament of Hope: The Essential Writings and Speeches of Martin Luther King, Jr.,* edited by James M. Washington. San Francisco: HarperSanFrancisco, 1990.

Klein, Gary. *Sources of Power: How People Make Decisions.* Cambridge, Mass.: MIT Press, 1998.

———. *Intuition at Work: Why Developing Your Gut Instincts Will Make You Better at What You Do.* New York: Currency Doubleday, 2003.

Krakauer, Jon. *Into Thin Air: A Personal Account of the Mt. Everest Disaster.* New York: Villard/Random House, 1997.

Kunreuther, Howard C. "Protective Decisions: Fear or Prudence." In *Wharton on Making Decisions,* edited by Stephen J. Hoch and Howard C. Kunreuther. New York: Wiley, 2001.

Kwasjniewski, Aleksander. "Victor Yushchenko: A Revolution for the World." *Time,* April 18, 2005, 86–87.

Lagace, Martha. "Machiavelli, Morals, and You." *Harvard Business School Work-*

ing Knowledge, June 25, 2001. Available at http://hbswk.hbs.edu/pubitem
.jhtml?id=2335&t=leadership.

Lao-tzu. *The Way of Life According to Lao-Tzu*. Translated by Witter Bynner. New
York: Perigee Trade, 1986.

Last, Jonathan V. "The Disaster Was a Movie." *Wall Street Journal,* January 13,
2006.

Lin, Anthony. "Criminal, Civil Charges Filed Against Three Former Tyco Officers." *New York Law Journal,* September 13, 2002. Available at http://www
.law.com/jsp/article.jsp?id=1030821213567.

Lincoln, Abraham. "Letter to General J. Hooker, May 14, 1863." *Abraham Lincoln: Speeches and Writings, 1859–1865*. New York: Literary Classics of the
United States, 1989, 447–48.

Maclean, James N. *Fire on the Mountain: The True Story of the South Canyon Fire.*
New York: William Morrow, 1999.

———. *Fire and Ashes: On the Front Lines of American Wildfire.* New York: Henry
Holt, 2003.

Maclean, Norman. *Young Men and Fire.* Chicago: University of Chicago Press,
1990.

Manly, Lorne. "Editors at Time Inc. Offer Reassurances to Reporters." *New York
Times,* July 13, 2005.

Manly, Lorne, and David D. Kirkpatrick. "Top Editor at Time, Inc. Made Difficult
Decision His Own." *New York Times,* July 1, 2005.

Marvel, William. *Lee's Last Retreat: The Fight to Appomattox.* Chapel Hill, N.C.:
University of North Carolina Press, 2002.

Marx, Karl. *The Eighteenth Brumaire of Louis Bonaparte.* New York: International
Publishers, 1963. Originally published in 1852.

McKibben, Gordon. *Cutting Edge: Gillette's Journey to Global Leadership.* Boston:
Harvard Business School Press, 1997.

McLean, Bethany, and Peter Elkind. *Smartest Guys in the Room: The Amazing Rise
and Scandalous Fall of Enron.* New York: Portfolio, 2003.

McPherson, James M. *For Cause and Comrades: Why Men Fought in the Civil War.*
New York: Oxford University Press, 1997.

———. *Battle Cry of Freedom: The Civil War Era.* New York: Oxford University
Press, 1988.

———. *Hallowed Ground: A Walk at Gettysburg.* New York: Crown, 2003.

Mehta, Stephanie N. "Cisco Fractures Its Own Fairy Tale." *Fortune,* May 14, 2001,
104ff.

Mello, Peter A. "Thirty Years with Sailing Training." In *Sail Tall Ships!: A Directory
of Sail Training and Adventure at Sea.* Newport, RI: American Sail Training
Association, 2003.

Metcalfe, Janet. "Cognitive Optimism: Self-deception or Memory-based Processing Heuristics." *Personality and Social Psychology Review* 2, 2 (1998): 100–10.

Meyer, John P. "Four Territories of Experience: A Developmental Action Inquiry Approach to Outdoor-Adventure Experiential Learning." *Academy of Management Learning and Education* 2, 4 (2003): 352–63.

Mintzberg, Henry. *Rise and Fall of Strategic Planning.* New York: Free Press, 1994.

Mizruchi, Mark S., and Linda Brewster Stearns. "Getting Deals Done: The Use of Social Networks in Bank Decision-Making." *American Sociological Review* 66, 5 (2001): 647–71.

Morris, Betsy. "Charles Schwab's Big Challenge." *Fortune,* May 30, 2005, 88–99.

Mullen, Harris. *10 Incredible Mistakes at Gettysburg: A Review of the Battle and How Blunders by the Generals Shaped the Outcome.* Tampa, Fla.: High Water Press, 1995.

Murnighan, J. Keith, and John C. Mowen. *The Art of High-Stakes Decision-Making: Tough Calls in a Speed-Driven World.* New York: Wiley, 2002.

Nagourney, Adam, and Janet Elder. "New Poll Finds Bush Priorities Are Out of Step with Americans." *New York Times,* March 3, 2005.

National Wildfire Coordinating Group. *Fireline Handbook.* Boise, Id.: National Interagency Fire Center, 2004.

New York Times/CBS News Poll. February 24–28, 2005.

O'Reilly, Charles A., III, and Jeffrey Pfeffer. *Hidden Value: How Great Companies Achieve Extraordinary Results with Ordinary People.* Boston: Harvard Business School Press, 2000.

Pace, Peter. "How the Marine Corps Trains Leaders." Interview by Jerry Useem. *Fortune,* June 27, 2005, 108.

Parrado, Nando, with Vince Rause. *Miracle in the Andes: 72 Days in the Andes and My Long Trek Home.* New York: Crown Publishers, 2006.

Paterniti, Michael. "Torched," *Outside* magazine, September, 1995, pp. 58ff.

Perlow, Leslie A., Gerardo A. Okhuysen, and Nelson P. Repenning. "The Speed Trap: Exploring the Relationship Between Decision Making and Temporal Context." *Academy of Management Journal* 45, 5 (2002): 931–55.

Pfeffer, Jeffrey, and Robert I. Sutton. *The Knowing-Doing Gap: How Smart Companies Turn Knowledge Into Action.* Boston: Harvard Business School Press, 2000.

Pillmore, Eric M. "How We're Fixing Up Tyco." *Harvard Business Review,* December 2003, 96–103.

Presidential Commission on the Space Shuttle *Challenger* Accident (Rogers Commission). *Report of the Presidential Commission on the Space Shuttle Challenger Accident.* Washington, D.C.: Government Printing Office, 1986. Available http://history.nasa.gov/rogersrep/genindex.htm.

Purdum, Todd S. "Imagining How Powell Might Still Have a Job." *New York Times,* "Week in Review," November 21, 2004.

Putnam, Ted. "The Collapse of Decision Making and Organizational Structure on Storm King Mountain." Missoula, Mont.: Technology and Development Center, U.S. Forest Service, 1995.

Pyne, Stephen J. *Fire in America: A Cultural History of Wildland and Rural Fire.* Seattle: University of Washington Press, 1997.

Quintanar, Ray. "Staff Rides." Memo of July 29, 2003, to Forest Supervisors and Directors, U.S. Forest Service.

Read, Piers Paul. *Alive: The Story of the Andes Survivors.* New York: Avon Books/ HarperCollins, 1974.

Redding Interagency Hotshot Crewmember Report. "South Canyon Fire Staff Ride, Glenwood Spring, Colorado, May 25–29, 2003." Redding, Ca., 2003.

Reilly, Brendan M., Arthur T. Evans, Jeffrey J. Schaider, and Yue Wang. "Triage of Patients with Chest Pain in the Emergency Department: A Comparative Study of Physicians' Decisions." *American Journal of Medicine* 112, 2 (2002): 95–103.

Rimer, Sara. "Professors, in Close Vote, Censure Harvard Leader." *New York Times,* March 16, 2005.

Rivlin, Gary. "Hewlett-Packard to Lay Off 14,500 to Save $1.9 Billion." *New York Times,* July 20, 2005.

Robbins, Royal. "Falling Up: Success Through Failure in the School of Hard Rocks." In *Upward Bound: Nine Original Accounts of How Business Leaders Reached Their Summits,* edited by Michael Useem, Paul Asel, and Jerry Useem. New York: Crown Business/Random House, 2003.

Roberto, Michael A. *Why Great Leaders Don't Take Yes for an Answer: Managing for Conflict and Consensus.* Cambridge, U.K.: Pearson Publishing/Wharton School Publishing, 2005.

Roberts, David. "Out of Thin Air: 75 Years Later, Everest Finally Gives Up Mallory's Ghost." *Adventure,* Fall 1999, 98–115.

Roper Center for Public Opinion Research. Survey by Center for Survey Research and Analysis, University of Connecticut and Heldrich Center at Rutgers and Center for Survey Research and Analysis, University of Connecticut, May 10–May 29, 2000. Retrieved June 22, 2005, from the iPOLL Databank, Roper Center for Public Opinion Research, University of Connecticut, http://www.ropercenter.uconn.edu.

Roth, Philip. *The Plot Against America: A Novel.* Boston: Houghton Mifflin, 2004.

Rubin, Robert E., with Jacob Weisberg. *In an Uncertain World: Tough Choices from Wall Street to Washington.* New York: Random House, 2003.

Ruggero, Ed. *Duty First: West Point and the Making of American Leaders.* New York: HarperCollins, 2001.

Russo, J. Edward, and Paul J. H. Schoemaker. *Decision Traps: Ten Barriers to Brilliant Decision-Making and How to Overcome Them*. New York: Simon & Schuster, 1990.

———. *Winning Decisions: Getting It Right the First Time*. New York: Currency Doubleday, 2002.

Salka, John, with Barret Neville. *First In, Last Out: Leadership Lessons from the New York Fire Department*. New York: Portfolio/Penguin, 2004.

Santamaria, Jason A., Vincent Martino, and Eric K. Clemons. *The Marine Corps Way: Using Maneuver Warfare to Lead a Winning Organization*. New York: McGraw-Hill, 2004.

Sears, Stephen W. *To the Gates of Richmond: The Peninsula Campaign*. New York: Houghton Mifflin, 1992.

———. *Controversies and Commanders: Dispatches from the Army of the Potomac*. Boston: Houghton Mifflin, 1999.

———. *Gettysburg*. Boston: Houghton Mifflin, 2003.

Shipton, Eric. *That Untravelled World: An Autobiography*. New York: Charles Scriber's Sons, 1969.

Simon, Mark, and Susan M. Houghton. "The Relationship Between Overconfidence and the Introduction of Risky Products: Evidence from a Field Study." *Academy of Management Journal* 46, 2 (2003): 139–49.

Sony Corporation. *Annual Reports*, 1997, 1998, and 1999. Available at http://www.sony.net/SonyInfo/IR/library/index.html.

Soros, George. "The Capitalist Threat." *Atlantic Monthly*, February 1997, 45ff.

———. *Open Society: Reforming Global Capitalism*. New York: Public Affairs Press, 2000.

South Canyon Fire Accident Investigation Team. *South Canyon Fire Investigation of the 14 Fatalities That Occurred on July 6, 1994 near Glenwood Springs, Colorado*. Washington, D.C.: U.S. Forest Service and Bureau of Land Management, 1994.

State of New York v. L. Dennis Kozlowski. Case no. 3418/02, June 4, 2002. Available at http://news.findlaw.com/cnn/docs/tyco/nykozlowski60402ind.pdf.

Stein, Nicholas. "The World's Most Admired Companies," *Fortune*, October 2, 2000, pp. 182–190.

Stewart, Thomas A. "The Leading Edge: Making Decisions in Real Time." *Fortune*, June 26, 2000, 332ff.

Sutton, Larry. "Leadership on the Line: Wildland Firefighters." *Wharton Leadership Digest*, January 2002. Available at http://leadership.wharton.upenn.edu/digest/01-02.shtml.

Swartz, Mimi, with Sherron Watkins. *Power Failure: The Inside Story of the Collapse of Enron*. New York: Doubleday, 2003.

Tam, Pui-Wing. "Boss Talk: Hitting the Ground Running—New CEO of H-P Immerses Himself in Studying Company." *Wall Street Journal,* April 4, 2005.

———. "Rewiring Hewlett-Packard—Before Attempting to Fix H-P, Hurd Had to Understand It." *Wall Street Journal,* July 20, 2005.

Tam, Pui-Wing, and Joann S. Lublin. "H-P CEO Won't Rule Out Breakup—Mark Hurd Says First Job Is Improving Performance." *Wall Street Journal,* March 31, 2005.

Tam, Pui-Wing, Joann S. Lublin, and Carol Hymowitz. "H-P Picks NCR Chief Hurd to Take Over Struggling Giant." *Wall Street Journal,* March 30, 2005.

Thamel, Pete. "Three Times a Charm for Pitino: Taking Louisville to the Final Four Comes Amid Personal Loss." *New York Times,* March 31, 2005.

Tocqueville, Alexis de. *Democracy in America.* New York: Signet, 2001. Originally published in 1835.

Trudeau, Noah Andre. *Gettysburg: A Testing of Courage.* New York: HarperCollins, 2002.

Trulock, Alice Rains. *In the Hands of Providence: Joshua L. Chamberlain and the American Civil War.* Chapel Hill, N.C.: University of North Carolina Press, 1992.

Tucker, Glenn. *Lee and Longstreet at Gettysburg.* Dayton, Ohio: Morningside Bookshop, 1982.

———. *High Tide at Gettysburg.* Dayton, Ohio: Morningside Bookshop, 1983.

Turtledove, Harry. *The Guns of the South.* New York: Del Rey, 1993.

Ulrich, Dave, Steve Kerr, and Ron Ashkenas. *The GE Work-Out: How to Implement GE's Revolutionary Method for Busting Bureaucracy and Attacking Organizational Problems—Fast!* New York: McGraw-Hill, 2002.

U.S. Marine Corps University. "Conduct of the Staff Ride." Quantico, Va.: Marine Corps University, 2004.

U.S. Military Academy. "Staff Rides." 2004. Available at http://www.dean.usma.edu/history/web03/staff%20rides%20site/sret%20pages/staff%20ride%20home03.htm.

U.S. Navy. *Standard Organization and Regulations of the U.S. Navy* (OPNAVINST 3120.32). Washington, D.C.: U.S. Navy, 2001.

U.S. Securities and Exchange Commission. Commission Announcements, December 17, 2002. Available at http://www.sec.gov/news/digest/12-17.txt.

U.S. Senate Select Committee on Intelligence. *Report of the U.S. Intelligence Community's Prewar Intelligence Assessments of Iraq.* July 7, 2004. Washington, D.C.: U.S. Select Committee on Intelligence. Available at http://intelligence.senate.gov/iraqreport2.pdf.

Useem, Jerry. "Decisions, Decisions." *Fortune,* June 27, 2005, 55–56.

Useem, Jerry, et al. "20 That Made History." *Fortune,* June 27, 2005, 58–86.

Useem, Michael. *The Inner Circle: Large Corporations and the Rise of Business Polit-ical Activity in the U.S. and U.K.* New York: Oxford University Press, 1984.

———. *Executive Defense: Shareholder Power and Corporate Reorganization.* Cam-bridge, Mass.: Harvard University Press, 1993.

———. *Investor Capitalism: How Money Managers are Changing the Face of Corpo-rate America.* New York: Basic Books/HarperCollins, 1996.

———. *The Leadership Moment: Nine True Stories of Triumph and Disaster and Their Lessons for Us All.* New York: Random House, 1998.

———. *Leading Up: How to Lead Your Boss So You Both Win.* New York: Crown Business/Random House, 2001.

———. "Corporate Governance Is Directors Making Decisions: Reforming the Outward Foundations for Inside Decision Making." *Journal of Management and Governance* 7, 3 (2003): 241–53.

———. "Behind Closed Doors." *Wall Street Journal,* September 23, 2003.

———. "The Essence of Leading and Governing Is Deciding." In *Leadership and Governance from the Inside Out,* edited by Robert Gandossy and Jeffrey Son-nenfeld. New York: Wiley, 2004.

———. "Corporate Governance and Leadership in a Globalizing Equity Market." In *The INSEAD-Wharton Alliance on Globalizing: Strategies for Building Suc-cessful Businesses,* edited by Hubert Gatignon and John Kimberly with Robert Gunther. New York: Cambridge University Press, 2004.

———. "Decision Making and Leadership." In *Encyclopedia of Leadership,* edited by James MacGregor Burns, George R. Goethals, and Georgia Sorenson. Great Barrington, Mass.: Berkshire Publishing Group/Sage Publications, 2004.

———. "Decision Making—the Problem of Proxies." *Harvard Business Review* 82, 11 (2004): 20, 24–25.

———. "Structures to Help Directors Reach the Point: Company Boards Are In-creasingly Adopting Formal Decision-Making Protocols to Ensure that They Address the Most Important Issues." *Financial Times,* May 20, 2005.

———. "In the Heat of the Moment: A Case Study in Life-and-Death Decision Making." *Fortune,* June 27, 2005, 125–34.

Useem, Michael, James Cook, and Larry Sutton. "Developing Leaders for Decision Making Under Duress: Wildland Firefighters in the South Canyon Fire and Its Aftermath." *Academy of Management Learning and Education* 4, 4 (2005): 461–85.

Useem, Michael, Mark Davidson, and Evan Wittenberg. "Leadership Develop-ment Beyond the Classroom: The Power of Leadership Ventures to Drive Home the Essence of Decision Making." *International Journal of Leadership Education* 1 (2005): 159–78.

Useem, Michael, and Jerry Useem. "The Board That Conquered Everest." *Fortune,* October 27, 2003, 73–74.

———. "Great Escapes: Nine Decision-Making Pitfalls—and Nine Simple Devices to Beat Them." *Fortune,* June 27, 2005, 97–102.

Useem, Michael, and Andy Zelleke. "Oversight and Delegation in Corporate Governance: Deciding What the Board Should Decide." *Corporate Governance: An International Review* 14, 1 (2006): 2–12.

Van Maanen, John. "Style as Theory." *Organizational Science* 6 (1995): 133–43.

Vaughan, Diane. *The* Challenger *Launch Decision: Risky Technology, Culture, and Deviance at NASA.* Chicago: University of Chicago Press, 1996.

Venables, Stephen. *Everest: Summit of Achievement.* New York: Simon & Schuster, 2003.

Vlahos, James. "Then Alive! & Now," *National Geographic Adventure,* April 2006, 46ff.

Weathers, Beck. *Left for Dead: My Journey Home from Everest.* New York: Villard/ Random House, 2000.

Weick, Karl E. "The Collapse of Sensemaking in Organizations: The Mann Gulch Disaster." *Administrative Science Quarterly* 38, 4 (1993): 628–52.

———. "Drop Your Tools: An Allegory for Organizational Studies." *Administrative Science Quarterly* 41, 2 (1996): 301–13.

Weick, Karl E., and Karlene H. Roberts. "Collective Mind in Organizations: Heedful Interrelating on Flight Decks." *Administrative Science Quarterly* 38, 3 (1993): 357–81.

Weisman, Steven R. "The Struggle for Iraq: The Transfer; U.S. Presidential Politics and Self-Rule for Iraqis," *New York Times,* February 19, 2004.

———. "Democrats Delay Final Approval of Rice for State Dept." *New York Times,* January 20, 2005.

Weisman, Steven R., and Joel Brinkley. "At Senate Hearing, Rice Cites Progress in Training Iraq Forces." *New York Times,* January 19, 2005.

Welch, Jack, with John A. Byrne. *Jack: Straight from the Gut.* New York: Warner Business Books, 2001.

Welch, Jack, with Suzy Welch. *Winning.* New York: HarperCollins, 2005.

Wharton Leadership Digest. "Leadership in China: Haier's Zhang Ruimin." March 2005. Available at http://leadership.wharton.upenn.edu/digest/03%2D05 .shtml.

Whitestone, Debra. "People Express." Case 9-483-103. Harvard Business School, Boston, 1983.

Wildland Fire Leadership Development Program. See http://www.fireleadership .gov, 2004.

Wildland Fire Leadership Development Staff Ride Library. See http://www .fireleadership.gov/toolbox/staffride/index.html, 2004.

Wildland Fire Leadership Development Training Courses. See http://www .fireleadership.gov/courses/courses.html, 2004.

Wildland Fire Leadership Development Values and Principles. See http://www .fireleadership.gov/values_principles.html, 2004.

Wilmoth, Peter. "Slowly, Slowly, a Corporate Strongman Climbs His Mountains." *The Age* (Melbourne), May 5, 2002.

Winik, Jay. *April 1865: The Month That Saved America.* New York: HarperCollins, 2001.

Woodward, Bob. *Plan of Attack.* New York: Simon & Schuster, 2004.

Yates, J. Frank. *Decision Management: How to Assure Better Decisions in Your Company.* San Francisco: Jossey-Bass, 2003.

Yermack, David. "Higher Market Valuation of Companies with a Small Board of Directors." *Journal of Financial Economics* 40, 2 (1996): 185–211.

ACKNOWLEDGMENTS

I must first thank the many people who have willingly and candidly shared their decision-making experiences, many but not all of whom are identified in the preface. I also want to thank the following individuals for rendering invaluable guidance and service during the preparation of this book: James Bailey, Penny Bamber, Maria Bartiromo, Alain Belda, Edwin Bernbaum, Aldo Boitano, Kate Bonamici, William Bowling, Leigh Buchanan, Peter Cappelli, Dennis Carey, Johannah Christensen, Jim Cook, Peter Cowen, Mark Davidson, Jonathan P. Doh, Kay Dowgun, Charles Elson, Claudio Engel, Robert Gandossy, Hank Gilman, Mark Hanna, Jack Hershey, Sarah Hershey, Paola Hjelt, Tim Hough, Anjani Jain, Rodrigo Jordan, Sandhya Karpe, Rakesh Khurana, Jeffrey Klein, Lynn Krage, Howard Kunreuther, Neng Liang, Connie Mack, James McPherson, Marshall Meyer, Kenneth Miller, Robert E. Mittelstaedt, Li-Chun Moy, Cait Murphy, Mukul Pandya, Kathryn Pearson, Eric Pillmore, Lewis Platt, David Pottruck, Michael Roberto, Joseph Rosenbloom, Sanjay Saxena, Paul Schoemaker, Harbir Singh, Jitendra Singh, Jeffrey Sonnenfeld,

Jon Spector, Thomas Stewart, Stephen A. Stumpf, Larry Sutton, Todd Thomson, Andrea Useem, Susan Useem, Yumi Wakayama, Chris Warner, Karl Weick, Evan Wittenberg, and Andy Zelleke.

For the chapter on firefighting on Storm King Mountain, I am grateful for the insights of a number of individuals who joined us during a daylong walk of the South Canyon fire zone on May 29, 2002. They include those working for government firefighting agencies: Kim Bang, Grant Beebe, Tim Blake, Jim Cook, Sarah Doehring, Pam Ensley, Deb Epps, Anthony Escobar, Jim Glenn, Jim Kitchen, Bob Leighty, Mark Linane, Nancy Lull, Greg Power, George Steele, Larry Sutton, and Steve Thomas; officers of the U.S. Marine Corps, Bob Baird, Eric Carlson, and Cheston Souza; John Maclean, author of *Fire on the Mountain,* a meticulous account of the South Canyon fire; and faculty and graduates of the Wharton School and the University of Pennsylvania, including Mark Davidson, Neil Doherty, Bruce Newsome, and Barbara Shannon. The visit to Storm King Mountain and another fire zone, Mann Gulch in Montana, are briefly described at http://leadership.wharton.upenn.edu/l_change/trips/SKM-fire.shtml and http://leadership.wharton.upenn.edu/l_change/Fire.shtml. I am indebted to firefighter Donald Mackey, whose decisions during the South Canyon fire have profoundly informed my thinking about decision making under stress.

A very special thanks is owed my agent, Raphael Sagalyn, personal editor Howard Means, and Random House/Crown Business editor John Mahaney. Their encouragement, direction, and backing during the development of the ideas behind the book and the book itself have been invaluable throughout. My colleague Evan Wittenberg requires special thanks for our numerous ponderings on decision making as we navigated terrains ranging from Antarctica to the Himalayas, and for his unstinting support on the more proximate grounds of our university. My wife, Elizabeth Useem, has lent her vital

personal support and guidance throughout the interviews, observations, and writing that followed, essential ingredients for completing
this enterprise. My son Jerry Useem and I held many helpful discussions on decision making; they shaped many of the ideas in these pages
and along the way they generated two jointly authored articles identified below.

Passages in this book have been adapted from several articles that
I authored or coauthored during the preparation of the book, all available upon request at TheGoPoint@wharton.upenn.edu:

"Oversight and Delegation in Corporate Governance: Deciding What the Board
     Should Decide," with Andy Zelleke, *Corporate Governance* 14 (2006):
     2–12.
"Developing Leaders for Decision Making Under Duress: Wildland Firefighters in
     the South Canyon Fire and Its Aftermath," with James Cook and Larry Sut-
     ton, *Academy of Management Learning and Education* 4 (2005): 461–85.
"Making Responsible Decisions," in *Handbook of Responsible Leadership and Gov-
     ernance in Global Business,* edited by Jonathan P. Doh and Stephen A. Stumpf,
     Edward Elgar Publishing, 2005.
"In the Heat of the Moment: A Case Study in Life-and-Death Decision Making,"
     Fortune, June 27, 2005, 125–33.
"Great Escapes: Nine Decision-Making Pitfalls—and Nine Simple Devices to Beat
     Them," with Jerry Useem, *Fortune,* June 27, 2005, 97–102.
"Structures to Help Directors Reach the Point: Company Boards Are Increasingly
     Adopting Formal Decision-Making Protocols to Ensure That They Address
     the Most Important Issues," *Financial Times,* May 20, 2005.
"Leadership Development Beyond the Classroom: The Power of Leadership Ven-
     tures to Drive Home the Essence of Decision Making," with Mark Davidson
     and Evan Wittenberg, *International Journal of Leadership Education* 1 (2005):
     159–78.
"The Essence of Leading and Governing Is Deciding," in *Leadership and Gover-
     nance from the Inside Out,* edited by Robert Gandossy and Jeffrey Sonnenfeld,
     Wiley, 2004.
"Decision Making—the Problem of Proxies," *Harvard Business Review,* November
     2004, 20, 24–25.
"Decision Making and Leadership," in *Encyclopedia of Leadership,* edited by James

MacGregor Burns, George R. Goethals, and Georgia Sorenson. Great Barrington, Mass.: Berkshire Publishing Group/Sage Publications, 2004.

"The Board That Conquered Everest," with Jerry Useem, *Fortune,* October 27,
2003, 73–74.

"Behind Closed Doors," *Wall Street Journal,* September 23, 2003.

"Corporate Governance Is Directors Making Decisions: Reforming the Outward
Foundations for Inside Decision Making," *Journal of Management and Governance* 7, 3 (2003): 241–53.

"Clear and Present Danger," *Fast Company,* July 2003, 29–30.

PHOTO, ART, CASE, AND SIMULATION CREDITS

Photographs, artwork, cases, and a simulation are used with permission of the following sources:

Introduction

Astronauts: Bettmann/Corbis
Tom Boatner: Tom Boatner
Robert Burritt: Marion G. Weiler

Chapter 1

Anatomy of a Tragedy: John Tomanio, *Fortune*
Firefighters cut a fire line: Tony Petrilli, USDA Forest Service
Donald Mackey's final decision: Photo by Jim Kautz, USDA Forest Service; graphic by John Tomanio, *Fortune*

Chapter 2

Gustavus W. Smith: Bettmann/Corbis
Rick Rieder: Lehman Brothers
Audrey Mestre: Despotovic Dusko/Corbis Sygma
Roberto Canessa, 1972: Roberto Canessa
Roberto Canessa, 2002: Pierre Merimee/Corbis
G. Richard Thoman: Mark Peterson/Corbis
Charlene Barshefsky: Reuters/Corbis

Chapter 3

Paul Grangaard: Paul Grangaard
Mark V. Hurd: Kim Kulish/Corbis
James McNerney Jr.: Caren Firouz/Reuters/Corbis
Dalai Lama: Bettmann/Corbis
Zhang Ruimin: Haruyoshi Yamaguchi/Reuters/Corbis
Arlene Blum: Bettmann/Corbis
Norman Pearlstine: Brooks Kraft/Corbis

Chapter 4

Jefferson Davis: Bettmann/Corbis
Robert E. Lee: Library of Congress, Prints and Photographs Division
Abraham Lincoln: Abraham Lincoln Book Shop, Inc., Chicago, Il.; all rights
    reserved
Joseph Hooker: Library of Congress, Prints and Photographs Division
George Meade: Library of Congress, Prints and Photographs Division
Richard Ewell: Library of Congress, Prints and Photographs Division
Strong Vincent: Massachusetts Commandery, Military Order of the Loyal Legion
    of the United States
George Pickett: Library of Congress, Prints and Photographs Division

Chapter 5

MBA student fire teams: Michael Useem
Carter Racing: © 1986, 2001, 2005, 2006 by Jack W. Brittain and Sim B. Sitkin
    and distributed under license by Delta Leadership Incorporated. All rights
    reserved. Not to be reproduced, modified, stored, or transmitted without
    prior written permission of the copyright holder or agent. For copyright
    clearance, contact Delta Leadership, Inc: carter@deltaleadership.com.
Rodrigo Jordan: Christian Buracchio/Vertical S.A. (Chile)
Approaching K2: Christian Buracchio/Vertical S.A.
Nearing the summit of K2: Cristian Garcia Huidobro/Vertical S.A.
Miguel Purcell: Christian Buracchio/Vertical S.A.
People Express fare card: Chris Sloan, CMedia
People Express Simulation: John Sterman, People Express Microworld,
    Global Strategy Dynamics Limited, Princes Risborough (http://www
    .strategydynamics.com)

Chapter 6

Dennis Kozlowski: Michael Appleton/Corbis
John A. Krol: Najlah Feanny/Corbis Saba

Peter Pace: SSgt D. Myles Cullen, U.S. Air Force
Peter Pace with photo of Guido Farinaro: SSgt D. Myles Cullen, U.S. Air Force
Sherron Watkins: Martin H. Simon/Corbis
Joshua Lawrence Chamberlain: From the original painting by Mort Künstler, *Salute of Honor,* © 2001 Mort Künstler, Inc.

Chapter 7

Edward D. Breen Jr.: Mary Altaffer/Associated Press
Jaime Irick: Nancy Warner
Madhabi Puri Buch: Madhabi Puri Buch
Liu Chuanzhi: Bobby Yip/Reuters/Corbis
Ann Livermore: Hewlett-Packard Company
Charles Elachi: Francis Specker/epa/Corbis
Seymour Cray: Cray Inc.
Damon Huard: Steven Senne/Associated Press
Eric Shipton: Royal Geographical Society
Tenzing Norgay on summit of Mt. Everest: Royal Geographical Society
Summit ridge of Mt. Everest: Royal Geographical Society
Edmund Hillary, John Hunt, and Tenzing Norgay: Associated Press

INDEX

ABOUT THE AUTHOR

MICHAEL USEEM is the William and Jacalyn Egan Professor of Management and director of the Center for Leadership and Change Management at the Wharton School, University of Pennsylvania. His university teaching includes MBA and executive MBA courses on management and leadership, and he offers programs on leadership, governance, and change for managers in the United States, Asia, Europe, and Latin America. He also works on leadership development with many companies and organizations in the private, public, and nonprofit sectors, and he has consulted with several companies on corporate governance. He is the author of *The Leadership Moment: Nine True Stories of Triumph and Disaster and Their Lessons for Us All, Investor Capitalism: How Money Managers Are Changing the Face of Corporate America,* and other books, and his articles have appeared in a number of journals, magazines, and newspapers in the United States and abroad. Additional information is available at http://www.wharton.upenn.edu/faculty/useem.html, and he can be reached at useem@wharton.upenn.edu.

Also by Michael Useem

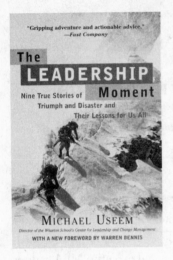

THE LEADERSHIP MOMENT
Nine True Stories of
Triumph and Disaster and
Their Lessons for Us All
978-0-8129-3230-0
$15.95 paper (Canada: $17.95)

LEADING UP
How to Lead Your Boss
So You Both Win
978-1-4000-4700-0
$15.95 paper (Canada: $23.00)